A MOUTH SWEETER THAN

a MOUTH sweeter than

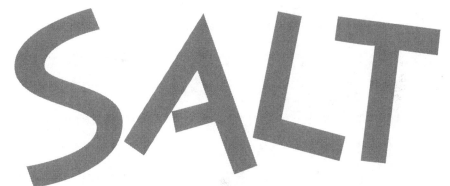

AN AFRICAN MEMOIR

by TOYIN FALOLA

The University of Michigan Press

Ann Arbor

Copyright © by the University of Michigan 2004
Published in the United States of America by
The University of Michigan Press
Manufactured in the United States of America
⊚ Printed on acid-free paper

2007   2006   2005   2004   4   3   2   1

A CIP catalog record for this book is available from the British Library.

Library of Congress Cataloging-in-Publication Data

Falola, Toyin.
    A mouth sweeter than salt : an African memoir / Toyin Falola.
       p.   cm.
    ISBN 0-472-11401-8 (cloth : alk. paper)
    1. Falola, Toyin—Childhood and youth.   2. Nigerian
Americans—Biography.   3. Nigeria—Biography.   4.
Nigeria—History—1960–   5. Nigeria—Social conditions—1960–   6.
College teachers—Texas—Austin—Biography.   I. Title.
E184.N55F35   2004
966.9′28051′092—dc22   2003026184

ISBN13 978-0-472-11401-6 (cloth)
ISBN13 978-0-472-03132-0 (paper)
ISBN13 978-0-472-02555-8 (electronic)

For JAMES ADESINA FALOLA

The thick rod that troubles the brass gong
The heavy rain that reduces the anthill to mud
The irresistible deluge, child of a warrior
The author of life who bestows blessings on others
The child of death who kills as he dies.

Offspring of the wealthy ones
Possessor of the machine that brings wealth
The boisterous one full of stomach like pregnancy
Adesina is more handsome than a woman, but for her beads and breasts
A deity that tempers drought.

Adesina, I shall call you three times more
If you do not answer, you will be like the wild bird who lives along the road
Let the farewell be long
As we meet only in dreams
An encounter between man and the wild bird.

ACKNOWLEDGMENTS

I waited almost fifteen years before deciding to write this. The pressure to write a memoir had been mounting for several years. I had been tempted to sign contracts in the 1990s when a publisher friend, now of blessed memory, traveled from the United Kingdom all the way to Austin in order to persuade me to write a first installment. The political aspects of my life that most interested the publishers are the least exciting to me, and they have not even been included here. The circumstances that compelled my change of mind will be narrated at the appropriate time, hopefully not as part of an obituary. Meanwhile, the present memoir covers my childhood years in the 1950s and 1960s. This was an era marked by the end of British rule and the management of the country by Nigerians during the First Republic. Extended families, the city, and the politics of the city and nation provide the larger context for the memoir. I am no more than an observer who saw more than enough, heard more than necessary, and listened to an excess of words.

This is the shortest acknowledgment I have ever written, but I cannot end it abruptly without thanking those who have encouraged me in various ways: Vik Bahl, Tayo Alabi, Rasheed Na'Allah, Ann O'Hear, Edgard Sankara, Paul Onovoh, Ben Lindfors, Barbara Harlow, Andrew Clarno, Niyi Afolabi, and Akin Alao. Rather than use mere written words to thank them, as is customary with most acknowledgments, I prefer to sing.

I swear to all that I am not a witch
The terror that kills friends and foes
I swear that I am not a snake
The thread that sews life and death
I belong to the company of life.

O! friends, people's mouths
Minds full of wisdom
Givers of wise counsel
By your authority
I walk not purposelessly,
 aimlessly, clumsily, slowly . . .

Honor me, I sing to you
Unaccompanied, we live in fear
Beautiful birds who strut in a sea
 of heads
I greet you first today
Let there be no trouble for what I say.

CONTENTS

CHAPTER ONE : : : TIME & SEASON

know when I was born; I mean to say that there are some people who know when I was born: the day, month, and even year. It is not that people who were born before me did not know all these pieces of information about themselves, and it is also not that those who were born after me know more or less about when they were born. But what we know does differ, as different generations of Africans tend to reckon and calculate time in different ways. My mother and father knew when they were born, but the answers they would have given about their own birth would not be the same, and these would be different from the answer they would give about mine. No one's reckoning is superior or more utilitarian than anyone else's; only the passage of time invests different meanings to each one. Time and season may go together, not always as friends or companions, not always working together; indeed, they can work against each other, and I have known of cases in which a season can kill time or time can survive the season.

If the information that my mother was born before the brother of her first cousin is not enough knowledge for the curious mind, then you have to travel to my cousin's compound and look for his brother. Talking to my mother would be a waste of time, as this is what she knew, what she could tell you, no more, no less. And, for reasons best known to you, it was important to know my mother's birth date, and you followed the instructions to the letter by looking for her cousin's compound. You were lucky to find him on his recliner, and after exchanging the normal greetings—long, ritualistic, tedious, and time consuming—you eventually reached the object of your visit.

"When were you born, sir?" you asked, expecting a short and quick answer.

Before an answer could come, many looked at you in wonder, amazed as to the kind of question you were posing. Although you are not a stranger, who is not allowed to pose such a question, as an insider you are certainly displaying bad manners. The answer you seek might even be intended for evil, some may say, as to know the precise time may be to manipulate the symbol of hour and day to destroy, to connect one's evil eye with the season of birth. But no one will accuse you of evil, as this is rather extreme. Thus, they begin to peel the onion from the outermost edges.

How old are you yourself?

Better not to think too much before answering, as someone would accuse you of misinformation. Or, if it took you such a long time to answer, it should take my mother's first cousin and his brother days to respond to your original question. Why should a question be used to answer a question? It should, as it may be the best way to arrive at the right answer, at the right time. Then you answered.

February 18, 1942.

And from the audience came a yell: "Alakowe, oniyeye" which you correctly translated in your mind as "the educated man is a clown." But you are not a comedian, so why have you been turned into one, and why is your education, the great investment in Western education, being ridiculed as a comedy? Well, you were spared from speaking, as another person in the audience stepped forward.

> Congratulations! I said congratulations, Mr. Alakowe. Fenmbuary eeeeteeni, nineteeen fortisomuteen. Congratulations. We know those who sent you to school, and those who sent you to school can-not ask us when we are born . . .

Your goal was not to fight, and you immediately apologized and begged to leave. As you turned back, to take the first steps to leave, someone asked you to stop.

> When you are not a radio, when you talk, you expect a reply. Or are you a radio who only talks to itself? The person you asked for his age is yet to reply, and you are leaving. If the question is not important to you, why did you leave your house and duties to come all the way here? It is true that you educated people are never serious. Okay, may I even know why you want to know? . . .

Now you asked yourself whether you were in yet more trouble or whether there was a solution to your trouble.

> Thank-you, Baba, it is just because I want to know when Toyin's mom was born and she directed me to the brother of her cousin, who was born after her.

Luck was now traveling your way, as the quiet old woman listening to the conversation was able to come to your assistance, blaming everybody for the confusion over such a small issue. She witnessed the birth of both Toyin's mom and the brother of her first cousin. She asserted that she was older than both Toyin's mom and the brother of her cousin and that this should be enough for you. To the wise, half a sentence becomes whole, a split word becomes one; only the fool requires assistance with complete sentences, with full words, even with the interpretation of sentences and the meanings of words. The wise do not carry a dictionary about.

> At least you know that I am older than the two of them, now that you know that they are younger than me. If they are not as old as me, then, you know their age. Don't you?

She was not mocking you; she was absolutely sincere. She was not joking; she meant that she had given you an idea of time. Time can be an idea, a concept. Time can be measured by comparing people, relating one event to another. Like logs of wood placed on top of one another, time can be determined by the placement of one log in relation to the other. My mother knew when she was born—she was even definite that it was before the brother of her first cousin. Why should this not be enough if she did not have to fill out paperwork, apply for passports and visas to travel, collect welfare and insurance money? Her knowledge of when she was born was enough, indeed, useful for her time and purpose in life.

But this is not enough for those with other purposes—scholars who need to understand society, planners who want accurate census data to make their projections. And it may not have been enough for those who wanted to plan her burial, who needed a date on the funeral program that mourners should know before they could reveal the full force of their sympathy, the dying reality of their love, and the excuse for drunkenness and food stuffing that would follow. For the mourners, what they needed to see on the funeral program was simple: "Mama was born over a hundred years ago." Since she aged enough to be proclaimed an ancestor, they could eat and drink and be merry after dropping the corpse in the six-foot-deep hole. For the scholars, you have to give them more work to do, as the longer the number of their footnotes the more respect they acquire: "She was born when King Akindele was on the throne." This is easy for them, to figure out when King Akindele ascended the throne of his forefathers. If one of them got the king list right and was able to determine Mama's birth date with a small margin of error, various awards would come, tenure and promotion would be assured, and citation upon citation would popularize the scholar's name within their own world, the tower made of ivory. As for the planners, since they have been planning, society has been going backward. Their data are useless, and even if they are useful they produce useless ends. "Mama was born in 1900!" You suddenly know the date, but you made it up so that the young man (you called him a small boy behind his back) can scribble 1900 on his pad and leave your house as soon as he arrived. It is not as if the young man, a representative of a government you do not believe in, actually believes in the job or data himself. Two people cannot lose from a lie: if the person listening to a lie does not know, the narrator has already discovered himself! Should he lose the piece of paper on which he scribbles Mama's date of 1900, he need not think at all before changing it to 1914. Who cares about the difference? Certainly not his boss, who will never read the reports or statistics. And, even if someone cares, what is the difference between '00 and '14? "Same difference," as the young official says to himself.

My father's situation is far different from my mother's, and his is different from mine, but it is too early to talk about mine. Be patient; your time is not about to run out; a wise person does not think of struggling for a bride until money has been procured to buy a marital bed. Not only did my father know when he was born, he was always more than happy to tell it, though not to write it down; to tell is to build a house, to see time as a narrative; to write is to see time as a single moment. How, then, can we begin the process, to learn when my father was born?

"Ask him," as my mother was said to have told a relation.

"Is it polite to ask?" The gentleman asked again and again before he could summon the courage to stop my father working on a new suit, halfway done. He was a tailor, among the many things that he did; not just a tailor but an "English tailor." To remove English from the full description of his job would be to insult him. After all, he was not trained to make Yoruba attire, which any of the illiterates in town could do, as his uncle used to boast about him with unmistakable arrogance; but even if some of his jobs appeared simple, they were "English" enough to be complicated. The gentleman had hardly finished asking the simple question about when my father, Adesina Falola, was born than an answer came from him:

Me, when was I born?

Son of Agbo, the warrior
Agbo who hit the grass in anger and the grass burned to become a
    desert
Agbo who hit the rocks and the rocks broke to become sand
Agbo, the thunder that hits to kill
Agbo, the lightning that strikes to destroy
Me, Adesina!

As he chanted his praise name, the gentleman looked confused rather than impressed. My father did not even notice the look on the man's face, which might have drawn attention to his possible state of mind. Then he stopped chanting and actually announced that many people had asked him when he was born and now was the time to tell. The gentleman was happy, stood up, waiting to hear the date, say "thank-you, sir," and leave for his business. He was right and wrong: the date came, but he could not leave so soon.

> I was rushed out of my mother's womb by war songs, the last war
> songs that the Ibadan army sang over and over again.

Again unmindful of the impatience of his guest, he changed from chanting to singing.

Before he runs,
Before he stoops down,
Club him down.

Before he stoops down,
Before he prostrates to appeal,
Slap him twice.

Before he begs,
Before he weeps,
Shoot him dead.

Before he stoops down,
Before he appeals to the chiefs,
Execute him.

Then he stopped singing, laughing so loudly that his army of apprentices looked at him and quickly resumed their jobs before he could ask them why they were looking at him. When he stopped laughing, he told the gentleman, "I was born on the day that the Ibadan people heard the last war song." Ever since, no such war songs had been repeated and no such occasion had come again. So strong was the linkage that he was nicknamed "Akin omo arogun tadi mehin"—"The courageous man who sees a war and ducks." Not that he saw a war and ran, as the poem made clear, but only held back. And to hold back is to reflect, to think, to pack the charms, to load the gun, and then charge like a horse. But he was not opportuned to show his courage, to shoot, slap, and execute before the victim rushed for an appeal. The last war song was loud, so loud that the pregnancy ended before the due date. It was not a miscarriage but a premature birth.

"And who does not remember the premature baby?" asked my dad. He did not wait for an answer, giving a lecture on the conventional wisdom between a premature baby and an abiku (the "one who is born to die," the victim of sickle cell anemia who was not expected to live long). He was premature not because of ill luck, but because of good luck, abundant good luck—to see the warriors, the friends and associates of his own father, to see his father, the war general, to hear songs of courage, to see the weapons before they rusted, the guns when they were still loaded, the sharp knives, the bows and arrows, and the horses, the great fighting force. He was the child who was in a hurry to come to the world, too impatient to stay further in the womb; a son with the script of life who had a lot of work to do and whose time was being wasted in the womb. He did not speak on the first day of his birth, as some "selected sons" had done before him to announce their glories to come, but he gave the sign of greatness: as the warriors were singing their last song, the baby was smiling. The more they shouted and sang, the more Adesina smiled in approval. Then, as the night fell, as the songs ended, he began to cry, not because he was hungry or sad but because the celebration was over. He wanted more. He kept crying until the soldiers and the general about to retire came to his mother's room, picked up the baby, and chanted. As they chanted and sang, he slowly stopped crying, he began to smile; he fell into a long sleep, his first sleep in life, and when he woke up, he was reborn into an era of peace. Eight days later, as he received his Yoruba name of Adesina (the crown that creates the path to success) he also received an English name, James.

Now about to return to continue with the suit he was making, he looked the gentleman in the face and asked,

Who does not know when the premature baby was born?

The gentleman, now either tired or overwhelmed or overpowered, was quick to answer: "I know."

But what does he know? Certainly not the date, the calendar day and month. My father had told him the accurate moment, the great event that marked the day of his birth. He had told him the absolute truth, one that everybody in the family had accepted and retold with varying emphasis.

I know this date, but he was not the one who told me, and I am absolutely certain that I was the first one in the world to discover it. To *discover* in this case is actually used in its real sense of working hard and with luck being the first to know something. My discovery is not like that of David Livingstone, who claimed to have discovered the Victoria Falls when it was actually Africans who showed him the place, later named by his fellow citizens as one of the seven wonders of the world. Neither was mine similar to that of the European explorer, Mungo Park, credited with having discovered the River Niger in the nineteenth century, a river that Africans had used for centuries to travel and fish, and one whose long banks had made many settlements flourish.

It was actually I who told others in the family the possible date: March 22, 1893. And when I told others, it was not secondhand information, like the kind picked up by Arab writers who stationed themselves in North Africa and waited for gossip and innuendoes to come across the Sahara Desert before they could write their pamphlets about the "bilad al Sudan." I told others what I had discovered, and cited myself as the source. How can a son cite himself as the source for the birth date of his father? Simple: because unlike the father who was a tailor, the son abandoned the work of working with hands and legs for that of history writing. If he could not invent suits, at least he could hunt for dates.

I knew the date, but not early enough to confirm it or tell my father. I knew the date when, as a graduate student in the 1970s, I began to study the event that he described to the gentleman. Time can be measured and presented as an event. People had been born in the year of famine, drought, hurricane, locust invasion, and other calamities. People had given as the date of their birth moments of joy and happiness, as on the day of the visit of Queen Victoria to Nigeria. I know of many people who were born on the day that Nigeria obtained its independence, which I could date to October 1, 1960, without having to share in the glory of any major discovery.

The essentials of my father's story were actually accurate. The Yoruba ended their long century of warfare in 1893, and Ibadan soldiers marched home. They did not lose their wars, but they did not win them either. They returned jubilant, faking victory, singing so loudly, in words that everyone remembers to this day. How long they sang I do not know. How loudly they sang, I cannot measure. Whether the song created joy or panic sufficiently to bring a baby to life, I have no idea.

Strangers mediated in the wars and dispersed the Yoruba warriors.

Rather than returning home with slaves, livestock, women, and the lucrative booty of war, they returned home empty-handed, after many years of war. These strangers from a foreign land, then and now called the British, decided to take Ibadan and others as their own war booty. In its long history of successful wars, Ibadan would take war booty but leave something for the defeated. Now when it was the turn of the British, they took everything, like the greedy and merciless thief who carried the victim's chair and asked his victim to carry the entire house and walk behind him. "Impossible!" shouted the victim. "No one can carry a house!" "Well, then," shouted the thief, "we can burn it down!" The British did not burn down Ibadan. They only imposed their first Resident, Captain Bower, in 1893.

This is the event, part of which I presented in my first book on the city-state of Ibadan. And the event can be used to produce a date, which was how I arrived at March 1893 for the birth of my father. Can I be dead accurate? We need to wait a little longer for you to see whether I am right or wrong. And it is for you to say, not for me to confirm, whether it actually matters to be wrong or right in matters like this.

As to my own date of birth, too many authentic records date my beginning to the first day of January 1953. More than this, they list the birth as having taken place in a hospital. Neither of my parents was born in a modern hospital, as probably none existed in their time. Delivery in their time was through the traditional midwife, a semispecialist woman who responded to emergency situations, quickly abandoning her regular occupation. It was most certainly a woman's job, as few men would accept other men probing into the privacy of their wives, even if it involved bringing out a new child from a hidden corner that professional boxers are not even allowed to hit. As modern medicine spread, men turned it into one of their main occupations, pushing women to teaching and nursing. Fellow men relaxed with the doctors who looked like them, and they can now deliver babies, mainly in less private hospital beds, and modern midwives can take care of them. By the mid–twentieth century, the hospitals were still not many, but my city had a few. By then schoolchildren knew of Florence Nightingale, the heroine of nursing. Mary Slessor had entered the elementary schoolbook as the pioneer medical worker in Nigeria who saved the lives of many twins destined to play for a while in the jungle. Traditional medicine was not dead, but those who had the means and education, like my father, were clever enough to combine both: I could be delivered in a hospital, but *agbo*, the multipurpose herbal concoction, was waiting for me at home to cure hundreds of diseases.

It was not modern medicine that insisted on recording the date of my birth. This was not one of the duties of a doctor. Hospitals only gave a piece of paper, a medical record indicating the place and date of birth for the baby's parent to take to the city council office for registration. The majority did not bother to collect the papers, and many who did actually threw them away as worthless papers disturbing their pockets, giving them the temporary illusion that they were carrying some paper currency to buy drinks to celebrate the birth of a new baby. It is indeed rare to find a Nigerian of my generation with a birth certificate. Thus it would have been a privilege for me to have one. Alas! I never did, and I had no such privilege. Apparently, no one considered a birth certificate important enough to keep in a safe. There was no reason to. The schools did not request a birth certificate to enroll, trusting the date supplied by the parents or merely inventing one. While the expectation was that one should be six years old to be in the first year of elementary school, only the parents who opted for private schools could guarantee this. In the public schools, the recruiting headmaster looked at the child to determine readiness. The hand must be long enough so that when stretched across the head, it reached the ear. If it did not, then the child was not ready for school. Late developers or short people were obviously at a disadvantage.

The real need for a birth certificate came after leaving school in order to start a job. For purposes of future retirement, a copy was obviously required. At this point, whether one was born in a hospital with a recorded date or privately in the traditional hands of the midwife did not matter. All could go to the city council or a public notary to swear an affidavit. The affidavit was a legal document, with a statement by one's parents or uncle giving the date of birth. I knew my date of birth from other family sources, but I had to obtain an affidavit. In cases in which an affidavit was not accepted, a city council could issue a new birth certificate for a few pennies.

Affidavits brought back my mother's answer and my father's narratives. Dates were arrived at by those stories, and the public notary, after listening to a story or an event, could invent a date. Even with people like me, with birth dates that were certain, affidavits connect the reality of documentation with the reality of memory. The new time can be connected with the old, as many ignore new documentation to invent changing birth dates on the basis of oral testimonies.

While combing the archives for various records in the 1980s and 1990s and during a brief stint as an administrative officer, the very first job that I had after leaving college in 1976, I must have come across over a thousand affidavits. Among this number, I must have seen hundreds of cases of a single person with different birth dates and records. None was fake, and there was no proof that the bearer was a crook. Many submitted the affidavits shortly before they rushed to the mosque for the weekly midafternoon prayer, and many others did so early on Monday morning, hours after leaving church to offer repentance in order to ask God for new favors. Many were just victims of stories and events that gave birth not to them but to dates. The story of the uncle might differ from that of the cousin, so that two new dates were possible. The outbreak of a flu epidemic could have been confused with that of a locust invasion so that dates had to be altered when the confusion was cleared up. When my father died in 1953, church records put his age at fifty-seven. He died in 1953, the very year that I was born. If his story was right, he should have died in 1950. Stories and events are not needed to confirm his death date: this is as certain as his death, recorded by the clergymen of St. James Cathedral, the church he attended and where his last rites were performed. He himself was baptized as James, but the church was named after the biblical James and not my father. The inscription on the tomb confirmed the date, as did hundreds of oral testimonies. If he was born in 1893, he should have been sixty in 1953. Perhaps the event that he narrated, which his historian son used to arrive at the date, was actually not correct. But the event was correct, as there is solid evidence to confirm it. Where could the three missing years be?

The process that created the need for birth certificates also created the need to invent dates, to alter dates, to associate events and stories with dates. Time and seasons were shifted and adjusted to accommodate dates and their documentation. Most of the events that people used, as well as the seasons in which they occurred, were real. If they took place during the nineteenth century, especially in the second half, there are actually documents to back them up or even to assign dates to major events. We know when all the kings died, when the major battles were lost and won, and when the army finally returned home. The events that gave birth to the dates could be a process, actually a long process, as in the case of the last war that Ibadan fought, which took seventeen years. The birth date that the new society demanded was one specific day, a particular day when someone came to the world. The day happened to be during an event that was a process, like the last war that Ibadan fought, a long window of seventeen years.

Seniority was valued in the older society when the events took place, and even long afterward. I knew not to disrespect those older than me, even when they were not members of my household. Within the compound, within the clan, within the village, everybody knew who was older, who died before whom, and who married after whom, all without birth certificates. Memory served them, and it served them so well that only an insane person would attempt to corrupt it.

By the time I was born, memory and money were becoming mixed. Memory and relevance were becoming altered. The multiple affidavits were not being presented to members of the village, clan, or household to challenge seniority and hierarchies, to become the elder with wisdom and responsibility. They were being presented to me, and others, as representatives of the government, as officials of the state. They were demanded by the police, who wanted to hand them over to the prison wardens, to the employers and recruiting officers, who wanted to give people jobs on the same day that they were asked about their retirement. They were being presented to those who wanted to probe into the numbers of their children and wives, cats and chickens. Those demanding the birth certificates were no different from those presenting; the officers, too, had been asked some years earlier to produce their birth certificates. If the person did not have one, the officer told him what to do, directing him to his own wife or friend who was a public notary with a typewriter and a sample letter to copy. There is no difference between the man who steals and the person who watches for him while he steals. Even if the officer knew that something was wrong with the birth certificate, he would remember his own past and his own steps and perhaps muse in his mind that a tree does not disapprove of itself because one of its branches is cut off.

The frog does not know that there are two worlds until it jumps into hot water. As Africans were being asked about birth certificates, they were moving into a different world, one in which the purposes of season and time are not always the same as their reality. My mother did not go to school, and no one needed to know when she was six years old. All that the interested parties were probably watching were her two breasts, to see when they had grown sufficiently for the parties to be thinking about her marriage. My father, who went to school, probably did not know that his age at the time of death was important information to a cathedral no longer satisfied with the information that one died young or old. The farmer in the nineteenth century stopped going to his farm when his eyes and knees gave way. In a new world, the government has appointed a timekeeper to check ages and give notice when someone is due to retire, when he has to renew some licenses, receive immunization, proceed on leave, or even die.

Those who asked for birth certificates have moved dates further away from season and time to money and opportunities. They ask the legs to show their importance by telling a man to stand on his head. They turned one single date into a commodity worth money and prestige. In 1981, shortly after I received my Ph.D., I got into the biggest trouble in my career, at least up to that time, since the years ahead are longer than those behind. A senior colleague had been elevated to the position of chairman (they added man, even when the occupant was a woman) of my Department of History at the University of Ife, Ile-Ife in Nigeria, the same school where I had completed the degree. So much was the chairman in love with me, and so sincere was he in boasting that I was the new star in the department, that he gave me his old office. He left a number of pieces of paper, some tagged to a board. Thrice I called his secretary to ask whether he had moved all his valuables, thrice I was assured that he had. I even left him a note, to which he replied that what he did not remove was worthless. Not that the pieces of paper were disturbing me, not that the various notices on the board stopped me from functioning, but the biblical Esu, mentioned below, asked me to collect all the papers and put them in one box. I did. Esu gave me other instructions, which I followed: "My son, take the box to the secretary and put it on his table." I did what Esu said. Impatient to rush to class to teach, I implemented Esu's instruction in a hurry. I walked to the secretary's office, put the box on his table, apparently on top of some "important files" he was working on, and left.

I finished the class to find the secretary waiting for me, not in my office but at the door to the classroom. As my students and I were trooping out, he was holding the box, not to give it to me but to throw it at me, to repay "an eye for an eye" the rudeness he thought I had displayed about two hours before. Sweating, agitated, and angry, he shouted:

> You were a student here before; because you are now a lecturer, you think you can become swollen headed. Who are you to put a useless box on my table? You better be careful, you rascal.

I was lost for words. I could not apologize for what Esu had asked me to do. He shoved the box against my chest, and I grabbed it with one and a half hands, as I needed the remaining half to hold my books and notes. I went to my office, not knowing what to do, not knowing what to say. My mind never told me that I was wrong. The secretary was probably right that I was swollen headed if I could not figure out my mistake. When a man thinks that he knows everything, his mother may be the only woman he can marry. I put the box in a corner, went to the office to check my mail, and walked past the secretary without the mandatory salutation. Because I did not greet him, he became even more furious and agitated. In a moment, you will discover for yourself the basis of his anger. He abandoned his task, dashed to the office of the chairman just behind his desk, opened the door without knocking, a sign of a great emergency resembling an earthquake, and complained that I had walked past him without greeting him. He added a lie, that I had rolled my eyes at him, a sign of gross disrespect. The chairman was angry. I am not one of the dead, who know about the friendship between corpses and the cemetery, but I know about power and the friendship between the chairman and the secretary. As both were men, we cannot accuse them of adultery. As the dean, rather than the chairman, controlled the bulk of the budget, I cannot accuse them of corruption. The water need not be clean to extinguish a fire. The chairman took the side of his friend, and the dirty water is ready to end the fire. Transitions can be swift, like droplets turning into rain, rain into a stream, the stream into a river, and the river into a sea: the office has become a box, the box is now an insult, an insult has become a fight.

The chairman gave me a long lecture about how my new office was a privilege, how he had told me that whatever he left behind was useless, and how I nevertheless went ahead to use such useless pieces of paper to disturb an innocent man doing his regular job, placing the box on the forms to prepare the budget, the most important forms, how I refused to apologize to the secretary when he politely told me what I had done, how by not apologizing I had ridiculed him in front of students who would now think that it was unnecessary to respect him. This is just the first part of the list. Now comes the second part, bringing an even longer list of sins. By the time his speech was over, carrying the box to the secretary's table had earned me close to forty allegations. The biblical Esu had sent me on a mission of self-destruction. I remembered, while still standing before him, that one could never sell trouble; it could only be bought. I had bought trouble from the biblical Esu. Misfortune had now fallen on my wealth, only sparing my health for the time being.

I had traveled on a path and come to a mountain. I was now about to sit down at the mountain's feet and cry. I could sob a little, get up, climb the mountain, and continue with the journey. The Yoruba Esu, whom you will meet later, intervened. Within seconds, the Yoruba Esu began to give me instructions: prostrate yourself, apologize in Yoruba, say that everything that had happened was because of the inexperience of youth, appeal to their older age and wisdom to teach you how to grow, and say that they will never see the box again. "As soon as I leave here, I will go and throw away the box." The apology was accepted, and the chairman himself asked me to throw away the box. I did.

The next day, at around five in the morning, there was a series of bangs on the door. Today in Nigeria, hearing such bangs on his door, a householder would reach for his gun, ask his wife and children to get under the bed, and panic in fear that armed robbers had descended upon his household. There were armed robbers, many already famous by then, but not at Ile-Ife where there was not much cash to take. The number of bangs was many, too many to count, but enough to wake me up. I opened the door. It was the chairman.

Where is the box?

He asked without the courtesy of salutation or apologizing for coming to the house so early. He was not a man anyone could honestly accuse of rudeness. It would not have been convenient for him to wake up that early, skipping his daily Bible reading and prayer with his family. I was not thinking when I said that the box was in my office. He was happy, thanked me, promised to pick it up two hours later when the offices opened for business. As he was about to enter his car, I beckoned to him to stop, then told him that I had thrown away the box. His face changed, his eyes turned red.

You threw away my birth certificate and affidavits of birth? You must be joking.

He drove off in a fury, speeding well beyond any normal speed limit, and this for a man who was noted for driving so slowly that people habitually joked that flies could land on his tires and play while he drove. I went back inside and put on the first shirt and trousers that I laid my hands on. I drove to the office. Now I was thinking, praying, that I could recover the box before it was removed by the cleaners. Trash was usually left in the office. The cleaners, mainly poor women without education, came very early in the morning to do their work. They were always at work, not that they were always thorough with the work, only that they were there during the hours when the contractors ordered them to report for duty. They could be fired at will if they did not show up on time, in rain or sun. Even though there was no transport to bring them from their faraway homes to the secluded campus in the jungle, they would trek miles upon miles just to show up for work. Underpaid by contractors, they saw the trash as made up of valuables to augment their income. They spent a considerable amount of time going through the trash, picking out bottles and cans that they could sell to small traders outside of the campus. The bottles were always in short supply, needed to hold palm oil, kerosene, medicine, water, and all forms of liquid. The cans were useful, as they could be melted or reshaped into bracelets, earrings, necklaces, or toys for children to play with. As to the papers, especially the newspapers, they were not to be wasted, but were sold to hawkers of peanuts and roasted corn and other edibles to use as wrapping paper. By the time the cleaner inspected the trash can, there might be nothing left to trash. One person's garbage was another's golden valuable.

The box was gone! I had not had time to think of my next move when I saw the chairman, carrying the master keys. For the first time in two days, we agreed on one thing: to come early to my office to rescue the box. I did not have to tell him that the box was gone. He could see my face; his eyes were sharp enough: the blindness that afflicted him came much later in his life and long after this incident. For the first time in forty-eight hours, we began to think alike: we needed to look for the cleaners. We moved from one office to another, covering three extensive buildings. We saw many cleaners, but not the woman we wanted. Each cleaner referred us to the next; each said that she had just seen her some two seconds before. Not knowing whether we were agents of the contractors, the university, or the government who could take jobs away from them in the twinkling of an eye, all the cleaners said something to cover their colleague. I never knew they had a guild. I never knew they had camaraderie. If anyone came looking for me, knowing well that I was probably in trouble, my colleagues would betray me rather quickly, even if that gave my enemies more evidence with which to destroy me. I was impressed. Poor people can be so helpful, so loyal to each other. Our cleaner could not be found.

The chairman was now impatient; but he was wise enough to realize that impatience alone could not ignite a fire. He was rambling on about the meetings he had to attend hours later and how busy his schedule was that day. I was quiet, dead quiet. He was rambling on about the documents. He was no longer referring to a box. Staff and teachers were arriving, one at a time; the crowd would come after 8:00 A.M. They greeted us and asked what we were doing, what had brought us together. He was older, and custom allowed him to answer while I could only greet. His answer was devastating.

Dr. Falola threw my documents away.

As he said it, he would look away from me.

Toyin threw my entire life's documents away.

Sympathy began to pour, and people began to mourn the loss of the documents. News spread. By noon, whoever said that he had not heard that I had thrown away the chairman's insurance papers, drivers' license, medical records, M.A. and Ph.D. certificates must be telling a lie. I became a bad man: the biblical Esu had achieved the great mission.

The cleaner appeared from nowhere, and she was even the first to say that she had heard we were looking for her, speaking in the most polite language, with a demeanor that reflected her lower social status. The chairman asked for the trash in my office.

I kan not knew the dustkbin for each okfice. I miksed dustkbin togeda.

Another puzzle. She had just said that there was no way for her to distinguish the collections from one office to another. She was right, as she carried a big bag along as she moved from one office to another, putting the contents of a smaller dustbin into her bigger bag. The chairman could be angry at me but not at her. He changed his style, deliberately speaking in a lower voice, cautiously, more slowly.

Madam, you need to help me. I am looking for my valuables.

The woman moved back three steps and in a raised voice said that she was not a thief. She had misread the loss of valuables as an accusation of theft.

"No, no, no. I am not saying that you stole something. Dr. Falola put my documents in the dustbin. I just want them back," the chairman said, again in a rather calm manner, as if appealing to someone superior to him.

"Won ti ko won lo gboro sir," she said in Yoruba, saying authoritatively that the trash had been taken off campus. We all knew what this meant. Petty traders had bought the papers from her. Looking for petty traders is like looking for a needle in the sea. The chairman's papers had gone, they had become valuables to wrap peanuts. If Ph.D. certificate was included, as he told those ready to listen, it would have been made out of cardboard, useful to convert into a fan to blow away hot air. His letters of employment, if they were in the box as he said, could be made into kites by kids who would try in vain to make light papers fly into the sky.

The birth certificates were gone, the affidavits were gone, all for ever. The bitterness began. As his story unfolded, he garnered more sympathy. As the story passed from one mouth to another, it was finally settled that I knew the contents of the box and had deliberately thrown them away to ruin the chairman, his exalted office, and his lifelong privileges. One person even told me that the box contained the handwritten draft of the chairman's inaugural lecture, the distillation of ideas to inaugurate the latest chair in African history. The prevailing climate at the time gave the rumor the wings to travel and a large capacity for authenticity.

The federal government, in an act of magnanimity and to find avenues to spend oil money, had made a law that allowed civil servants and university teachers to merge all the years they had worked, to add them up to arrive at a generous pension. The longer the years the bigger the pension, and many were beginning to dream of a glorious world in retirement. Many began to look for papers of previous employment, with some saying that they had started to work at the age of six, at a barber's shop, the barber that cut the white man's hair during the colonial period. If they wanted to work longer, they could age more, changing their dates of birth, all in order to collect more retirement money. The chairman had one age for his wife, another one for the school, and a different one for the baptismal record, and he probably invented yet another to benefit from what was being called the "merger of service." When he said that he did not need the box, when he asked me to throw away the box, he forgot that it contained his important documents. Perhaps he was hiding them away from his wife, a woman much younger than he. By the time he remembered, it was too late. I had lost what he needed to make money: I had thrown away his birth records, real and fake. I had thrown away the pieces of paper he had collected from previous employers to show that he had worked for them. I was responsible for his misery, the loss of fortune.

Ten years later, the same government made a law that whosoever had worked for thirty years must retire. People fell into another round of misery and shame. A professor who had worked for thirty years and more complained that he was being asked to go in his early fifties or late forties, when he still had a lot to contribute to society. Could they have obtained their Ph.D.s at the age of ten? Of those in the first and second generations who went to school, a large number started elementary school when they were well over ten years of age. By the time many of them completed their education, they had to reduce their ages in order to work long enough to enjoy pension plans. No one could determine their real ages. Within a decade, two conflicting government policies had necessitated changing ages and birth papers.

On the day the box was thrown away, my only son, Dolapo, was born.

I do not need a birth certificate for him. He was born on the day that his father threw away the documents of his chairman. You can use the event to determine his real age. I have given you the clues. Perhaps one day I will seek help to learn the date on which I threw away the box, and I expect sympathy from you. If my son protests, asking for his birth certificate, criticizing me for my carelessness for not keeping the one his mother obtained on the day of his birth, I will stay calm, musing to myself that when a lion becomes old he is a toy for little flies.

A day may be so fragmented that there can be no confusion as to time or season. A wristwatch or clock is not essential to the understanding of this fragmentation; it only serves to ornament the habits already in place. Work merges with time, time and work merge with people, all combining in elaborate greeting forms that denote boundaries of time, season, gender, occupation, and space. It is important to know who comes to the world earlier than others in order to maintain social hierarchies and the order of greeting codes. Greeting forms can easily be mastered; their violations, when voluntary, can be a deliberate act of protest. An elder who finishes his bowl of pounded yam all by himself, so goes a warning, will carry his plate by himself, as the angry youth will watch and stand by, violating the moral ethic of respect, which insists that the elder should not carry the bowl. Next to knowing the location of the mother's breast to obtain milk, the child learns how to greet.

In learning how to greet, I and others were being cleverly taught the concepts of season and time. Day and night are delineated not only by the changing sunlight but by changing greeting forms. The dry and wet seasons are marked by different greeting forms, again different from the harmattan period or when climate and weather are confusing. As events change, so too do greetings. Good laughter is generated when a novice greets someone with a new child as though she is newly married. Sadness is compounded when sympathy is offered to one who is rejoicing or joy presented to one in sorrow. A small child can be forgiven for the carelessness, but not an adult. A stranger can use in the evening the form of greeting meant for afternoon without facing sanctions. One way to know how a stranger is acculturating is through his or her understanding of the codes and language of greeting, the appropriateness of word choice, and the adequacy of response to the responses of others. Strangers provide simple but great jokes when they say "Amen" to a greeting that merely asks them a question: "How are you today?" returned with an Amen!

One wakes up in the morning to a cacophony of sounds and words, greetings to welcome one to the day, asking about the night and the sleep, the state of the body, the physical alertness to start the day. To each question, one must answer, sometimes in simple forms of "yes, thank-you." But in waking up one prays not to first see one's enemy or someone one dislikes. A house or a compound is not exclusive to a nuclear family, small in number, so small that one can count the members. A house can have a large number of occupants, a man, his many wives and children, visiting relatives, a fluid population of strangers. Tensions and conflicts are ever present, depending on how the major householder is able to manage them. If the house is free of such enemies, one may encounter them outside the house, as the first neighbor one meets. The wish is to meet a good person first thing in the morning. If a day has a tale of bad news, a legitimate question would be, "Who did you see first this morning?" If it was a good person, the bad news is attributed to another evil agency; if it was a bad person, he or she must have been responsible for ruining the day for the innocent fellow.

To be greeted in the morning and not respond is a sign of conflict. But it is a conflict among the immature. For the mature, to perform the customary morning greeting does not mean that the conflict is over, only suspended for some time. And to greet is to claim, when accused of animosity, that it is not so. "After all, I greeted you this morning. What do you mean saying that I hate you? If I hated you, I would not have said good morning." Greetings are not the same as prayers, but they may be combined, as in the common one in my household and many others: "May today bring you prosperity." If greetings bring a prayer, one says an amen, unless one is again dealing with an enemy whose prayer is intended to work in reverse, the wish from one who hides blood in the body to spit white saliva in deception. Many neutral forms exist through which one can pose a greeting as a question, to which one must answer, "Did you wake up well?" to which the response will be "yes" in an appreciative form. An affirmation is similarly common to indicate that things are well. "Good morning" is a common one.

As the society ages in time but not in wisdom, elaborate greetings become a nuisance to a small number of the new generation, mainly products of formal school systems. An economics teacher, when economics was itself a new discipline in Africa, began to calculate the amount of time that was wasted on greeting and to regard it as a form of inefficiency. The teacher obviously did not have a television in the early 1960s to show how watching a thirty-minute television program would waste more time than the equivalent of one month of greetings. The economist-teacher was a lone voice in a society that quickly turned to greetings as one of the ways to test the commitment of its youth to values, respect, and love. For an elder to walk in and not be greeted by a child is to invite trouble, so serious that some parents may even ask the child not to go to school until repentance is assured, remorse is shown. Serious spanking is taken for granted and may not be sufficient punishment for the disrespect already shown to the elder. If the elder is a visitor, the embarrassment becomes far more serious, since there is a courier to take the message elsewhere that the family is too tolerant, too loose, and so decadent that one of them does not even greet. One attraction of city life, and only in such cities as Lagos, the federal capital of Nigeria for a long time, associated with the fast life and decadence, is that it enables many of its citizens to escape greeting one another. A house in Lagos may be full of tenants, all strangers from various other cities and cultures, disobeying the rules of age and genealogy, without an elder to enforce authority, without sanctions to punish miscreants. Even then, they greet in Lagos in fast forms, in new ways that reveal their restlessness, in short answers that betray their rising cosmopolitanism. A rushed "hello" is usual, and one need not wait for an answer. One may even be exchanging greetings with a ghost in Lagos: the homeless, the strangers without addresses, may just as well be visitors from another planet.

If Lagos is having problems with greeting forms, it definitely will never cope with their full versions. All along, I have been dealing with the shorthand greetings, the most basic, the elementary ones that one can easily grasp after a little effort. One may not know how to change the tone, so that even the short greetings can communicate tension rather than friendship. But to know the words is important, and the tones may come much later.

The elaborate greetings are the cognomens, the panegyrics reserved for each individual, family, and city, the long lines that are difficult to memorize and use. My one-word short praise name is Isola. In seconds, I can teach anyone to pronounce it, although it is much harder to pronounce than Toyin, which at the very worst can be converted to a Chinese-sounding name as my colleagues at the University of Texas did when I moved to Austin in the 1990s. The pronunciation can never be part of the real problem with the name Isola, as the meaning is the real issue. Isola can be but a trick to hide my history from many, those outside the boundaries of my family. They can never fully understand me; my life in its totality is but a mystery to them. They cannot motivate me, as what they have is rather tangible, too artificial. They cannot inspire me to greatness, to show loyalty to compound and clan. They cannot reward me enough; the best they can do is to give me a university diploma, which can get me a job, one that is devoid of history. Honors may come with the degrees, but they are inadequate to move me. The university diploma does not say who I am but only what I know. When the gentleman asked my father his age, he started his answer with his cognomen, to psyche himself up. When you call me Isola, you connect me to him, to the poem whose recitation he was unable to complete.

To call me Isola is to move me quickly past the recent years, back to the nineteenth century, the beginning of time for my ancestors, and I mean the recent ones. The history of the distant ones is now hard to tell, only communicated in the archaic words that have become harder to read, decode, interpret. The older ancestors did not belong to the realm of ghosts, but the living, only that in the last years of the eighteenth century and the early nineteenth they were swept away by a hurricane of political disorder and wars. The wars of kings and chiefs had the same impact as the wars among elephants have on the grass. The kings and chiefs of different Yoruba cities failed to maintain order; within the big states such as Oyo, the power rivalry of the period was too intense. As they fought and raised deadly resources to fight, many people became victims of needless wars. Thousands within the region fled, relocating to mountains and other safe places. Thousands were chained, walked to Lagos, dumped into a ship, into a journey of no return. Some actually returned later, men like Bishop Ajayi Crowther, whose face and that of my father look so alike that one can mistake one for the other. Thousands of others were displaced to new, bigger cities such as Ogbomoso in the northern part of Yorubaland, Ibadan and Ijaye in the center.

We remember those displaced to Ibadan in the nineteenth century. As to whether they faced a serious adjustment crisis or not, I already know they did, since I profited in life by studying their experiences. As to whether they could recall their own ancestors, whom I can no longer remember, I can confirm that they did. But they did so in memory. Memory can be short; where death does not kill the man and his wisdom, old age will terminate the memory, incapacitate the brain, mangle the words. The ancestors came to life too early to be able to communicate in writing, as only their successors could write in Yoruba or English. They could have sought another medium if they had fully understood the importance of Arabic when it was introduced to them. With many of them running away from Islam in order to protect their ancient gods, it never occurred to them that they could take Arabic, together with the mullah's long beard, and avoid the preaching of the Prophet and the sayings of those who tried, in various guises, to present and interpret the message, to use the Prophet from the desert to construct a new vision for themselves and others.

The cognomen of Isola moves me to the dead, much closer to memory, opens the door to a history long forgotten, creates puzzles in language and vocabulary, and provides a daily mental exercise. When I learned to play the game of Scrabble in the 1970s, I mastered it not by memorizing English words whose meanings I cared not to know, but by simply telling myself that this was much simpler than Isola's *oriki* (poem). For one thing, I need not string the words together, just dump them thoughtlessly onto a board after calculating the points. No one ever thought that Isola's *oriki* would be written down, as it was meant to be chanted not read. No one knew that the lines would end, as it was supposed to be elongated with the passage of time. Just a few lines for you, to leave the rest for my chanters:

Isola, the scion of Agbo
He who dreams daily of wealth
He who thinks daily of the good things of life
He who looks unto the sky and says, "I can hold you if I want to"
Isola, spare the sky.

Isola, the scion of Agbo
Isola, spring to your feet
The guinea fowl flies up as free as the air
The woodpecker taps the tree with a rattling sound
Isola, heights never make the monkey lose his breath.

Isola, the scion of Agbo
The Agbo who cages the tiger
Isola, the mighty tiger
The elephant that shakes to disturb the forest
The gallant masquerade moves, the crowd shakes
Isola, do not shake, do not move
Not to terrify the strong and the cowards.

Isola, the scion of Agbo
If you shake, do not frighten me
Isola, if you move pardon me
The tiger, Isola
Isola who says he is not ready to marry

When he is ready
Girls will line the street from here to Hausaland.

We shall chant more, in life and in death.

I was in such a hurry to talk about Isola that I slighted the shorthand greeting forms. As I said, they are simple, made up of short sentences. Unlike the cognomen, one cannot be excused for not using them. If a cognomen changes with fresh additions and recitations, the regular greetings change with time and season. Except in Lagos, not too far away from Ibadan where I spent the greater part of my childhood, for someone to notice that two people did not exchange greetings and keep quiet is considered immoral. Indeed, the person who noticed that the two people did not greet and failed to report it has done more damage than the two parties. For not to greet is the first sign of trouble, an early warning sign that relations are waning. The observer can mediate, by asking the two to talk, to explain their problems, to pressure the one who refuses to talk to please state the reasons, whether trivial or substantial. Elders may be asked to mediate if the problem is bigger. Like a small fire that turns wild, ignoring the early signals of the avoidance of greetings or the use of a negative tone to communicate them may lead to more conflicts among families and could divide the compound.

The opportunities to notice problems are limitless. Within the interval of one hour, one may be greeted "E pele o" more than a hundred times by a hundred people. "E pele" for someone older in age or the mere "Pele" for one's peers and juniors is not bound by season or time; it neither affirms nor negates time and season. Its fluidity is broad, its application is limitless. You have to say Pele to me if I sneeze, cough, hit my toe against a rock, or get bitten by an insect. If the insect is a mosquito and I unsuccessfully seek revenge, you have to greet me twice, once when the mosquito bites me, to sympathize, and yet again when I make my short drive to "bite" the mosquito in return, to use my toe to mangle its small body into pieces and see the blood in me being wasted. You have to say Pele when I am sad, angry, moody, depressed, lonely, and dealing with my mind in ways that I am unable to reveal. When I am happy, you still have to say Pele to accommodate my temporary elation, the effectiveness of the caffeine that the kola nut has released into my system. When you knock on my door to check that I am home, Pele replaces the doorbell; when you do see me, Pele is an appropriate sign of friendliness. If you think you are talking to me and I am not paying sufficient attention, say Pele, which is far more polite and friendly than "Excuse me." For each Pele that comes my way, I must always answer, thanking you for greeting me. I can return your Pele for Pele. One Pele does not cancel another, only creating a rhythm that may be danceable with bells and gongs.

About an hour away from my city is Oyo, one with greater claim to history and culture. But this is not the Oyo that many know as the metropole of that empire of genius, the Oyo that spread so fast and vast. Its king, the Alafin, was so powerful that modern military dictators such as General Sanni Abacha, who came much later to rule the much bigger kingdom of Nigeria, would envy him. The Oyo add "Eku, eku" to their Pele. Like Pele, one cannot stand on a street corner of Oyo without hearing Eku many times. It actually sounds better than Pele, and I traveled to Oyo one afternoon in the 1990s just to hear it. I was happy, and on the return journey to Ibadan I turned off my radio just to be repeating Eku. I could not have been the only one impressed by the sound and the word. In faraway Sierra Leone and Liberia, and further away still in the Americas, those who were more impressed than me did not call the Yoruba, my nation, clan, and group, the Yoruba, but the Eku or Aku. They were smart to have adopted this name, and I could have suggested Pele as well. Thus the Eku people have turned a greeting form into a name, a collective identity outside of their homeland.

The Eku country and its people do not, however, see Eku and Pele as enough. How can it be? Daily activities are so many that Pele does not fit all. Whatever the work I am doing, any activity denoted as work must at least earn me a short reward of " E ku ise," which the people with some contact with English have translated as "Well done!" E ku ise is not commending you, as in "Well done," for it is only celebrating the process of work itself, your endurance, your ability to choose work over laziness, your desire to overcome poverty by refusing to toy with work, the morality of not opting for a life of robbery, as one who can work but does not can be called a thief.

E ku ise's tone can be altered, using the same words to criticize: meaning that the process is in trouble, that laziness is overtaking the mind and body, that the end product is not impressive, that one is paying too much attention to the work itself, that one has been misled into thinking that aggressiveness leads to riches, that the path of slavery is glorious. The perfect E ku ise tone is the one that celebrates the end of a task, the literal "Well done" translation, that commends one for accepting the reality that work does not look for workers but it is workers who look for work, that one may start late but hard work may cheat time, and that it is better to die while working than to die when indolent.

E ku ise is too generic, connected to all work. An occupation can be well defined as its greeting form. One may not know how to greet a professor, an engineer, or a medical doctor, as these occupations are too new to have evolved their specific stamps. Older occupations come with their own symbols, codes, and greetings. E ku ise is not enough for a hunter, for all the troubles he has endured by looking for game, for the ability and luck to survive the snakes, for the failure to come home with any game, on a day when the animals are much smarter than he is. Neither is E ku ise adequate to praise the palm wine tapper who climbs a tall palm tree with a mere rope. On reaching the top to collect the gourd with the juice already secreted into it, he is met by deadly bees. Avoiding the bees, quickly descending the tree, he finds a python waiting for him, challenging him to a fight, pushing out its tongue ready to dart and discharge the killer venom. The palm wine tapper needs to save his life. Should he drop the gourd, he has nothing to sell to make money for the day. He clings to the rope and gourd, but there is no third hand to hold the ax. Then he remembers that he can use magic, but in panic he forgets the incantations. Before reaching the snake, he jumps, clever enough not to lose everything. The gourd breaks, the snake disappears.

No one needs to tell me that E ku ise is not enough for this tapper or for others who toil in other occupations. Before the end of my first decade, I knew how to greet a tapper, a hunter, and a farmer, as one was regarded as uncultured for confusing them. A few years later, to be uncultured in the new circle of urbanites was to hold a fork with the right hand—the mechanics of moving food from the table to the throat became more important than moving the yam from the forest to the home. I was cultured in both. In any case, I respected the sanctions that came with confusing occupational greetings, and I was a master of them, dropping E ku ise and Pele for the more specific and more dignified lines for each person, such as greeting a trader arriving home after a long day as E ku Oja (Welcome from the market) differently from the trader when at work as E ku tita (Happy sales), E o ta bi? (Are you able to sell?) or more commonly Aje yio wo igba o (May money come your way today). To our dear tapper, still nursing his wounds, cursing the snakes and the bees, wondering why the bees cannot sting the snake or the snakes swallow the bees, I know that I have to say Igba a ro o (May the climbing rope show greater flexibility).

I mastered the seasons and time quickly, again thanks to greeting forms. When the sun rises, the greeting forms for the morning have to be dropped, replaced with those for midday and the afternoon, which in turn give way to those for the evenings and nights. If someone is not about to sleep, one does not use the form for night itself. To be ready to sleep is to be ready to receive greetings in the form of prayers rather than statements, appealing to the spirit not to interfere too dangerously in dreams and for the person to wake up. Of course, quite a number never woke up when I was growing up, people who made the quiet transition from sleep to death without the courtesy of saying farewell, without notice, without warning. Rain and showers, cold air, hot weather, famine, food shortage, all bring out their own forms, their own specificity.

Through greetings, I received my first lessons in geography, the brilliant use of space, time, weather, and events to teach. Greetings were my first lesson in values, the appropriateness of each to denote respect and social hierarchies: the child who is not afraid of anyone will develop bad manners, the manners that can endure for long and follow one to the grave. With the corpse and bad manners wrapped together, the soul is in trouble, deciding whether to wander back to the world, sneaking out of the grave. Should it sneak back, it may enter the womb of a pregnant woman, the unfortunate one receiving a bad soul with bad manners, to bring to the world yet another bad person. Or the soul could decide not to torment the innocent pregnant woman and choose to mix with the air and stay in the sky, reflecting on what to do next.

As I cross space in time, changing the seasons as I travel, moving to Lagos, and from the airport there, the only "international" one that services Western Nigeria, my part of the country, to other lands, near and far, separated by the sea and sky, I begin to interact with those who do not know how to greet, whose vocabulary is handicapped. Slowly, painfully, I learn not to say Pele and Eku, not to greet the cashier at the department store, not to exchange smiles with the technician, not to laugh loudly in seminars. My vocabulary, too, begins to shrink, my face begins to look sterner, my neck is less flexible, as it no longer needs to turn the head to look at the palm wine tapper about to fall. When people greet me, I thank them, and they wonder why they deserve the gratitude. A Pele can no longer be returned for another Pele.

Birthdays and greetings are united in names. Names capture time and season. Season and time give birth to names. Names evoke cognomens. The unity should be clear to see. My names embody the unity of time and season. To my maternal grandmother, I am Abiodun, someone born during a major holiday. Anyone could give me a name, and I collected seventeen of them, all now in disuse, a few being activated now and then. To my paternal grandfather, I am Isola, but he was definitely not the one who gave me this, as he would not have had the authority and right to do so. He only chose to use my praise name in order for him to be able to open the window into history anytime he chose. And by my parents, more likely my father than my mother, I was given a major name that referred to the Supreme God, Olorun.

God is not new, but Olorun has a new history. When the missionaries came among the Yoruba, with Yoruba agents active in the process, the Bible was translated into the Yoruba language. This was a major challenge, as the translators were searching for equivalencies. Some gods were unlucky in the process; they could not enter the Bible since the disciples in the New Testament and the prophets in the Old Testament were human beings with real names that could be converted by merely adding additional letters to make them meaningful. David becomes Dafidi and Solomon becomes Solomoni, easy enough to follow. One god was particularly unlucky, the respected gatekeeper to heaven, the king of the crossroads, Esu, the chief, the rebel was retained in the Bible as Satan. Esu can never mean the biblical Satan—their homelands and power are far different. As Esu got into the Bible and spread with Christianity, the old Esu suffered in the process, with his name soiled and damaged, destroyed for ever. The Supreme Being is luckier than His subordinate officer, Esu. The Yoruba used to call Him Olodumare, and one of His attributes is to define His abode as the sky, Olu Orun, the king who lives in the heaven. With so-called pagans clinging to the use of Olodumare, Olorun creeps into the Bible as the translation for God, no longer the homeless spirit, but now identifiable in the sky. Then, there were no airplanes, so no one could conceive the possibility of reaching Him if only to seek a favor or to check if He had relocated elsewhere.

Thus I am linked to God, the biblical one as well as the Yoruba Being whose abode is the large and unreachable sky. Olorun cannot be a full name by itself. Something has to follow, to indicate His bigness, invincibility, immortality, and power. It could be Olorunmbe (God exists), as if to remind the community each morning to be on the lookout for God. It could be Olorunbusola (God amplifies my status) to announce the abundance to the family made possible by God, although they are not ready to share it with others. The possibilities are limitless and may include gratitude to God, His attributes of compassion, forgiveness, the giver of fortunes, wealth, long life, and work.

My name is simple and ambiguous: Oloruntoyin (God is enough to praise). The ambiguity is not in the name itself, but in the motives of the name giver. It is an affirmative statement that does not create opportunities for debate; one can praise God without even believing in His existence. Motives are not permanent; they change with time and season. The earliest version of the story I heard, when I posed the question as to why I had been given the name, was that it took a while for my mother to have me after several years of marriage without a child. Since she herself was the only child of her mother, the long wait was troubling, the uncertainty worrisome. When I came, the sky God needed special praise. My mother married rather young, and I never understood the rush for a child. Later on, in the 1980s, I did. The expectation after marriage was that a woman should be pregnant within the first few months. Not to be pregnant was to create panic about her possible infertility, the sin of bringing an unproductive woman to the household. Childlessness was regarded as a curse. As a curse, it afflicted mainly women, since the man could find various tricks to solve his own problem. As my mother lacked the power to impose a name on me, it could be that she influenced my father to choose it. When I asked others what my father told them, it was that I came to the world after he had survived an illness. In a period of ten years, the reasons and motives multiplied, changing from one person to another. One day, when I began to talk and disturb others, creating a nuisance for adults, I was told that the motive for the name was to thank God that I came to the world so as not to cause too much trouble in heaven. One day, I may, but for now I only cause trouble on earth. The very first trouble I caused was to remove Olorun from my name, except when I am forced to fill out forms that will move me to and from time and season, and from and to stories and events, testimonies and affidavits, birthdays and dates of birth.

CHAPTER TWO : : : BLOOD & MOUTH

ust as I have a praise poem, my city also has its own. Not just my city, all Yoruba cities have their pane-gyrics, the *oriki orile*. No one knows who composed them; no one is interested in their authorship but only in their rendition. A city poem is collective prop-erty, to be recited by anyone who cares. When I used some lines from the poem for one of the cities in a manuscript, a publisher asked me to obtain permission from the author who holds the copyright. "From whom?" I asked the editor.

From the author and publishers; you know we cannot use more than two lines without permission.

I was cooperative, reminding myself as we spoke on the phone that who-ever attempts to catch a cricket must move slowly and that even fools do not try to eat chicken before it is cooked.

"Sure," I said, "but kindly give me the address so that I can contact the author and the publisher." I thanked her and left things to time. Three days later she called back, saying that she was told that many searches had yielded no positive results. I was amused, asking myself what voids and blankness the search engines must have been revealing and when technology begins to disappoint those who have been clever enough to reach the moon. It was time for me to give a lecture, now speaking like the patient dog enjoying the fattest bone after the fellow dogs, so much in a hurry to eat, had run away with the small bones with little meat. Whoever claims to be an author of the ancient poems for cities must be a thief, just like the modern scholar who wants to receive credit as the source of proverbs that were recited before his grandfather was born. His father told him a proverb, he went to school to learn En-glish, he translated his father's poem into English, and the rogue now wants us to cite him. Where is the father to witness the rogue he gave birth to? We cannot blame the bad son who has gone to school to learn strange notions of property and theft from the intellectual agents of imperialism.

By the time I was six, I could recite Ibadan's poem, fascinated most by the first two lines, which celebrate the wild fruits the people enjoy, and their creativity in using snail shells as cups with which to drink corn porridge. It was not until much later that I took an interest in other lines, some of which have appeared in print, translated by "sons of the soil" and their admirers from faraway lands. Let me use one credited to a visitor whose name no one can tell me since I have began my inquiries after I was asked to memorize and recite it in a play. Perhaps the visitor was a missionary in one of the early churches or one of those scholars in the only university in the city. Or the visitor could even be a way to accord agency and power to a "son of the soil" who mastered the white man's language and put it to a good use, if only once.

> Ibadan!
> The spirit of the rock protects the town.
> Ibadan, don't fight!
> We must ask for permission before we enter the town;
> Because this is the town in which the thief is innocent.
> And the owner of property is guilty.
> Here peace is lying exhausted on the ground
> And belligerence dances on its back.
> Ibadan, the town where the owner of the land
> Does not prosper like the stranger.
> Nobody is born without some kind of disease in his body.
> Riots in all compounds are the disease of Ibadan
> You may look at this town whichever way you wish
> You will see nothing but war.

"Nothing but war!" Yes. An oríkì is a distillation of history, the compression of multiple events into lines that summarize the character of a city. When Nigeria obtained its independence in 1960, it inaugurated a First Republic with civilians in power. The order and stability of those days now appear like a fairy tale, compared to what followed when soldiers replaced the civilians. The republic fell within five years. Ibadan was at the center of the politics that led to its failure, assuming the fearsome character of the "Wild Wild West." When the Civil War that almost ended Nigeria began in 1967, the intellectual leaders of the secessionist movement plotted some of their moves in Ibadan. All the major challenges to modern authoritarian rule in Nigeria must have the stamp of Ibadan before they can become serious matters. The careful person knows to heed the warning, to "ask for permission before entering the town."

The poem was not composed after 1960. By then, it was over a hundred years old. Ibadan was just acting out its manners. The poem is no longer about the summarizing of a past long gone but about the future still unfolding. The city can no longer be gentle, the rocks cannot be moved, the thieves must come, claim their innocence, leaving the property owner feeling condemned.

Peace lies exhausted on the ground, and as people step on it they drive it further underground. Peace fights back, attempting to resurface, but a multitude of bodies with iron legs hits back, as if in stampede. To know about the soil, you must speak with a squirrel. If telling you about Ibadan requires my becoming a squirrel, I am ready. Each year, the British ordered that a celebration must be held to worship their queen. Offices and schools were closed; students were forced into long practices and rehearsals. On the day, the big day that they had been prepared to expect, they all trooped to a stadium to perform, sing, display gymnastic skills, and affirm their loyalty to the queen. In the late 1950s, I paid my dues, saluting the queen, whom only a few people had seen even in a photograph. Then came the country's independence, and the worship of the queen was converted to the worship of Nigeria.

Reciting the national anthem was part of the school rituals, and everybody knew the first stanza until they decided to change everything in the 1970s when the brain had lost its sharpness for storing fresh lines. People not only knew the old anthem but mocked it as well, changing "Nigeria we hail thee," the first line, to "Nigeria we hate thee." I could sing both, the real and the fake, with the same rhythm and deep commitment.

So I sang both in October 1963, the real one at the stadium for official reasons and the fake one as part of the joy of the long walk back home. I am sure, absolutely sure, that what we all enjoyed were not the events themselves. The practices before were too much of a punishment, the marching was chaotic, frustrating the teachers who had to arrange boys and girls by height, choosing those who were amenable to a mediocre military practice. Walking many miles to the stadium and locating the collection points for each school was an ordeal for the students and their teachers. The sun was harsh, biting the students and their teachers as they waited for long hours for the event to start, for the governor and his commissioners to show up. By the time it was over, the release from the stadium was like opening a prison house. We all rushed out, changing the songs, the tunes, and the plays. Teachers and students parted ways. We all regrouped into our comfortable smaller friendship circles, leaving behind the larger union with its schedule and syllabus.

It was time to look upon Ibadan, and whichever way we looked the anonymous poet warned us to expect a war. Three boys began to play, all now men still alive. They traveled home, in the same direction. A small argument ensued, each boy making a separate point for a total of three. Nobody had warned them about what to expect on the streets of Ibadan. Perhaps no one ever told them that a marriage tree can be killed by its own fruits. The argument was now turning bigger, no more three separate points by three small boys, but two points made by two opposing forces. Toyin and Philip on the one hand, in alliance with their point, and Yusuf on the other. There should never have been such serious issues for ten year olds to argue over, but they found them. A fight ensued; Toyin looked on expecting Philip to win. In a rush for a knockout, Philip retreated, picked up the first rock he saw and threw it at Yusuf. The effect was immediate, with blood all over Yusuf's face and his shirt, some dripping on the ground. The fight was over. Adults spanked Toyin and Philip. Not knowing that our house was many miles away, they asked us to rush home and for Yusuf to go and treat his wound. No one spoke. Yusuf was holding onto a part of his head to stop further bleeding. As we moved nearer home, after a long walk of over an hour, we all parted ways. The event was over.

I was reporting the success of the day's celebration, with the usual embellishments, when Yusuf and his parents arrived, angry and cursing me, my family, and ancestors. Yusuf's mother grabbed me, hit me violently, threatened to kill me. She was overpowered. She was crying, I was looking. It took another person to announce that Yusuf had lost his eye. The left eye was damaged beyond repair. The rock had hit it so badly that the chances of recovery were gone by the time the damage was reported.

Yusuf had done me a favor. When they asked him who did it, he mentioned Philip. They only came to our house because they did not know where Philip lived. Ashamed by the encounter, my clan held a short meeting and decided that Yusuf's parents should take me with them to determine any appropriate punishment and the revenge most satisfactory to them. They did not give me up for adoption; they gave me up for execution. This is Ibadan's idea of instant justice. A hundred years before, I could have been marched to one of the altars of the gods for an appropriate sacrifice, my blood shed both as revenge and as a prayer to the gods to spare the eyes of others in Yusuf's family. Two hundred years before then, Yusuf's parents could have sold me into slavery, on that very night in one of the private slave marts, the first stage in a long journey to Brazil or South Carolina.

I never knew what was going on in the mind of Yusuf's mother. Miserable Yusuf could not have been thinking about anything other than pain. I knew what was going on with me, not with my mind but with my body. It was the first major beating of my life, with blows coming from all directions, from various people. I saw blood, but I had no hands or towels to wipe it away. After a while, I stopped thinking, as my brain had left my skull. A drowning man in the sea would clutch anything to survive, even a serpent or a hungry whale. I held on to my enemies, and another enemy would pounce on me. I held on to Yusuf, but there was no help. I was dead, the first time that I would die. Jesus Christ is not the only one who was resurrected after death, he is only the most holy. I was not an intermediary between God and humankind, and my resurrection was not important for divine purposes.

I saw the stars and the angels, but was too dead to describe them. My resurrection was made possible by Yusuf's mother. She revived me before I could be buried. Not that she loved me; even if she had read the Bible with her Quran, there was no passage that would have convinced her to forgive me. A bee with honey in its mouth has a sting in the tail. Yusuf's mom gave me the honey in order to use the sting. The person she wanted to kill was Philip. I was useful to her alive, as a guide to Philip's house, as evidence to prove that Philip should die.

Yusuf had told his parents that he did not know where Philip lived. Yusuf became the first camel to pull the caravan, but it is the last camel that gets the beating so as to drive the caravan. A cow learns not to be at the back of the herd if it does not want to get the strokes that force the other cows to move. I am no longer the squirrel telling you about soil, but the cow at the end of the herd, the last camel to be flogged so that the caravan will move forward. Yusuf knew where Philip's house was but told a lie. Later in life I asked him many times, too many times to count, why he did so. He gave me the same answer over and over again: he did not know. When I told him that he must have led his parents to our house because he thought that since I did not throw the rock they would spare me, he will always say that he did not know. When I insisted that he was trying to protect Philip, his answer was the same. When the three of us meet, and we have met too often, I will joke that it was because he was afraid of Philip that he refused to disclose that he knew the location of Philip's house. As if provoked, he would look for a rock to show that he, too, could throw one.

If Yusuf actually had time to think about his answers in 1963, I was unable to. Like a walking corpse, I led Yusuf's party to Philip's house, some two miles away. A pocket with one coin does not make any noise. The pocket of Yusuf's mom was full of coins making too much noise. The news of a young boy losing an eye, about to start a lifetime career of begging, the only job available to the blind, was like honey that catches more flies than vinegar. The news had traveled, from one house to another, on street corners. By the time we reached Philip's house, the entire membership had congregated outside. Philip himself had disappeared. This was the first real magic I saw in life; previous examples had all been fake. It was after the dust had settled that Philip revealed the secret: he ran to the raft, a sort of attic. He must have learned the trick from a lizard, for there was no ladder to reach the raft. It could not be reached from outside the house. Within the house, one would have to climb onto a tall person to touch the raft. Even if it were possible to get to the raft, only a brilliant mind could conceive the idea of hiding there, keeping company with rats and roaches, mice and snakes.

The anger displayed at my place was small compared to what followed here. It was an open fight, but Philip's family could not hit back. They wanted to deliver Philip, but he was nowhere to be found. It was in the midst of the commotion that someone suggested that they should take Yusuf to the hospital, which they did. Not that Yusuf's parents were stupid, but their anger had not allowed them to even think about this. The hospital was left to deal with the wound. The eye was gone, never to come back.

This was not my first encounter with a fight, not the last either. It was the most dramatic, the most memorable. The poet already warned us:

Nobody is born without some kind of disease in his body.
Riots in all compounds is the disease of Ibadan.

The poet was not describing the riot that broke out in Philip's house. He was long dead and did not observe it. He was talking about the nineteenth century. Street fights were so common in Ibadan then that an observer remarked that it was considered unmanly to go a day without a fight. Young men saw knives and charms as part of the routine of dressing. Samuel Johnson, a patriotic Yoruba in spite of his two English names, lived in Ibadan during the nineteenth century. He loved Ibadan so much that he thanked God for creating the city, although he was a son of another one. He was the first to document the extensive street fighting in Ibadan, the passion for wars, the demonstration of courage at the slightest opportunity.

The chiefs, too, could be tough, not shy about inviting a rival to a fight, an open duel if possible. One prominent chief, starting as a mere private in the army, rose to become the general and commander in chief some years later through sheer bravery. Even as a private, he was known to have provoked his most senior superior to a duel. He would climb a tree, like a monkey, to add to his short height and gain attention. Below the tree was a drummer singing his praise name.

> Ogunmola, the brave
> He who does not know him is yet to meet him
> He who has met him does not know him.

> Ogunmola, the brave
> Ogunmola, of a civil fight he shall die
> Die for sure, sure, sure.

> Ogunmola the brave
> He keeps kegs of powder a rolling, rolling, rolling
> With a jackknife in hand he is looking heavenward steadily, steadily,
>   steadily.

Ogunmola was tempting death, "looking heavenward steadily," but he was lucky. A large number not only looked at heaven but reached there, unable to use their jackknives and kegs of powder to save their lives, to muster enough followers to fight their wars.

Knives and guns defined Ibadan's modernity during the nineteenth century. Always a step ahead, the city-state redefined the meanings of tradition, the boundaries of space, the character of individuals. Yoruba cities before Ibadan had grown over a long period of time, most of them for many centuries. Their founders and early kings had become mythical heroes, some even worshiped each year as gods for the protection of the cities. The cities before Ibadan had paid much attention to the power of kings, the influence of chiefs and nobility, the wisdom of diviners, and the generosity of the wealthy. Not to disturb social and political hierarchies, events could move slowly, individuals could settle into a life of routines.

Ibadan first modernized itself before settling for traditions. During the twentieth century, the plea to Africans, if they wanted to enjoy life and alienation as westerners, was to abandon tradition and rush to modernity. The chiefs of Ibadan, now long buried in their graves, would be laughing at the suggestion. As they were about to move to the post-modern, the British came to force them to abandon modernity. Ibadan was not planning on tradition, it was the British who forced them. Ibadan did not even want a king with a crown, like other Yoruba cities and kingdoms, with the powerful half man half god idling away at the palace with his harem. The British encouraged Ibadan to replace a warrior with a gentle king.

Knives and guns moved Ibadan into the modern era in the snap of a finger necessary to stab and see blood. The Yoruba were adept at wars;

indeed, they fought many wars to build and expand many of their king-doms. Gentle wars, quick handshakes with enemies, exchanges of jokes at parleys, small tributes as tokens of surrender. When it was Ibadan's turn to fight, it was like Yusuf's mom, with intensity and fury beating the enemy so badly that he had to die and be resurrected within the same hour. When my ancestor was going to a war in 1860, the bard sang his poem in praise and as a stern warning.

> My Lord is going to the field of the heartless,
> I said the field of the heartless, o! o! o!
> Listen, my Lord is about to move to the field of the heartless,
> Where the parent of two will be left with but one,
> Where the parent of one will be left all forlorn,
> Let him whose mother forbids him to go return from following my
>   master,
> Let him whose father forbids him to go return from following my
>   master,
> My master, my Lord, the King of the camps.
> Let him whose betrothed is of age to be wed return from following
>   my Lord,
> The Lion of the Master of camps.

Is this not a sufficient warning? War was no cocktail party. Ibadan fought to win, not to negotiate. This was the major business in town, where the chiefs and generals made their money. Young boys did not want to spend their entire lives on the farms, waiting slowly for yams and okra to grow. The poems reveal the stress on knives and guns, courage and endurance. The praise is not about wisdom and aging slowly, as with other cities steeped in tradition. As my ancestors fought, they built one of the largest empires in Africa, turning Ibadan into a flourishing metropole. The Ibadan empire redefined the notion of citizens and sub-jects, of colonies and metropoles. The chiefs at Ibadan had worked hard to attain their glory, and the colonies must do their share by maintaining Ibadan's glory, ensuring that the chief would not be provoked into rest-lessness. Goats and chickens, with oil to roast them, must be constantly supplied for supper, palm wine for entertainment, women for relax-ation. The chiefs envied the gods and began to demand sacrifices. Even the peace that followed Ibadan's victory was turbulent. As the army marched back to the city, the poet warned the victims.

> It is true that the war with Ibadan has ended, but its aftermath—
> hatred—remains like the seed of tobacco in the hearts of men.

Philip threw the rock; Yusuf's mom dealt the blows; Philip ran to the raft. History is now becoming poetry. When the orange tree at the back of your house begins to produce bitter grapes, it is not enough to pluck all the fruits. Cut the tree, uproot the stump. To the colonies, Ibadan became the orange tree with the bitter fruits. It took time, but it happened: formidable alliances emerged, and a war broke out in 1878. Strong wars, fierce battles, difficult peace negotiations. My father believed that he was born on the day the wars ended, as a son produced by one of the war generals.

The genes were passed on to me, the genes of war, of restlessness. Like Ibadan, I can be impatient, thinking that it is better to resolve a conflict by war sooner than later. Diplomacy is more costly, such a waste of time. Peace is an illusion, the message of imams and pastors massaging your ego so that the tithe and offerings can be bigger. Fear has no meaning in my world. Depression is strange: pimples attack the faces only of the gentle, stress the minds of the restful and lazy. Once I know the conclusion of an argument, I want to rush there to contest it, and we can use the process to complicate the conclusion, rather than the conclusion to eulogize the process. Intrigue does not bother me, as I once told my colleagues at Ile-Ife in the 1980s. Intrigue actually inspires me, moving me not to seek alliances and words but to check the knives in my pouch, the bullets in my gun, and the charms in my pocket. I never respond to gossip, as I see it as a sign of weakness. Like Ogunmola climbing a tree with his drummer boasting below, I dismiss gossip as the pastime of the idle and the weak who cannot confront Isola, the tiger. I only need to shake! As I shake, I have pity on those who want to fight me, who want to gossip. Empty sacks who cannot stand upright, they bend too many times before Isola, whose body, hardened with the genes of battle and war, fears no rain of words, the only weapon of intrigue. Isola and Ibadan are connected, not as twins but as history.

Ibadan was never at war with itself. Yusuf did not fight Philip; Yusuf did not pounce on me. He even said that he did not know where Philip lived, and when he was forced to lead the way he went to the house of the innocent. I have never been at war with myself. Ibadan did not believe in alliances in the process of forming its huge empire; it could have saved the empire by adopting a strategy of alliance and diplomacy, but it refused. Isola never forms alliances, buying people to fight his battles. Never. The gene is in him, and as Isola walks behind Ibadan he becomes like animals who, by walking behind an elephant, avoid being drenched in dew.

The street fights that fascinated Samuel Johnson, the pastor, the pioneer agent who wanted to turn the war empire of Ibadan into a new Christian kingdom, were preparations for wars and greater glories. Constantly at war with others, the individual needed to be battle ready. Ibadan started as a war camp in the 1820s. As many settled to a life of farming, others began to practice for war, initially to revenge the sack of their older cities, which had turned them into refugees. Then they discovered that they could build a bigger city, and they did. Then they realized that seeking revenge was a small reward, and they sought a bigger trophy: an empire. The cities and kingdoms before Ibadan did not have boys like this. They built armies only when they needed them, when a war chief begged for recruits. As soon as a war was over, the war chief would disband his boys, who were forced to return to a dull life of farming. Ibadan abandoned tradition yet again. Recruits could be obtained from the colonies, trained rapidly for combat. At Ibadan itself, soldiers could be promised a lifetime job, trained to fight, retained to fight, used for conflicts. As they practiced and fought, the serious ones were promoted with firm assurances that privileges would come. The rewards in ego, money, and captives were immense. The boys who carried knives about in the city made it possible to build an empire.

In making the empire possible, they sought entitlements and rewards. It was their knives and kegs of gunpowder that turned a war camp into an empire. One of these boys was taking a casual walk one afternoon and came across a freshly killed antelope. He saw the bullet; as a soldier he knew that the antelope did not die by accident. Soldiers did not shoot antelopes; only hunters wasted their bullets in this way. He carried the antelope away, stealing it. To steal was bad enough; for a soldier to steal was to tarnish his honor significantly. He arrived home with the stolen antelope. People knew he had stolen it. As they were spreading the news about a brave soldier now a thief, he was butchering the antelope. As many were thinking about what would happen to the thief, he was roasting the antelope. As his neighbors were leaking the news to the chiefs and judges, he ordered palm wine and called for a small banquet. It was a great party, a good meal, interrupted by city guards who came to announce that the chiefs-in-council wanted to see him. "The chiefs-in-council!" he screamed. He sensed trouble, and he needed to think fast, at the speed of light. If he miscalculated, he would become like the prince who grew too big for his underwear and had to dance naked.

"All the leading chiefs were called to an emergency meeting because of an antelope?" He spoke as if asking a question. "Well, then, give me a moment to change." When the chiefs send for you, better run, as the longer they wait the angrier they become. He knew not to keep the chiefs waiting. He was still in his house, but he was wise enough to know that one should not spend an entire evening in a house where one is forbidden from staying the night.

There was no need to waste time. He only changed into his uniform, the attire of war. It was a heavy jacket soaked in blood, with many pockets full of charms. As he moved out, he refused to follow the guards. Rather he mounted his horse and raced. The guards had been bitten, twice within five minutes. They had allowed him to change his attire when he should have been arrested on the spot and delivered to the chiefs as he panicked, like a rat who ran into a cat. The guards had been robbed of the glory of delivering their captive to the chiefs. The guards could not boast of the difficulty of their mission, the hardship they had encountered in arresting a difficult omo ogun (war boy), the name they gave to him and his peers. As the horse ran, the guards ran after the man on the horse's back, praying that they could pull him down, set the horse free, and carry their prisoner. The horse ran faster, the guards were tired, but they continued to run, even if slowly.

"Was he planning an escape, an exile?" wondered one of them. They probably thought so. Those in trouble at Ibadan, including even chiefs, had sought exile when in trouble. Modern Ibadan even encouraged voluntary exile. It was offered even to their prominent chiefs. Should they refuse, the other chiefs would order the public to loot their compounds. When the compounds became empty of beds and chairs, of food and clothes, of goats and sheep, they could set them on fire. Then exile would follow, and the next words that would trickle in would be those of suicide.

"He must have escaped in the direction of Ijebu," concluded one of the guards, to the region south of Ibadan, the area outside of Ibadan's control. The guards were probably thinking about how to present the escape, what lies would cover their carelessness. Their story was already formulated, a leader appointed to narrate it, others to take the questions.

The "war boy" did not escape. He arrived at the meeting of the chiefs-in-council before the guards did. The chiefs were more than impressed; as their guards walked in, they looked at them with contempt. The basorun (the boss of all the chiefs) asked three of the guards to bend down to form a bench, and he ordered the war boy to use the human bench as a seat. Exerting the power of his full weight, the war boy sat on the comfortable chair; the guards were now like a dead man arranging his own funeral.

"You have been accused of stealing an antelope." The basorun read the offense, pointing to the angry hunter who came up with the charges. Only diplomats tell lies, cowards whose only weapons are words. An Ibadan warrior would find it undignified to cover a mistake with a lie. The war boy said that he had taken the antelope. He thanked the hunter for killing it, but could not imagine why a cat who has successfully chased a dog should now see himself as a tiger. He chastised the hunter for wasting the bullet on an antelope when he could have used it to kill a man of his age, reducing the number of Ibadan's enemies and carrying the fresh skull of the dead man to the city for all to see. If the hunter was afraid of a fellow man, the war boy did not know why he killed the antelope as if he were afraid of the animal. He faced the hunter, pointing a finger at him, looking at him with scorn, and said, "Why not run after the antelope, capture him alive, bring him to the city to let goats and sheep mock him before slaughtering it?" The war boy was changing the story, making new wheels, spinning the story from theft to bravery. He praised himself, reminded the chiefs of his contribution to the city, and made a closing remark.

> What is an antelope to me? I have carried corpses and wounded soldiers from battles. If I can carry a dead soldier without permission, why should I spare the antelope, an ordinary animal?

All the chiefs were impressed. The basorun paid the hunter for his animal and asked the war boy to go home and finish his meal, to continue with his party.

My city did not punish bravery but cowardice. Occupations that moved toward courage and bravery received more respect and stature. The hunter had respect because he could fight; the war boy was just telling him to kill men instead of game. After all, whosoever is not happy with the position of the moon can make a long ladder, climb it, and move the moon around. The war boy was telling the hunter to move up the courage ladder. The hunter was more important than the farmer. The hunter would argue that anybody could fight, but how many could wait for a lion in the jungle, for a long duel between man and beast? To the war chiefs, merchants and traders were important for profits, part of which they must relinquish as gifts and taxes. When a successful merchant who was the most prominent woman in the city during the nineteenth century was becoming too mean for their liking, they set the mob on her.

All good dancers dread only one moment: no matter how good they are, they have to yield the floor to others on the day when better dancers emerge. Warriors and their war boys are like the ripe fruits that can never hang on a tree for too long. As they ripen, they rot. It was on the day that my father was born that my city, too, was reborn. It was reborn into tradition, losing its modernity. Rather than becoming postmodern, it regressed into the neotraditional. The wars came to an end. It was clear that my father would not become a soldier, except in the colonial army or police. Only those without status, courage, and identity chose the colonial army and police created by the British to impose their power and majesty. It was much later, after the country had become independent, that military officers realized that they could use their guns to stage coups and stay in power. It was only then that men of status and education regretted their decision to go to school, to become doctors and professors instead of joining the army to become state governors and diplomats who drive around the city in a convoy of cars with sirens to disturb all, to announce the presence of power.

As to my father's father, he and his generation and the thousands of war boys actually believed that wars would still come. They had to conclude the wars that came to a stalemate and fight to regain the colonies that were lost because of an unnecessary peace settlement. The belief became a dream. They created as much tension as was possible so that the British would leave; they even antagonized the pioneer colonial officers, provoking them into riots and conflicts. But the wars never came.

Ibadan moved into the twentieth century without wars. The war boys had to find other occupations, even as laborers in the building of railways. They had to take up farming, accepting a lower status position. Cocoa came, and those who could devote energy to its cultivation made some progress. They neither ate chocolate nor drank coffee. They only knew that some people in faraway lands found cocoa beans useful for reasons that they did not know or even care about. Money from cocoa came too slowly; a blessed tree would take seven years to produce its first baby. Many others went to school to receive a Western education, but the missionaries insisted that they must take Christianity as a mandatory gift with it. They knew what they wanted to do with education, but the gift was a problem. My father took education and the gift. As for my mother, she was more interested in the gift than in the education, collecting the gift through other intermediaries, native agents who spoke Yoruba to communicate messages from lands far away, from the Holy Book that my mother could not read. God had to be interpreted for her.

No one waits to be told to discard a pot that can no longer boil water. Slowly, the war boys began to leave their knives at home. Not being hunters, they did not need the kegs of gunpowder anymore. The warrior chiefs were aging, and they eventually died. They struggled to keep the memory, through moonlight stories of wars and bravery. I heard so many war stories, too many to count. Only a few of the elders knew that their stories and experiences would later become useful. Many of their children who went to school and received the story treasures poured cold water on them. The stories refused to go away. The stories became the truth that hides by becoming converted to oil; as more water is poured on the oil, so does it float. As the oil floats, the past comes back to haunt the present. New Ibadan is only new to the extent that it accepts the old. New Africa is like Ibadan with a destiny bound to its past. Each time Ibadan rebels against its past, it fails; like the chicken practicing for when its owner will order her to stand on one leg, it tries and fails. Each time Ibadan tries to stand on the one leg of the new, it stumbles, to be rescued by the second leg of the old.

If Isola gives you the road map to navigate history, to unravel the cognomen, his city, too, has just one name, which you must know to understand the full complexity of its character: Mesiogo. No other city in Africa, indeed, in the world, has this name, can ever claim this name. No other city can duplicate it. The twig can try; try as it will to lie in water for as many years as possible, it will never turn into a crocodile. Other cities, other people, can attempt to become like Ibadan, but they cannot be Mesiogo.

Mesiogo is a combination of two words pronounced as one, actually two words that should have been hyphenated in order to prevent confusion. Mesi is "to reply," but it is more than that; it is to be very quick to reply. To be quick does not indicate the content of a reply. Ogo means "a fool," someone stupid. In combination, Mesiogo communicates an ability to reply quickly to a fool, with actions and words that will communicate or disguise intentions. By joining the words, the meaning is hidden, the intentions are further compounded.

If wars and bravery are clear, Mesiogo is about the ambiguity of words, their capacity to multitask and create many exit points for an individual. Mesiogo sees a human personality as an embodiment of words and actions that shift like time and season. Fools are many, stupid people are legion, acts of stupidity and folly are countless. The Mesiogo, which is the Ibadan personality, must be ambiguous enough to cope with the exigencies and unpredictability of foolishness and stupidity and to survive the routine of interactions with fools.

Today, Ibadan is a city of over five million people. Not all the five million are Mesiogo. Those who are not, and the floating population that visits, know who the Mesiogo are. The city has turned yet again to its habits and manners to define itself. What the non-Mesiogo know first is the most trivial. Many Mesiogo have difficulty pronouncing some letters, notably the phonetic /s/, which may be swapped with the Yoruba tonal s. Chicken becomes ciken, cushion is turned into kusin, television is telifisan, cinema is shinima. As each of these and other words are lumped into sentences, they generate laughter. When the Mesiogo go to school, they learn to correct this. Knowing two ways to pronounce words becomes an advantage. They can use the new ways to mock others, to show off, to ridicule other Mesiogo as well. They can use the old ways to disguise themselves, misleading others into thinking that they have not been to school; or they may simply be affirming their peasant roots, a way of identification with others, a signal of nonelitism.

When those who mock Mesiogo speak, they betray themselves as well, revealing their own inadequacies in speech, like the man who beats a drum for a madman to dance to and turns out to be no better than the madman himself. I must have met hundreds of people, the non-Mesiogo who have problems with the letters l and r. "I want to go and pray" becomes "I want to go and play." When they are ready to play, thinking that you are invited to join them, you find them heading to the mosque or church to pray. Elect and erect may be swapped, and a politician who has won an election may be introduced to you as someone who has just had an erection.

Judging the book by its cover, visitors and strangers misjudge the Mesiogo. They throw out more words to amuse themselves with possible mispronunciations. They give the dog a second bone before it finishes the first. They empower the Mesiogo who is less interested in how the words have been pronounced than in their effects. To break off the meeting or to terminate the discussion, the Mesiogo says "Mo nbo" (I am coming), which is wrongly interpreted as taking a small break. As you wait for the Mesiogo, your patience runs out, darkness descends, and you give up. The Mesiogo never returns. Then you run into him the next day, launch your accusations, make your anger known. The Mesiogo can simply reply, "When I said that I was coming, did I leave my keys, my bags, and my shoes?" You understand the message: if someone has packed his baggage, why expect him to come back?

The Mesiogo does not always see yes as the opposite of no. The Mesiogo does not always see yes and no as avenues to express lies or truth. Lies are not the opposite of truth. Truth is not necessarily to be celebrated as a virtue when it can do more damage than lies. Lies should be condemned when, in serving as the opposite of truth, they discredit the individual. To say yes to a proposal, to all proposals, may be to remove a burden from oneself and to buy time to engage in further reflection to enable one to say no. In other words, yes may be a route, the right pathway to saying no. The shout of "yes," they always warn, can never be loud enough to destroy the throat. Yes is a timesaver, allowing people to leave you alone. No opens the gate to arguments and excuses, rationalization and explanation, and yes is the best antidote.

I cannot count the number of times that I have witnessed an encounter between two people, one seeking a favor from the other, usually money. About to create a "favor bank" or withdraw from the established one, the person walks in, looking dejected, sweating, worried. The host sits down comfortably, relaxed. A conversation ensues. The host starts the conversation.

> Why are you in a rush, behaving as a goat being pursued like a lion? We thank God that you escaped, and our door is open. The lion has been chased off. Do you want to drink cold water? I have one cold bottle of beer if you care about it.

The visitor replies immediately, even before the host can finish the last sentence or even begin it.

> Cold water, beer? My case does not require that. I have plenty of cold water and beer in my house. If you go to my house now, you will see people drinking, waiting for me to join them. Beer and cold water cannot solve my problem.

The host adjusts his chair, leans forward.

> Lord have mercy! My friend, if you can reject the offer of cold water and beer, then the matter must be serious. What is it? Tell it straight.

The visitor tells a long story, a really long story. The first part is how successful he has been until recently. The second part is how the success of the host has overtaken his own. The third is how he is about to begin another journey to success. The fourth is the reason for his current predicament, the extravagance of his third wife, whom he was advised to marry by their mutual friend. He recaps the story, with the stress on success, problems, and new journey. Then he moves to the last part: "I need £50 to solve an emergency." Then he closes by praising his host, massaging his ego, praising him for his many achievements, his record of generosity, and his contribution to society. "I know there is a heaven," he concludes, "It is meant for good people like you."

The host listens, but he knows never to buy a goat only because of its voice. As he listens, the Mesiogo reminds himself of those who bought a goat just because of the good voice only to discover, on slaughtering the goat, that it is all bone. He ponders an answer, as he reminds himself that whoever thinks everyone is good has not traveled much, has not seen the entire human population, has not even ventured to England. He listens to the story with attention, with concern. He is patient, telling himself to listen, to become the small egg that waits many months just to give birth to a large bird. He does not ask questions, he does not interrupt. When the visitor finishes, he hands him a cup of cold water, the cold water that was previously rejected. The visitor accepts and drinks the water. The host rejoices, thinking that anyone who can drink a glass of cold water will have a cool temper to listen. He stands up, thanks his visitor for the good words, sympathizes with all the troubles, and asks him to return the next day, with a tone indicating that he will solve the problem, with an assertive demeanor that suggests the problem is actually not as big as the visitor thinks. Before he leaves, the visitor criticizes the host for offering him cold water instead of cold beer. The host apologizes and offers the cold beer. It is not enough beer to become drunk, but enough to be thankful for, to even begin to think that part of the £50 to be collected the next day can be used to buy more beer. He leaves, thanking his host, thinking that before long it will be the next day.

The host forgets about his visitor for a little while and pursues other things, not wasting his time finding £50. The host needs to think, to review the history of the relationship between the would-be creditor and debtor. His answer must be based on conclusions derived from history. Has the visitor repaid previous loans to others and to himself? Is the visitor one who helps others when they are in trouble? Does the would-be debtor have a history of ingratitude, of betraying friendship? Is the reason for wanting a loan serious enough? It is much easier to raise a loan to bury one's father; in the entertainment that follows, the creditor and his friends will drink as much beer as they want and eat as much food as their stomachs can take, all in order to collect interest on the loan. It is more difficult to give a loan to someone to start a business—why can't the lender take the idea and make use of it?

Let us rush to the next day, murdering sleep in order to reunite the visitor and the host. The host takes the initiative in greeting, an extended greeting to make the visitor most welcome and relaxed. Breakfast may even be offered. Then our host, the Mesiogo in his positive mood, begins to speak.

Yesterday's matter, the issue you brought here yesterday, is a great matter indeed. It is a great mark of friendship, for if you did not like me so much you would not tell me so much. I know that you cannot approach me and ask another person at the same time. I have never seen a chicken who uses its two legs to scratch the soil at the same time. As soon as you left, I promised myself that just as you trusted me so much, so too will I help you. I could not tell you yesterday that my pocket, too, is shallow, so shallow that a small boy could empty the contents with two tiny fingers. Telling you yesterday about the shallowness of my pocket would only have compounded your problem. The beer you drank was the only bottle left in the house, and I am glad you drank it to cool yourself down.

The Mesiogo has already told the visitor the conclusion, but he is not about to stop talking. The face of the visitor is turning morose, like someone who has been told of the loss of a family member but refuses to cry in public. The visitor cannot stop the host from talking; he has no such right. He is too sad to drink, to ask for a beer as a technique of interruption. His world may be collapsing around him, as he has already planned how to spend the £50. The host, refusing to be a moneylender, not about to become the eager antelope with the elephant shoes who can no longer run fast enough to discourage being killed by a hunter, continues with his speech.

As soon as you left, I took off, visiting all my other friends. Too much work, too much travel. Baba Simeoni was not home. I left word, but he has not contacted me. Two other friends, the two friends of mine who you know who work at the Sekritariati [the government office] said that they were yet to be paid. Then I went to my cousin at Agbeni quarters who said that he was expecting some money in a few days. I came home dejected. My senior wife was worried, warning me not to allow my dejection to turn into a serious illness. I went to bed, unable to sleep, asking myself what I would tell you when you showed up. Your creator is my witness that I tried my best; your destiny will judge me if I betray you. I am so sorry that I cannot help you at this time.

Case closed, hours wasted, and no money changed hands. I happen to know that the host had £50 to give. Indeed, I know that on the same day on which he was requested the loan he spent over £75 buying a variety of items. A day later, he gave me £5 as a gift for good behavior. This Mesiogo was not poor. The reader, as a stranger, might wonder why the host did not say no and close the matter on the very first day. Ibadan does not encourage the habit of kanjuko, words and manners that say no in a careless manner. The Mesiogo said no not when you wanted him to but in his own time and with a demonstration, call it a pretense if it makes you happy, of compassion.

If your world is built on saying a sharp no and yes, take a deep breath and accept other realities. The world will not change because you ask it to. The Mesiogo can say no on the spot, depending on the politics he is playing with the visitor. I have seen the same person saying no quickly, asking another would-be borrower why he approached him, mistaking him for a bank. "Am I the government?" he once replied to a visitor. The Mesiogo can become the small pepper with the sharp taste whenever he chooses. He never promised his visitor £50, only begging for time to consider the request. When the time came, he needed to dress up his no with a story of trial and failure. There could have been trial and triumph. Baba Simeoni could have given him the money. In this case, bringing Baba Simeoni in does not even mean that the host has no money, only that the visitor must repay the loan at the appointed time since it was borrowed from a third party.

Be more patient. I have only told you that the host has money. I can also confirm to you that the visitor who came for a loan is known in the neighborhood for financial recklessness. He is so quick to spend money that only a small amount can stay in his pocket at any particular time. He is such a nice guy that his house is always crowded with guests. His two wives live permanently in the kitchen, cooking for guests all day. The host knows this, that the £50 is meant to entertain guests, not to invest, not to solve the problem that his visitor described to him. The host knows that the visitor has little to lose by not repaying the money. To say no to him on the spot will circulate as bad news: a nice man, temporarily short of cash, was humiliated because of the small amount of £50, two pieces of paper, not enough to provide an enjoyable evening.

The Mesiogo must ponder the consequences of words and actions, the damage that no and yes may cause. The Mesiogo will try to anticipate enemies, and how words will further empower them. If yes will weaken the enemies, the Mesiogo will offer it. Living in a huge city, the largest in West Africa, the Mesiogo are too brilliant to misread the intricacies of intrigue and conflicts. Words and actions must factor intrigue and conflicts into human relations, into the daily contacts between visitors and hosts. Human behaviors are not permanent, and the Mesiogo relies on the fluidity of words to deal with the plastic beings. *Koburu* (okay, not bad) allows the Mesiogo to make just one word so elastic as to provide an answer without offering a conclusion. One cannot stay in Ibadan for even a few minutes and not hear "*koburu*" as an answer to thousands of requests, a response to all sorts of behavior, and a resignation to all cases of disappointment. *Koburu* combines no and yes at once, leaving the receiver to use a set of other circumstances to decipher the meaning, to arrive at the accurate answer intended by the speaker. If you like this book, I can say "*koburu.*" If you do not like this book, I can say "*koburu,*" and thank you with a smile. If you like one part and dislike another, I can say "*koburu*" as well.

"*Koburu,*" please read on. A positive response does not mean that the intended answer is positive. *Koburu* is an example, which in tone and meaning actually sounds positive. *Oda* (it is good) is even more positive. "*Oda*" may be an answer to a proposal that the listener does not agree to, to a piece of advice that is annoying, to a behavior that should be condemned. There is *be gan lori* (it is exactly so), which may in fact be a negative response to a most foolish request. How can "it be exactly so" if a fool calls you a monkey? Yes, it can be exactly so, as you will one day offer the fool a banana when he most needs your help.

All the examples of positive responses and short equivalencies of yes have layered meanings. In the 1980s, by which time my classmates were successful men and women in society, they developed multiple ambitions. One wanted to become an honorary chief of my city so that he could use the title to advance his political career. I know the king of the city (now called the *olubadan*). Indeed, I know all the kings of the cities so closely that many of them have sent for me to run errands for them. The kings have even offered me titles, which I have rejected, as I do not want to be a chief for now. I know one chief who, in the process of wanting to become a king, lost his life.

The king in power in the 1980s, King Asanike, a Muslim who did not go to a Western-style school, was one of the most astute Mesiogo of the twentieth century. He came to power as an old man, and his successors were expecting him to die within a few months. He refused to die for many years, actually living far longer than anyone could have imagined. He must have had the magic to conquer death. As he had not gone to school, those who did, like some members of my generation, mistook him for a dunce. Presenting the image of a dunce, he conquered the educated elite, confirming the adage that the wisdom of the educated is in their wrists and not in their heads. As he was a Muslim, he was portrayed by the Christians as a nonmodernizer. King Asanike agreed with them. When they built a new palace for him, he refused even to live there, reminding his critics that he was accused of not paying too much attention to new buildings. In reality, the magic that he used to conquer illnesses and hold death at bay had been buried in his old palace, and the magic maker had warned him not to uproot the medicine. Should he live in the new palace, his life would be cut short. So he believed, and I am not sure one can argue that a short life in a new palace is better than a long life in an old palace. Even the pastor who preaches about the rewards of working hard so that one will go to heaven prays for his own long life.

I took the friend eager to become an honorary chief to the king who could grant his ambition. One does not go to kings and chiefs empty-handed. Only a tortoise knows where to bite another tortoise; if the crab tries, it only bites the shell. I know what the king wanted—nice-looking goats, several bottles of hard liquor, cash, and clothes. The king's salary was not great, but his expenses were large, for he had to maintain hundreds of dependents and visitors. My friend procured all. He even added tobacco, which did not offend the king, although he was no smoker.

I knew the palace very well. I had been there many times to conduct interviews, to listen to proceedings, to observe traditional practices of power, and to show the palace to visitors from foreign lands. I had mastered the shortcut to the palace. I knew the tactic of going through the back door after giving the right tips and making the right statements. My friend was impressed. Getting into the palace through the back door, I knew the procedure for moving up in the appointment book, unless the representatives of federal and regional powers were visiting. Within ten minutes, we moved up the list.

My friend was happy, as he moved closer to the king who could make him a chief, turn him into an elder in his thirties. The courtesy, behavior, and words required to greet a king are different from those for ordinary folks. On sighting the king, one must prostrate oneself, with the chest on the floor. In those days without cement floors, one would take dust from the ground and sprinkle it on the head. As one lies flat on the floor, the head is raised to allow the mouth to greet.

Kabiyesi
May the crown last on the head for long
May the sandals last on the feet for long
May your era be prosperous.
May Ibadan not be spoiled
May we your children not see harm
May you not see harm
May harm not see you, Kabiyesi.

As we greeted, the king determined when it was time for us to stop. Using his fly whisk, he commanded us to get up. There were chairs around, good chairs probably donated by many with ambitions similar to those of my friend, but we could not sit until we were told to. Again, the fly whisk commanded us to take our seats. To sit was not the start of business, as we could not initiate the discussion. The king turned to another set of visitors. Doubling as an office and living room, the space in which the king met us was large and could hold about a hundred people. It was the prerogative of the king to determine the order in which he would talk to guests and dismiss them. If the king was tired, all the visitors could be dismissed without apology and asked to reschedule for the next day. We were lucky.

"My children, what can I do for you?" the king asked us. To the king, everybody is his child except his parents.

My friend stood up. I also stood up. Unless asked to, one could not speak to the king while seated. I forgot to tell my friend that part of my job was to represent him. I never knew that he had memorized a speech to request the title. He began to speak, to make his request. He spoke about his achievements, reciting a curriculum vitae more suitable for looking for an administrative job in a university. I could not stop him. The king allowed him to finish. The outcome was more than we were prepared for.

"My son," the king began to respond, "you are a very successful young man, a worthy son of the land. I have my staff to blame for not bringing your name to my attention. Your reward is coming late, but I am glad that it comes when you are still young to enjoy it. Your wish is granted."

A huge amount was determined as a fee to cover part of the expenses of the ceremony associated with the chieftaincy as well as a gift. My friend was carrying a checkbook, and he issued a check to the king's staff in another part of the palace. We left. I claimed victory. My friend hosted a small party two weeks later to announce that he would become a chief in a few months. His wife was worried, and she told me so, that the new chief would abandon monogamy.

The season to award fresh titles arrived. The palace released the list of new men and women to receive titles, to be conferred by the king. My friend's name was not on the list. I was out of the country when the list was released. My friend located my address and telephone number and asked me to hurry back home. I was yet to give the lecture for which I had been invited. I had to cancel it and rush back home. Who does not know that a friend close by is worth more than a relative in a distant land? A lecture on an academic topic cannot be compared to the crisis of missing a title. Only a few people in the academic world could understand the lecture anyway. If they were worried about my decision and choices, I had created new topics for them, questions for their students to answer in examinations, ideological options for them to articulate. Isola has entered their discourse, not in footnotes but in the body of the essay itself. This was not the time to shed the Mesiogo genes.

We rushed back to the palace. We were even luckier this time around. My friend was also ready with a speech, much longer than the one that had won him the award. The king allowed him to speak, not interjecting once. His fly whisk lay on his right thigh, his two eyes fixed on us. When it was his turn to speak, he offered only a sentence.

My son, I forgot.

This was classic Mesiogo; the king had killed the enterprise without shedding blood, without making any move, without saying much. Only the fool visits the house of the goat to beg for lessons on wisdom. My friend needed another animal to offer help. To say that one forgets is to say that all my friend had said, not once but twice, was useless. The king had successfully used the art of forgetfulness to terminate the narrative of memory. You cannot tell the king or anyone who forgets to remember. It is hard to wake up a person pretending to be asleep.

My friend tried again, listing episodes and events to remind the king. "Dr. Falola was here with me, your Royal Highness. I brought some gifts. I left a signed check for the amount I was asked to pay. Your Excellency, I said this, I said that." The king did not reply. Case closed. The ambition had collapsed. I said not a word, telling myself that my friend's head contained too many lice and he was trying unsuccessfully to use just one finger to remove them. One finger could only press the lice on the head; he needed two fingers. The king moved his hand toward the fly whisk. He lifted it, and he used it to dismiss us. The meeting was over.

As my friend went into mourning, I embarked on learning why the case had failed. It was my first research into Mesiogo manners. I knew much about them, but I had never studied them as a system of thought, a philosophy of life. When the king said yes at the first visit, it was a yes to indicate no and to dismiss us without wasting our time. This I understood; we forgot to pay attention to the king's physical actions, the expression on his face, the importance he attached to the brief encounter. When he said that he forgot, it was to tell us to make a second trial, to hint that he was leaning toward yes by saying no. It was our task to seek the means to remind him. I needed another chief to tell me what to do. I rushed to my friend, telling him that I had discovered the means to remind the king. It was easy enough: we started all over again. We paid twice, and his name entered the list before it was too late.

The king did not want to say that we had not paid enough, that he had not seen the benefits of making my friend a chief, that when my friend was making his first speech he forgot to add what he would do for the king and the city. He wanted to be rewarded on the basis of his past achievements without announcing the start date of a new future and the achievements of this future. The king was actually generous in forgiving my friend for representing himself, denying lower chiefs income and gifts. He had to be punished; indeed, he was. My friend was not the only one whom the king forced to learn new lessons, to run back to history and culture as I did to save my friend.

Mesiogo is a strategy of knowing when to fight, when not to fight, and how to fight. It is about understanding the codes of behavior in a highly stratified society. One must know the answers to give to satisfy those in power and authority. One must factor age into the answers. How does one say no to a king or an elder? How does one say yes to a cheat?

Mesiogo factors the agency of destiny and the future that only the greater forces can see and manipulate into interpersonal relations and the dialogue to sustain them. If someone wants to relocate to Lagos, how can you give the right advice if you have no clues to the person's destiny? The choice, as the Mesiogo would make it, is to create an eclectic response. If you advise the person to go to Lagos and things do not work out, you become part of the problem, the bag to punch for making a big mistake. If Lagos turns out well, you take credit and gifts can come your way.

Mesiogo is about the ability to plot revenge by avoiding violence. Words must fight words. To fight back, one must allow the opponent to use the tongue to get himself into trouble, just as the bird gets trapped in its wings. Whosoever is not ready to learn words, to bring together fascinating sentences to win a case, is advised never to engage in a fight. It was much easier for the soldier to steal the antelope and escape a punishment that could have been as severe as an execution than to make a case for the theft. The injured person may be the loser in a judgment if he or she lacks the ability to narrate, to summon words in self-defense, to create words to demolish the enemy. One's mouth is one's lawyer.

Learning words, expanding vocabularies, and putting words together is one of the essentials of growing up in Ibadan. There is no syllabus for it, no end to learning, no limit to the sources of wisdom. For me and those of my generation, we had to start quite early in life, mastering codes and signals. We must know when to leave the room without being told. We must learn when not to leave the room even when words are used to send us away. Once when I was being a nuisance I was sent on an errand to collect an object, an *arodan* (stand still), from a neighbor. Eager to run to the neighbor's house and run back, I delivered the message, stretching my hands to receive the object. "Oh, yes, *arodan*," said the woman. She asked me to sit down. I did. She said she would quickly make one. I sat for six hours. I was sent on an errand with an accompanying code to keep me away from home for long hours.

One must learn proverbs. Without the ability to use and interpret proverbs, one cannot be a Mesiogo. A proverb is regarded as the "horse" that carries words to a different level, investing them with meanings, enrobing the user with the garment of wisdom. Just as a man's character cannot be washed away by the rain, so, too, a true Mesiogo can never be drowned in a sea of proverbs. Proverbs allow contradictions to attain a meaningful status, for the wise to escape being caught in a lie. One must learn idioms, sentences so complicated that the elders might be summoned to help.

One must understand memory and history. A stream may flow for long, a river can be as long as the Nile, but they never forget their sources. The Mesiogo thrives on memory to understand Self and Others. One must weave history with idioms to create effects. As the Mesiogo speak, they intertwine proverbs with history, presenting the listener with clues to understanding the issues at stake or even suspending judgment.

The Mesiogo also use silence for effect. Single words such as *koburu* and *beni* are used to create effects similar to that of silence, that is, talking without revealing anything. The Mesiogo with the skill to talk can use many words, and many sentences, to say little. Piling one proverb over another, the clever Mesiogo exhaust the listeners. A ride in a bus, a visit to the market, an encounter in offices can turn into long and endless chats and discussions on a wide range of subjects.

A thousand words cannot fill a basket. As each drops into the basket, it disappears like water. The purpose of talking is to create an effect. Ibadan went to war, and a defining characteristic of courage and bravery developed. As in words, there is a reason to stress bravery and courage. When Ibadan was born, in the very first week, the pioneer leaders sent for a *babalawo* (diviner). The old man appeared, with his divination apparati. He chanted, making a long incantation that only a few understood.

The *babalawo* demanded that the city chiefs must produce two hundred snails. As the snails were delivered, the diviner made another round of incantation, this time longer than the first. He held the snails, moved in a circle, and released the snails one at a time. As the snails crawled to the bush, he announced, "Ibadan will spread as far as the snails can travel, in all directions." His prediction has come to pass.

Men and women had to work for the prediction to become history. The first ruler began to work to impose a lasting character.

> Oluyole, I salute the Mighty
> The wicked as he is equally kindly
> The fulsome who sent the intriguer on a difficult errand
> As if to urge the intriguer to commit suicide on his father's farm.
> Mighty Lord, Iba!
> The descendant of blacksmiths and possessor of an abundance of
>   wrought iron
> When he marches, he produces the sound of a thundering rain.
> Iba! The proverbial heavy rain
> Owner of a quiver that is full of instantaneous and efficacious prepa-
>   rations
> The cruel and the gracious alike.

The ruler's successors became greater in fame, larger in ambitions. To recite the poems of Ibikunle and Ogunmola, two leading war generals, will take time. Ibikunle was

> The captain who disgraces men as would the dearth of money.

The poet even went as far as comparing him to God, the Supreme Being, calling him

> A strong-witted man with incomprehension comparable to that of
> Olodumare.

This is blasphemy. Ibadan's ambition became so large that men were being compared to God in wisdom and accomplishments. Eager to expand the scope of individualism, Ibadan became a place to visit and settle. It became the largest city in West Africa in the nineteenth century, and as the snails travel the city spreads. Combining action with words, I saw, as I grew up, both citizens and strangers trying to manifest their ambitions. Words and actions are needed to generate conflicts and mediate them as new ones are created.

The ultimate goal in the city has been to seek success, individual success that will translate into public notice. For one's poem to become longer, one has to seek to become a *borokinni*, a famous person. The famous person needs wealth and titles. The sources of fame have changed over time. My earliest recent ancestor was a diviner, giving the permanent name to the clan, Falola, one who attains prosperity through the ability to divine. Falola used esoteric knowledge. He passed magic to his successors, who added the ability to fight in wars. Then one segment of the family branched off to Western education during the twentieth century. One of the snails that the diviner requested when Ibadan was founded probably crawled to the coast, dropping into the sea and swimming across the Atlantic. Ibadan has expanded beyond the sea, bringing Toyin to the United States.

Changing definitions of fame and its sources have yet to change Ibadan manners and the ambitions of Ibadan's people. An ever-expanding city wants its citizens to seek an abundance of everything—of bullets, crops, food, and books. My father sought abundance, through nine children of whom I am the last. Not knowing whether there would be food and beer in heaven, he and his last son developed great habits of eating and drinking and their stomachs became larger than the rest of their bodies. As Adesina witnessed the birth to his last son, they called the old woman from the family to perform the naming rites. The woman prayed for an abundance of wealth and titles, of wives and children, of honor and rewards. Olorun was added to Toyin to placate the sources of fertility and abundance.

When the old woman finished praying, she passed the baby around, to be touched by all those in attendance, all from Ibadan. As the baby was moved from one hand to another, each begged Olorun to give him force, energy, vitality, power, and drive. All prayed for abundance, stressing the ideals of pragmatism so as to act out the character of the city. No one in the audience prayed that he would be a historian. No one knew that such a job existed. They were too preoccupied with three things—health, wealth, and children—to consider the ways in which these would come about. They prayed for Toyin in the image of his father, but to a Christian God, to make him a successful Ibadan man, one with many wives, children, and long life to enjoy his wealth, wives, and children. It was too early to pray for his death and decent burial. But they hinted at the theme of death by praying for Toyin to live long enough to bury his parents. The old woman even announced that I came from heaven, a visitor, but they would keep me at Ibadan for a long time, as I seek all the means to attain wealth and immortality.

I never understood any of what they were saying. They did, which was why they were talking to one another and not to me. They believed in the contents of the prayers they were all offering. They all, even the Christians among them, believed in the concept of *ayanmo* (destiny). They did not ask a diviner to unfold my own destiny, only praying that the positive destiny should manifest itself in due course. Toyin's father was already successful. The new child was yet another proof of the glory that the gods had promised him. Adesina's life was good: he was begetting children, he was acquiring money, he was feasting friends and relatives to celebrate the birth of his son. More children were expected to follow. The new one was the first of his new wife, the fourth wife. Adesina could never be private; he was already assured by his diviner that wealth, wives, and children would keep him from obscurity.

An elaborate party followed the naming rituals. The new baby must produce the evidence of his father's success. A new child had come to expand the family and the city. One day, the baby would become an adult and follow the snail. The baby's father must entertain lavishly to demonstrate to his fellow citizens that he was a *borokinni*. With his new occupations, modern as they were, he was doing what Ibadan had asked him to do. He was not a warrior like his father, but he had created the instruments to break new ground. He was a Mesiogo who was able to deal with the crowd and think of answers to requests that would be presented to him. Spending so much money on that day, he could not say that he had no £50 to lend. He even recorded in his diary the huge amounts of cash he received as gifts from those who came to rejoice with him. As he was counting his cash, using his memory, he was also probably telling himself that the best way to improve his memory and knowledge of others was to lend people money. His relations and friends knew his ambition to become an important chief and possibly a king. He was already a minor chief; he had to work harder and live longer to become a king. He knew, ever repeating a saying to himself, that one who has enough money can buy a road in the sky.

This was January 1953 at Ibadan. I still knew nothing, not even the date that I just told you. I only had the genes of Ibadan growing in my body, as I relied on my main foods: milk and corn pap. I also had the prayers, with their set contents, added to my being. They repeated part of the prayers each morning. They began to call me Isola and to recite my poem, adding that of the city when they had the time.

Then came May. Another loud noise, this time of mourning. Adesina died. He never lived to realize all the prayers, certainly not that of long life. I was still a baby who did not know that he was dead. By not being able to bury him, entertain all my relatives and friends, show off my abundance, I broke the first promise I had made to Ibadan, which was sealed in a prayer. I broke the promise rather early, the first in a series of Ibadan's mandates that I would break, of manners that I would forsake. As I have broken each mandate, the city has been cruel and unforgiving in seeking its revenge. Toyin Falola started life by staying close to a river and abusing the crocodile. As the hungry crocodile watches to make its move and swallow its prey, the poet begins to chant.

Isola, run, run away
The river contains the scorpions that sting
The bank contains the bees that sting
There are night adders that can bite.
Isola, look at the vipers
The crocodile is ready to swallow.
Isola, leap
Be kind to the kind
Be cruel to the cruel
Do not say what is bad is good.

Each time I remember the leap into the future, following 1953, I take Ibadan, Adesina, and the crocodile with me.

CHAPTER THREE ::: SNAKE & BIBLE

hen I was nine years old, I entered the bowels of the longest snake. To me, it was a real snake, one that I courted and tempted until it swallowed me. Angry that I was not edible, the snake showed its merciful side, vomiting me in a strange land, grudgingly crawling away, leaving me behind to hide in a jungle to deal with life and salvation or death and redemption. The snake was not cruel; it was generous, amiable, and powerful.

This longest of snakes was a train, with coaches that crawl on railway lines. I must have played with toys and soil, as did all children. Certainly, I must have ridden in cars and trucks, carted by adults as if I were part of their luggage. None made such a notable impact on me as did the train. My curiosity first came with the whistle, a loud and prolonged trumpet-sounding noise, repeated and interrupted as the train approached the station about five miles from my house. As the train moved, a different noise followed and turned into a song that we kids would sing until the sound faded away.

Mo ti gun
Mo ti so
Oke talajapa ko le gun
Mo ti gun
Mo ti so.

I have climbed
I have descended
The hill that traders cannot ascend.
I have climbed
I have descended.

This was a song in praise of the train, the powerful machine that moved faster than the caravan of traders, climbing hills, weaving through valleys without any sweat or sign of fatigue. As the sound stopped, we sang more, adding a chorus of three words that were differently pronounced for effect.

Faka fiki faka
Faka fiki faka.

As we repeated the chorus, we behaved like the train. When the train was no more to be heard, we created toys of train and rail lines, stringing together discarded tins of milk and tomato paste, beer bottles, small pebbles, pieces of clay, and other objects. In praise of the real and fake train, we would sing yet again.

Jagunjagun o le mu reluwe duro
Ika owo kan o le mu reluwe duro.

The warrior cannot stop the train
One finger cannot bring the train to a halt.

The urge grew stronger to see the train. Descriptions came from friends and classmates, repeating old stories. When an errand is important, the most reliable person to deliver it is oneself. I could never be satisfied until I saw the train. The station was too far away to run there and run back without getting into trouble. The railway lines were a little bit closer, easier to see than the train. The lines did not move, day and night, unlike the train. In twos and threes, other small boys and I would walk the distance to see the rail lines.

Seeing the rail lines itself was an act of conquest. To sneak away from the house and school for about two hours without being discovered was a victory. We began to repeat the stories we heard from the older boys, while adding new ones. The rail lines introduced us to the idea of suicide at an early age. Whosoever was fed up with life could lie down to be crushed by the train. We actually practiced the drama of death, not because we wanted to die so early, but to practice for the future, talking about how easy it actually was to die whenever we chose. Boys who wanted to punish their parents would leak the information to their mothers that they knew the road to heaven. The mothers would panic, beg the boys for forgiveness. Were they to tell their fathers, they would be encouraged to pack their bags and travel on the glorious road, if only to reduce the household expenses.

Our stories, like the songs, praised the train for being able to travel many miles, from east to west, south to north, without complaining, without being tired. The older boys told us that a train could take over a thousand people, all sitting down, without crashing. "What a load for one person to carry!" I once said. When we put rocks into our toy train and pushed it, it collapsed. We would use bottle covers to make tires, and the train would collapse yet again. We got brighter, making stronger tires, better tracks, bigger trains, and they actually began to move on the toy tracks. Like our toy train, the real one was vulnerable to accidents. We believed that magnets and needles could bring down the real train. We would carry needles, stolen from the bedrooms of unsuspecting parents, to drop on the rail lines, waiting for news of the train crash. No such news arrived. Then we believed that as the train moved a powerful broom swept the lines to remove our magnets and needles, crushing our dream instead of the train. We could not defeat the train.

One afternoon, as we were pretending to prepare for imminent suicide, a loud noise came from nowhere. Four boys panicked. This time around, we could not sing. We ran as fast as we could and then stopped. I saw the train for the first time. Coaches upon coaches, moving slowly, following the crooked and winding lines. I thought it looked like a snake. We never knew when the train would appear or the schedule that guided its operation. We knew when to expect the sound from the neighborhood and we knew that this could change for reasons that we did not understand. I myself saw the train, the snake. As it moved away, I marveled. Then we all ran back to the rail lines, to touch them, to feel the heat. Another victory, actually a bigger one, as we could carry the story to school and to our friends.

Still eager to learn more, we did not turn to adults or books. We wanted to see the "Station" itself, where the train stopped. This was a journey to the city center, the crowded downtown to which parents had warned us never to go without adults. Among the items in the "lost and found" list were small kids who had wandered away as their parents and market women were haggling over prices. For us to get to the Station, we needed an adult. Boys older than us had begun their careers as businessmen by taking younger boys to the Station. They would collect one's lunch allowance for a whole week, in addition to which one had to deliver their love messages (in words or letters) to the girls they very much admired. Love words I could deliver without a problem, even when the occasion included a slap from a girl who felt insulted. Money was my main obstacle, as the food allowance was paid directly to the teacher. The older boys accommodated this easily. I would collect the food and hand it over to them. To go hungry for five days to see the Station was worth it. To look for one's black goat, one must begin the search in daylight. I began to pay during the middle of the week, too anxious to see the Station. After five days, my guide announced that I needed to pay more. The older boys could take you to the Station, but the contract did not include bringing you back. Another five days of payment. I paid. Then he asked for more, to protect me from the crowd, the thieves, and the police who patrolled the Station. What started as a contract for a week became a contract for a month. Our desire to see the Station was a lucrative avenue for the bigger boys to make money or get free meals.

I saw the Station! I knew how to get to the Station from my school, and I knew how to reach the school from our house. The older boy had overcharged! There were only two turns to know. The older boy was no braver than me. He, too, was scared of the crowd and the Station. We reached the Station, but the older boy would not cross the road, only pointing his finger at the Station. We stayed for a minute or so before he promptly ordered me to follow him on the return journey. I saw the Station, but not the inside or the snake taking its normal rest. The younger boys had been cheated—we bought a cow and forgot to buy the rope to tether it. All that the older boys had known were two road stretches. One of them we all knew, only we did not know how long it was or that there was a fork on it that led to the Station.

In any case, it was a story of success. To know how to get to the Station, to survive the return journey, and to come up with a reason to escape from the house defined the bravery of the adventurous. Boys who had never seen the Station were weaklings, undeserving of respect. The teachers awarded their good grades on the basis of learning by rote, but the students were graded on the ability to see the Station and the stores and people on the way and all around. At the age of eight, I had acquired respect among my peers. I had the credentials to boast, to declare my boyhood. I could even set up my own business, eating free meals and collecting cash from those who were too young to see the Station. Some there were who had seen the Station, taken there by their parents, brothers, or sisters. These boys were not to be respected: they were cowards who could not play truant, goats led to the house with ropes tied to their necks. It was shameful for one to declare that he had been led to the Station like a goat. The shame was so much to bear that even those who had seen the Station had to lie about it unless they had done it on their own, paying the older boys for the chance. Seeing the rail lines, pretending to sleep across the tracks, and sneaking to the Station uncaught by parents were the early determinants of success, of courage. I made it.

Soon afterward, I visited the Station on my own. I braved crossing the road to enter the Station. I went inside, looked around for a while, and left. The crowd was big, the goods were bigger than the crowd. I felt successful and wiser, like the goat who regarded growing a beard as a sign of wisdom. The secret leaked out that I had made it to the Station on my own. More respect.

About a year later, at the age of nine, I became the goat with the long beard, too full of wisdom. I wanted to make the run to the Station, stay on the other side of the road, and return home as I had previously done, looking at people, traders, and their wares. I made the trip but did more than stand by the roadside staring at the Station. I crossed the road, coming closer to the Station. I entered the Station, a step further than the big boys had ever taken. I saw a crowd going beyond the offices and goods. I followed them. They boarded the train, whose doors were open. I followed them and occupied a seat. I was now in the belly of the train. I was not thinking about any journey or trip. I was thinking about how well my story would be received in the school. No one had gone to the Station to board the train all by himself. This was the first time I would make a top rating at our best sport. I would be the most important boy in the school.

The train moved. People waved inside and outside. Some even wept for reasons that I did not know. I was happy. The train moved slowly at first, passing places in the city that I did not recognize. Then it picked up speed, moving through the forest and over hills. There was light inside and darkness outside. The train began to travel, with me as one of its passengers. I was happy, more than happy, to be in it. Everything I saw excited me, the people inside the train, those outside the train. Things were new, or they appeared so.

Only when the neighbor is harvesting does the lazy man remember that he forgot to plant his seeds; I was hungry only when I saw people bring out their food from their containers. Some chewed hard meat or kola nuts as snacks. Some had brought the kind of food I could recognize. I was offered free food, and I was not hesitant to accept. My stomach was full, the scenery was new, the crowd was noisy. Then and now, one cannot start to eat without inviting others. It is customary to reject the offer, but with a greeting and prayer that the food should not miss its way in the journey to the belly. Occasionally the food makes a detour in the throat, creating a cough or hiccup, arousing suspicion that one's friend or relative is sad that one has the means to buy food; or it could be punishment for being too greedy, starting to eat without inviting others.

After many hours, running to half a day or so, a ticket officer came to our coach. "Wey yor tiket?" he demanded, speaking in an authoritative voice, demanding that each passenger should produce a ticket. The women removed their wrappers, to dip into the pockets in their underwear. Those without underwear hid the tickets in their bras, and dug underneath the breasts to bring out the tickets. A man in front of me removed his right shoe to take out the ticket lodged inside his sock. They all produced their tickets except me. "You must commot at the next staktion," ordered the ticket officer, declaring the end of my stay on the train. He even gave me an exit paper. He mustered some angry words at my parents, who, he thought, wanted to cheat by having me use a coach different from theirs. Perhaps he had seen such kids and tricks before. Perhaps he thought I would take the exit paper to my parents who would be forced to pay for the ticket. I had to do what he told me, as he might come back.

The next station was Ilorin, which I could read on the signboard. I had heard about Ilorin at school, in storybooks that spoke about wars. And I had been told many times at home that the rock salt (natron), called kaun, which we added to tough meat as a tenderizer and used to cook okra, came from Ilorin. I had been deceived once by a playmate who gave me natron to chew, calling it something else. It was so bitter that I almost threw up. Now I could see Ilorin. The first thing I looked for was the natron, but it was nowhere to be found. I had taken the first trip of my life on my own to a distant part of the country, a place that even my mother and father had probably never visited. If they had, no one had ever told me about it. The Ibadan diplomats and traders reached Ilorin during the nineteenth century, walking for about ten days in one direction with no long breaks except to sleep at night. The train delivered me to this place in one day. I was not praising the train for its speed at the time, as I had no idea how fast it had been compared to the trek of the diplomats and soldiers. I was happy, not to get away from home, as no one was maltreating me, but to see the Station and be closer to the train.

I was not afraid. I was not thinking of home. The mongoose that wants to catch a chicken must not be afraid of the dew. The boy who wanted to go beyond the Station must see more. He had survived the snake. I followed the crowd, left their Station. I could not go back in the direction of my school, to head back home. I looked at the crowd. Their language was different, but I could hear a number of the people using words with which I was familiar. I noticed that they were talking a lot. Even now, they still do. So much do they love to talk at Ilorin that the city's poem eulogizes the power of words.

Ilorin, the city of Afonja
The mouth is much sweeter than salt
Only the person with two mouths can live in Lagos
One needs four mouths to live at Oyo
At Ilorin, the city of Afonja
Only the person with eighteen mouths can survive.

As the poet affirms, to doublespeak is not enough at Ilorin; a sentence must have about eighteen different meanings. I needed only one sentence with just one meaning in my first stray. I could not even understand everything I heard. The poet was not thinking about the deaf and lost like me, but about those who heard what was said at Ilorin yet found it difficult to understand. So famous has Ilorin become in the art of doublespeak that people are advised to go there for lessons in *jamba* (havoc making and multispeaking). A famous city with a complicated history, its rise to fame came with the relocation there in the early nineteenth century of Afonja, the *are ona kakanfo* (generalissimo) of the Old Oyo Empire. As he and the *alafin* (emperor) fought for power, the general withdrew himself and his forces to an advantageous location. While the *alafin* was consulting his magicians to look for the charm to kill his general at Ilorin, Afonja mustered the support of Muslims and together they established an army to overrun Oyo and many parts of Yorubaland. It was their wars that led to the creation of my own city. Unknown to Afonja, the Muslims had their own agenda. Their leaders, dan Fodio and Bello, in faraway Sokoto, in the northwest of Nigeria, gave them the authorization to stage a jihad in Ilorin. With their horses and soldiers, they betrayed Afonja and his men. The Fulani and Hausa began to move into Ilorin in greater numbers, regarding Ilorin as home. Swollen headed with their victory, the Muslims wanted to create a larger caliphate through other wars. It was the army of Ibadan that stopped their southern march in 1840, the famous war that prevented the conversion of all Yoruba to Islam, paving the way for half of them to listen to the Christian missionaries when they began to visit in the 1850s. Ilorin has exacted its revenge. It stands as an obstacle to the northern expansion of Christianity, erecting barriers to stop the missionaries from reaching its gates and crossing to the north.

The Yoruba never left Ilorin, insisting on their identity and language. They became Muslims, and the few who listened to the missionaries did so at their own risk. Ilorin has never had much use for the Bible. By the time I reached Ilorin, they had Yoruba and Hausa Muslims, each defining the religion to suit their purpose and politics. The city had those who spoke Yoruba, which I could understand, and those who spoke Hausa, which I could not. They had their emir, from a Fulani lineage, but the Afonja family continued to press for power. Ilorin's poet agreed with them, calling Ilorin "the city of Afonja," if only to remind the Hausa and Fulani that they had stolen a crown that did not belong to them. At the age of nine, I did not know the history that I just told you. I studied it years later and then realized why I did not understand many of them on my first visit and why they have to doublespeak, as their poet continues to remind us.

I saw many, many young people hawking items, and I wondered why they were all truants like me, running away from school. Truancy I fully understood. Many big boys in my school had tried this and gotten into trouble, receiving countless strokes of the cane to stop them from repeating their truancy. One big boy who repeated it was made to put his two legs in hot water until he could stand it no more, crying for mercy. Coming to school with the band aid and pain, he never missed any class again in his life. I knew that the punishment for truancy would be much pain, but this could not stop me from pursuing my friendship with the train. Daily school songs warned about the consequences of truancy. Without coming to school, one could not hope to become an adult with shoes that make the ko ko ka sound, as one walks confidently, wearing a suit and tie.

Were the truants at Ilorin looking for the Station? They did not even call it a station as we did. I heard them refer to it as Oju Irin (the abode of metal), which was actually appropriate, naming the place after the rail lines made of iron. I saw women with veils; I had seen a few where I came from, but here I saw many of them walking in different directions, wearing black attire, as if they were mourning the death of their husbands. Their husbands were alive, and they, too, were wearing veils, so I thought, only that I could see their eyes. What I regarded as veils were turbans, and it was the first time that I saw numbers of them. The turbans were competing in color, size, and height. I thought that the men with the tallest turbans must be the most important, and those wearing the ordinary caps, common where I came from, must be the small men among them. I kept walking, moving away from their Oju Irin, hearing strange words such as Albarika and Alihamudu, Arabic loanwords sandwiched into Yoruba sentences. I stopped here and there. I spoke to those who looked as small as me, but they did not understand me. I was not afraid I was not thinking about home. I was not thinking about food.

The first moon appeared, followed gradually by the first darkness. I could read the signs in English, which were not many, all for stores and small shops. Many had closed for business. I crossed the road to one of the signs and shops. I saw a bench and sat. What I heard next, at the same time that I saw the rising sun, was an angry female voice, calling on the "useless boy" to leave the bench so she could open the store. I probably yawned and stretched my body. I kept walking.

Suddenly someone stopped me. No one can choose his mother! This woman was about to adopt me. She was not wearing any veil. I could see her face clearly. She did not say hello or greet me, which was strange. She held my arm, not so tightly as to make me panic. She spoke. She spoke the language I understood, a dialect of Yoruba that sounded funny to my ears, but I could still make out words. "He asked you to come," pointing to a man not too far away. I followed her. The man first spoke in a language I did not understand, probably Hausa. I did not respond. Then he spoke in Yoruba.

"Would you like to be my stick boy?" I agreed, although I did not understand what he meant. I knew what a stick was. I had used them to fight in my school, with boys for play, threatening one another or even engaging in harder battles. I knew what a boy was. I was one. I could not combine the stick and the boy. It was my first job in life. "Stick boy" was an occupation, a great job for that matter. The job started immediately. The man, tall and able, would pretend to be blind. I would hold a stick, with him at the back holding the tail and I holding the head. I led, and he followed behind, whispering to me, giving me directions where to go, telling me to move to a person sitting quietly in front of his house. The blind man would beg, offering prayers. I would repeat the prayer or offer my own. Alms would come, we would give a short thanks, and quickly move on to the next person, who might not be so kind. I would collect the alms and pass them on to him. He never missed my hands as he received the money; he never missed his pocket as he put it there. At the end of the day, he would give me my allowance. This was easy to understand.

I had seen beggars in my city, especially on Sundays when they came near the cathedral, some blind, some crippled, begging for money. Adults would give them pennies. I never knew that blindness could be faked to create a living. My master was not the only beggar, and they had a large congregation with rules and procedures about where they could go and the severe punishment for stealing the stick boys of fellow beggars. Perhaps the woman who recruited me was a commission agent, making a living by looking for truants who needed temporary jobs. Later, in the 1970s, when I was taking college-level courses on historical methods, I would return to this experience to mock the teacher behind his back that he didn't know what he was talking about with regard to the nature of evidence. At the age of nine, I already knew the practice of deconstruction, only no one had told me there was a theory behind it. And years later some scholars made big names for themselves by talking about the multiple realities of an event, the multiple interpretations of an episode. Like my first master, they forgot to add that fortunes may come by saying the obvious, their own way of faking blindness. I also did not know then that I was actually valuable in the city of Ilorin, where a small class of small boys, known as *almajiri*, was in the process of creation.

Students of Quranic teachers, their masters released them to the streets to seek alms, to offer them labor to make some kind of a living. Perhaps people did not notice the trend, the damage that urbanization was creating. When the trend was noticed in the 1980s, it was through the evidence of violence. The *almajiri* had become an underclass, millions of young and poor people who became involved in all the cases of religious violence. Whenever their masters want to create urban wars, they already have an army ready to fight.

The *almajiri* learns to pray and sing. I could sing, but not Ilorin songs. I did not know those songs. I could pray; the lines were short.

Whom God has blessed
Give me, please!
Allah will not dispossess you of your eyes
May your eyes last you till old age.

Many actually would give, in sympathy for the blind, for the boy who had to be fed by the blind father, thanking God for not making their lives as hopeless as ours. They were obligated to give, as a mandatory condition of going to heaven when they died. Islam enjoins them to show generosity to the poor, help to the needy. Alas! the Quran does not provide the clues needed to discover the fake. My master was telling them that he had caught a frog by its tail, and they had no means to discover the lie. A frog with a tail? With a small kid in front, as the proselytizers for the Jehovah's Witnesses do, sending small girls ahead to knock on your doors, my master could fool the public.

I saw about three suns rise and set, about five moons show up in a clear sky. I lost count of hours and days. I assured myself that I could not have stayed at Ilorin for a month, as the time to prepare for the examinations was not near. All students had an instinct for the examination period, which always brought fear: the teachers came up with surprise questions, and the parents with the cane should one fail. The job offered food, since the master promised that he was saving my wages. A poor dancer blames the drums and the music; the master blamed the stick boy for poor collections. Moving along the same routes and street corners, the job quickly lost its attractions. I wanted to go home, eager to tell my stories to my friends. I was still thinking of my school. I was telling myself that the big boys could not have stories as great as mine. They would flog me for truancy, but the joy of seeing the snake was worth the temporary pain.

It was on a Wednesday that my job ended. If I worked harder, I could even research the exact date and time. I knew it was a Wednesday because, unlike my master, I could read, and one of our donors was reading the newspaper when I approached him, the same newspaper that was delivered to our house in Ibadan. I actually caught a glimpse of the headline, day and date. As soon as we left the donor, I saw the mailman coming in our direction. My master forgot to instruct me not to talk to him, as he had always done whenever the police or others in uniforms came our way. The man facing me looked exactly like the mailman who visited my street every day. He was carrying letters in one hand and his bag in the other. I could not have mistaken him for another person. I spoke without thinking.

"Can I send a letter?" The mailman looked confused, perhaps shocked. I spoke in English, which was probably the source of his strange look. A stick boy speaking in English at Ilorin? Perhaps this was the first time this had happened. I did not know the language that he expected the stick boy to use. I simply spoke in English, as this was what I had used in communicating with the mailman in my city.

"Yes, I can take it now." He stopped, looking me all over. It was then that I also looked at myself. My clothes had become dirty, tearing apart in places. I had not combed my hair since I left home. I had not taken a bath. I had not changed clothes or pants. I had not brushed my teeth even once. Then I told him I had not written the letter and I had no address at Ilorin. Before he could talk further, my master, sensing trouble, suddenly experienced a miracle: his eyes opened. One does not begin to dig a well when his house is already on fire. My master could not explain the miracle to the mailman. Rather, he appealed to his legs for help. He fled, running as fast as he could. A small crowd had gathered around the mailman and the stick boy. I told my story, the short version. I told my story to the wrong person. He was not like the big boys in my class who would laugh, ask questions, clap for me, and carry the story around the school for everyone to see the boy who could do what they could, who had the wisdom of a teacher.

"Grip him!" "Hold him!" "Do not let him run!" Everybody was advising the mailman not to let me escape. A woman grabbed my stick, broke it into four pieces. The mailman gripped me. He put the letters he was carrying into his bag, held me so tightly that I could feel the pain. He walked fast, dragging me along. I was now at the back, like my master, but the man in front was not holding a stick, the bridge between the master and me. He was not praying, not asking for alms. He was not even speaking with me. He walked me to the post office. Very quickly, he put me in a storage where letters and parcels were collected. I had already told him my zip code, SW6/456, Ibadan.

When I woke up, I was now near another man who wanted to pack me in with the mail. I was loaded into a van. No one spoke with me. No one offered food. I began to miss my master. At least he would talk to me. He once promised me that when I grew taller he would release me and get me my own stick boy. He confided his ambition to me; he would raise money to start a small business. His job, he told me, was too hard, too painful. His joints were weakening, the heat from the sun was too much, and the people of Ilorin were too miserly. He once assured me that the majority of them would go to hell if they were so mean as to give only small pennies. I had already heard about hell so many times, and I believed him when he said that the people were sinners. Even if he was pretending to be blind, how could they know?

I could see the roads through the window. My interest came back to life. I did not know the direction or destination. I was happy each time we passed through a city or big village. The van would slow down, women and children selling food would come closer, offering their wares. I felt like grabbing the food. We drove. Then I saw the Station, my Station. We drove past. The van stopped. It was the post office, the main post office close to the Station. Six men appeared, not to unload any parcels or letters but to unload me. One held me by the left arm, the other by the right. One stood in front, the others at the back. I did not have to be told that I was in some kind of trouble.

As we walked into a room in the post office, the first thing I saw was my photograph, in a notice announcing my loss. I had seen such notices before, pasted on walls, light poles, churches, all available spaces. They were usually of obituaries. They were effective. Whenever a person died, notices were printed and pasted around the city, on house walls, electricity poles, church notice boards, and stores, to announce the death and funeral arrangements to all city dwellers. People took the notices very seriously, as this was the fastest way to find out what was new and to prepare for their social commitments. I had read many notices even before the glue had dried. We would gather around each new one, reading it line by line, looking at the photograph of the dead man, the long list of wives, children, and grandchildren who had survived the deceased. When an uncle's name was omitted, he would be angry, printing his own notice to remind the public that the deceased had an uncle with income to print a notice in which his name would not be forgotten. I saw myself, the first notice I had seen of a missing person. I could read. I was not missing, I told myself. I knew where I was. I had gone from the Station to Ilorin and moved around the city with a blind man.

As if to display me to the public, the post office staff decided that I had to be taken home on foot, taking the same road that had led me to the Station. Two of them held the posters that announced my loss for people to see. People lined the streets to look at me, many shaking their heads, some abusing me, others cursing me. As we moved closer to the house, the crowds became larger, the curses became more severe, as people added the worst of them all, "omo ale." For a Mesiogo, "omo ale" was the ultimate insult, communicating the negative notion of a bastard, the illegitimate son who would create troubles for the family. In real life, no man could actually produce a bastard, as all wives were legitimate, even if the man had yet to pay the dowry when the woman became pregnant. A monogamous man could not even produce a bastard with a mistress. The British must have introduced the notion of a bastard to my people, who confused their own mistresses with the ones an Englishman would keep. A father who was angry with his child could even use the insult to communicate the depth of his anger, although he knew that his wife was legally married to him. We passed the cathedral and my school, descending into the valley that would lead to the bridge over the Ogunpa River, which passed through the city to join other small rivers that dumped their water into the Lagos Lagoon. From the bridge, one could see our house to the right.

I had never seen such a huge crowd gathered in front of our house, including visitors from other places, near and far. The post office must have sent an advance messenger to tell everyone to wait for my delivery, the parcel they could not put in a bag and carry. No one could have been inside the house. The mailmen delivered not the usual letters but me. An adult signed some papers, as people looked on. Everyone was talking, giving advice—wisdom does not live in the head of one person, and all the wise heads had mouths that decided to talk all at once. The stuffed nose disturbs both the nose and the eyes. I am the stuffed nose. The family was obviously embarrassed, ashamed. A small boy had drawn them into the public eye.

My family wanted to take me inside. Members of the crowd refused: why should hunters argue about selling the skin of a lion they have yet to kill? The crowd who had distributed the notice, who had read the notice, who had kept vigil, wanted to know my story. "Talk." "Say something." "How did you get to the town of Ilorin?" I refused to talk. These were not my friends or the big boys who needed my stories, who would rejoice with me. These people only wanted to kill me. After a while, someone suggested that they should wash me, a purification rite. There was consensus on this. I should not carry shame and sins into the household. This was my first and last public bath. I was stripped in public and washed many times with an herbal mixture and soap. People kept praying. More suggestions, more advice: "Do not beat him." "Treat him gently."

It was later that I heard that my family had given up hope of my return, not even knowing how to mourn. "My child is dead is better than my child is lost," was a saying that I had heard many times, even before I was nine, to warn about the problems that truancy might cause. They had moved beyond the idea of truancy to the bigger problem of magic. The belief was strong, and I heard it many times in my life, then and now, that one could become rich by conjuring money. *Ogun owo*, the charm used to conjure money, could be custom ordered. I once compiled a list of cities where the money doctors lived for my friends who were in a hurry for wealth. This belief survived the twentieth century, and it is destined to last yet another century. Were one to become rich without showing much evidence of work, the rumor would spread that one had made a successful *ogun owo*. A successful trader could make the *awure* magic, a lesser type, to attract customers at the expense of competitors. The most potent *ogun owo* or *awure* uses body parts. The money seeker would go to the magic maker, who presumably has the power to make money but is not yet ready to become rich or has been warned never to use the esoteric knowledge for personal benefit. The magic maker would ask the money seeker to bring a human being—a wife, a son, a stranger. This person would receive the magic to make him or her lose consciousness. In the most common story that circulated, the money seeker would carry the unconscious being to his home. In a room that only the money seeker could enter, the unconscious being would be made to kneel down with a calabash on the head, held in place by two hands. Whenever the money seeker needed money, all that had to be done was to call the name of the unconscious being, open the calabash, and take out the cash. The cash was limitless. Perhaps my family was closely watching the neighbors to see who suddenly grew rich before accusing anyone of stealing me. I have actually seen people accused of becoming wealthy by making *ogun owo*. I returned from Ilorin. No one had used me to manufacture money. They recovered the "stick boy" because of the mailman. Had my blind master loaded me into a truck and shipped me to the northern city of Kano, I would have been gone forever, roaming the street, nameless, homeless, without history. History does not like us to pose the "if" question, and what would have happened to me in Kano is just my own fantasy. Because I had returned, the interpretation of my existence and reality had to change. Indeed, it did.

Unknown to me, I had acquired a new status, a new life. I was now an *emere!* Everybody had proclaimed the boy and the trip as mysteries that brought misery. Even the respected clergymen at the cathedral confirmed that the boy's character was out of the ordinary, a mystery that only God could unravel. *Emere* was a child who could come and go at will, an unpredictable sojourner among the living. *Emere* was a category above the dreaded *abiku*, "the child born to die." An *abiku*'s death was and is considered unnatural, even when research confirms that it was caused by sickle cell anemia. An *abiku* was a punishment of the cruelest kind delivered to a family by a baby who knew well ahead of time that it would not survive. The *abiku* knew their game plan. In anger, their corpses were treated very shabbily. In the past, as recently as some decades before I was born, the *abiku* would be carried to a faraway forest to be buried among insects and rodents, in retaliation for the grief he or she had willingly caused. If the *abiku* was one of those with a soul that could reincarnate, the corpse would be cut into many pieces to prevent the reorganization of the body into a soul to torment yet another unlucky woman. Isola was certainly not an *abiku*. Such signs had not been presented when his mother was pregnant, and he had survived the age of infancy. He had actually grown taller than was expected for his age. Were he an *abiku*, rituals would have been offered to the gods to ward off his death. There were names to present his survival as a victory over death, such as Igbekoyi ("the bush refused this one"), Durojaiye ("stay to enjoy life") or Kuti ("he refused to die"). He would also have acquired an instant nickname: Ayorunbo, "the one who sneaked to heaven is back on earth." He never had any of these names, and he had returned from a great journey. He must be something else.

An *emere*, which is what he had become, was certainly worse than an *abiku*. Unlike the *abiku*, who was honest with his intention to live in the world for a few days or months, the *emere* would not give any clues. So deceptive was he that he would show great promise and courage in order to prevent his parents and the diviners from preparing the necessary prophylactic comprising a rich arsenal with which to oppose death—the *ase* (verbal commands to ward off death), the *ofo* (spells to fight the messengers of death on the way to kill the child), and the *ogede* (powerful incantations). The *emere* tricked the parents into a false sense of security so that they would not go to the diviners to make *egbogi* and *agbo* (herbal medicine) and *ero*, the balm to appease death. The *emere* was also potentially at war with Iku (Death), cleverly refusing to be represented as Iku itself in order to take Death by surprise. On the other hand, the *abiku* was honest in representing Iku, but in a respectful and subdued manner. An *emere* was a spirit in disguise, misrepresenting death as life. Since an *emere* was clever enough to disguise his objectives, it was hard to placate his spirit. An *emere* would scheme a death that was hard to prevent to deliver the maximum punishment to the family and community at a time when they were most at peace. Since the *emere* might not be planning a possible reincarnation, as the predictable *abiku* would do, an *emere* wanted a total death and a total burial, a deliberate tactic to ensure that sacrifices were not performed to seek reconciliation with Death and end the conflict between Earth and Heaven. Earth and Heaven were always engaged in a fight over supremacy, with Heaven showing its superiority by not releasing rain to wet Earth to produce food. Without food, Earth would lose its support, as human beings, now angry, would beg Heaven to open its doors to receive new members. The *emere*, living on Earth, gave unconditional support to Heaven, distorting the balance of power, betraying the Earth and its followers, annoyed that Earth did not allow visitors from Heaven to show their identity and walk around without question. Rather than confiding in Earth, his spirit sought communion with Heaven, leaking secrets, even telling Iku whom to take, including his parents and the classmates doing better than he was at school. An *emere* would accomplish so much within a short time in order to be loved and to attract praise. An *abiku* might do far better, but he could never be praised. Even when an *abiku* died, he must never be mourned, as he had been mourned before he was born. An *emere* would never fully reveal himself, his spirit hard to placate. It was when you thought that he was most active and healthy that he would disappoint you. A small headache that the normal person ignored could become his exit point from Earth, all in a premeditated plan to leak to Heaven the secrets you had long been holding to end the fight over the leadership of the universe and all its planets.

The family was in shock and confusion, and even the church had confirmed their fear. The family had not produced an *abiku* before, but it was jumping the hurdles to something greater. It had produced *ibeji* (twins) before me, and the first (Taiwo) died, leaving the second (Kehinde) behind. They mourned, but they were not troubled by that. *Ibeji*, too, were feared, and they brought their names of Taiwo and Kehinde from Heaven, allowing their parents only to give them an *oriki*. The baby that followed in the family, also bringing a name from heaven, Idowu, was no reincarnation but a separate being, not linked to any dead twin. When the baby twins became full-grown adults, the female twin could decide to kill the mother and the male twin could take the father. One could not visit Ibadan or any Yoruba city without seeing the mothers of twins singing and dancing in the streets and markets, like beggars, to seek donations but more to appease the spirit of the twins. Like *abiku*, twins demanded sacrifices although they were not gods. If one of the two was angry that he was being treated with inequality or disrespect, he or she could reject the sacrifice and proceed to heaven. Even after this voluntary death, a wooden figure must be dedicated to the dead, dressed like the other twin, who chose life, and propitiated in order to prevent anger that would lead to the death of the other one.

Twins made themselves understood, an *emere* did not. An *emere*'s breath had power, not just to give him oxygen to live but big wings that could fly outside of his body to anywhere they liked, probing the minds of others. If the breath decided to imitate an *aje* (witch), it could cause severe damage on its path, killing innocents and sinners alike. Twins asked and obtained sacrifices; the *emere* was too cunning to let you know what it wanted. The *abiku* might name a god for the parents to worship. The *emere* did not tell you who the deity should be, making you run from the goddess of the sea to the god of the hills, confused, exasperated. You could be angry with an *abiku*. When an *abiku* chose to die, you could burn the body or cut off the toes as a punishment, to tell the baby that even in death he would be punished. With an *emere*, you did not know the part of the body to mutilate, as it might release its breath to cause more damage. An *abiku* only preferred life in Heaven, ignoring the parents' desire that he should at least live for many years on Earth. An *emere* wanted to enjoy Earth and Heaven at the same time, traveling in both whenever he chose and with absolute ease. An *emere* wanted you to smile and cry at the same time, to shed tears of the torture of labor mixed with the laughter of life. When you laughed, an *emere* wanted you to remember that tears of deprivation might follow, turning the tears of birth into the agony of life. An *emere* wanted you to wail and smile, to seek comfort in sorrow, to endure wealth as if you were in poverty, to travel on a road that keeps the bees alive with the honey you seek.

To use an *emere* for money magic would not work. Not everyone believed my story that I was lucky to have returned home. The accident of speaking to the mailman was regarded by some as a myth. One-third child, one-third evil, and one-third god, the mailman was a messenger to deliver the *emere* after the colossal failure to make money out of his being and soul. Existing rumors confirmed this belief. Not all attempts to make money through magic were successful. A money seeker, known in the area to some people, used his wife for money. The magic failed, the wife died, and the man became mad. It was bad luck to have picked an *emere*. The process would work for a while, until it was time to go to the calabash on top of the unconscious; then the *emere* showed up, not leaving an empty calabash but suddenly regaining consciousness. The *emere* would overpower the money maker in the privacy of his room, bite him in the neck, and suck his blood, slowly, painfully, leaving all the signs to tell whoever cared that an evil man was around and had used magic that failed. The *emere* would simply walk away to his own house, appearing in wonder, as he had disappeared in mystery. The problem that the money seeker faced was that in supplying the human body to the money maker, he could not discern the person with multiple souls. The money maker manipulated the soul to conjure money, and the body only delivered it. With the *emere*, not only could the breath disappear, making it very difficult for the money doctor to manipulate, but he had multiple souls. There was one, the *ojiji* (shadow), that followed the *emere* about. When an *emere* acted as a member of the Earth, the *ojiji* stayed quiet, without a function. When a money maker used an *emere* for money, the *ojiji* became activated, frustrating the magic. All the money maker knew was one soul, that of the *eleda*, the one that controlled destiny, associated with the *ori* (head), which he had the power to manipulate, but the others, the *emi* (breath) and *ojiji*, were hidden, defying the power of charms and incantations, actually stupefying the money seeker and the money maker.

Once you discover an *emere*, you must act. My family acted. As I had no eyes at the back of my head, I could not see what they did. My two eyes, located where yours are, saw the front. I received no flogging for truancy. No morality lesson, not even one of those stories on the misadventures of the tortoise, an indirect way of teaching. Soon after the public bath, I fell ill with malaria and pneumonia. It has remained my longest illness, dwarfing the number of days that I now lose to back pain and hangovers from excessive alcoholic consumption. My head was shaved to remove the lice that had turned my head into a safe abode. I changed schools, as other parents were afraid to have an *emere* hang around their children, who had regular names and souls.

I saw more. Anyone who boasts of being able to fly must first know how to stand. Emere wanted to live in heaven and earth. He needed to commune with God so that he could opt to stay only on earth. The family chose the Christian God. More prayer, more Sunday School, more singing lessons. I stayed in the choir for some years before finally bailing out. The songs were wonderful, not the sermons and the prayers. Sunday School was an ordeal, one of early rising to go to church, of memorization of Bible passages, long psalms. It was not all that bad. To be in the choir for a wedding or a funeral came with its reward: good food and small coins to thank us. Emere learned slowly how to drink, sipping small quantities of communion wine. One could drink the wine meant for God. The rock in the middle of the sea cannot fear the rain. Stealing wine in the house of God came with instant forgiveness—as I drank the last drop, I only had to say that I was drinking to the glory of God and make the sign of the cross for repentance and deliverance at the same time. God listens to prayers, as we were told all the time, which might be why I was never caught taking small quantities of the wine meant to celebrate His glory.

My new school was fun, far away from home. I had to walk eight miles a day, passing through crowded streets, shops, the bank of the Ogunpa River. Emere began to see more, to learn more, to discover the city, to know that there were other places more exotic than the Station, and to notice even animals, which often mingled with people in public. Emere now knew the people from different parts of the country, places where nightclubs were located, areas where truants from school congregated, places where one could spend one's allowance before reaching school, amusement zones to be visited on the way back from school. No one can hear a broken drum. Emere was learning the tricks required to prevent the drum from making noise when it was beaten.

A twisted hand finds it difficult to grip well. To grip Emere, it was not enough to perform surgery on the hand, but it had to be performed on the mind as well. Not on Emere, but on the hands and minds of those who wanted to grip him. His people forgot to take into account the forces at work, forces that they did not control, whose consequences they must interpret. The train that took him to Ilorin and the road that brought him back were part of the changes that the British introduced after 1893. By the third decade of the twentieth century, the new railway system had connected Ibadan to the rest of Nigeria, to the north in 1912 and the east in 1927. Ibadan was part of the heartland of the cocoa-growing belt. From far and near, millions of cocoa bags were deposited in the city, to be carried by train to the port in Lagos, for onward transmission to Europe so that its people could enjoy their beverages and cakes. Ibadan was in the heartland of the production of palm oil and kernels, which must find their way out of Nigeria. The villages of Ibadan produced huge quantities of food, and the markets received supplies from there and other parts of Yorubaland to feed millions of people in the city and to send to Lagos and other places where people no longer needed to farm. The train that Emere took did not end in Ilorin; it went further north to bring to Lagos peanuts that would find their way to far-flung places such as New York and London. New roads were built, the arteries to supply blood to the railways, moving goods in small quantities from the most remote corners of the country to the various railway stations. Emere did not create the trains or roads; he only used them for small geography lessons.

With its history and central location, Ibadan became one of the few colonial headquarters. Throughout the twentieth century, it remained a regional and state capital, a famous city. The trains and roads have deposited millions of people in Ibadan and taken millions to other places. No one can count the number of visitors, no one knows the number of those who stayed at Ibadan or returned to where they came from. My family only knew of one Emere who went to Ilorin and returned home. There must have been thousands of them. As more people arrived, they stayed in the southern part of the city, creating many new neighborhoods defined by ethnicity, race, and education. Along the railway lines and the road that returned Emere were many new settlements created by strangers.

A fault line emerged. Indigenous Ibadan, the city of the Mesiogo, remained intact, also expanding. Before I was born, the strangers' areas had also become fully developed, well populated, vibrant. The new city center emerged far away from the indigenous areas. The Mesiogo had to troop in thousands into the new city center to shop, buying textiles from the Lebanese, Syrians, and Indians. The new areas were the first to acquire the modern amenities of electricity and pipe-borne water. Mesiogo who wanted cold beer and prostitutes had to travel out of their base.

The Ibadan landscape had been transformed so rapidly that the warriors of the nineteenth century would not recognize many parts of the city were they to wake up in their graves and take a walk. The warriors wanted to create a heterogeneous city, and they did so. Their concept of expansion and accommodation was different from the later concept. New people, usually young and restless, would identify themselves with a host and compound and be absorbed as family members. In the Ibadan of Emere's time, the city was more than heterogeneous, but the strangers created their own paths, brought their own goods, and created their own gods. Ibadan after the death of the warriors was seeking cosmopolitanism and all the troubles that came with it. Banks, schools, markets, churches, and stores had to be created in large numbers and within a short time. There was money to be made, by both honest and criminal means.

The Ijebu and Egba came from the south and quickly established a great impact in business. They invested their money in more businesses and the education of their children. Their wealth was visible in their modern architecture. We had a successful Ijebu as a neighbor, with a mansion, and some others as tenants. They worked hard, avoided too much leisure and pleasure, and took the Bible very seriously. Many who had lived long in the city were active in party politics, and Ibadan gradually became resentful of their success. Yoruba from other ancient kingdoms also came, with similar motives, men and women from virtually all the cities, towns, and villages. They could speak Yoruba, and the school system taught them to adopt the Ibadan-Oyo dialect. Millions of people could understand one another, and they could survive even if Yoruba was the only language they understood.

The roads brought to Ibadan thousands of Igbo, Edo, Urhobo, Ibibio, and others from the southwestern and eastern parts of the country. They had to work for the railways and federal government agencies. There were thousands of jobs for those without education as cooks, gardeners, drivers, and maids. They enriched the language, contributing to the use and spread of pidgin, the rotten English that survived on words borrowed from Nigerian languages. The beautiful girls among them civilized the social life. They did not have to hide under the cover of darkness to work as prostitutes; migration to Ibadan had already given them the anonymity they needed to engage in selling their bodies to the thousands of bachelors with some coins to spare. The street that faced our house might actually see a car that missed the T junction to crash into us, but generally the cars drove slowly, with their drivers looking for car parts, household utensils, domestic supplies, and occasionally women.

Facing our front, two miles from Emere's house, were the stores and homes of Indians, Syrians, and Lebanese. I did not know the difference between them, as we called them all by the same name, Koraa. When the airplanes deposited them in Lagos, they hurried to Ibadan to buy cocoa, sell textiles, and establish pawnshops. Emere saw them and became so fascinated that he later wrote essays on them, the so-called peer-reviewed essays that the university demanded for his promotion. The Indians we saw in the movies shown in the cinemas close to Emere's house were lean and tall. Those at Ibadan were short and fat. The Indians in the movies spoke and sang about love and friendship; those at Ibadan spoke about money, credit, and debts.

The road from Ilorin brought Hausa from Northern Nigeria. Not all the Hausa traveled by truck. A large number actually walked hundreds of miles from the far north, moving the cows that trekked along with them. Reaching the south, they sold the cattle. The process of returning home was not always pleasant. Many stayed behind, and many others walked back slowly. When they ran out of money, they could fake blindness, like my master at Ilorin, to recoup their losses or gather some cash to inject capital into a dying business. They created their own quarter, the Sabo, independent of others, with their own market, government, and mosque. They even had their own cinema, hotels, and prostitutes, whom they imported from the north because they did not want to come near the women of Eastern Nigeria.

The white colonial officers had created their own zone, the Government Reservation Area. So that the natives would not come near, they created a large forest reserve as a buffer between them and the old city. I heard the story of animals living in a zoo, and the Government Reservation Area looked like one to me. However, when I began to go there, I saw mostly black people and just a few whites. The Nigerian elite had been moving to the Government Reservation Area in the decade during which I was born. Elitism was being redefined. The first university in Nigeria was created at Ibadan, named after the city. It was then almost as young as me, only some five years older. The train would not stop there, but the road to Ilorin passed in front of its gate. It was a huge reservation, another zoo, containing humans and animals. Its impact was sudden. The teachers told us that if we were bright we would end up there. If we survived the University of Ibadan, we would pack our luggage from the hostel and move to houses in the Government Reservation Area.

Rotten wood cannot be carved. The old city was being abandoned, left to rot, becoming the useless piece that the carver discards. The fault line was being defined and marked—the old city was no longer elitist, and its bright kids must move to the new city. Later, in the 1970s, a ring road was completed, to move the elite and strangers out of the city without having to pass through the old city.

I never knew whether my father entered the bowels of the snake as I did. He had two legs. He put one in the old city, with ambition for a title and with connections to an extended family in the compound of the ancestors east of the city. His lifestyle reflected a partial survival of the traditions of old, as he had four wives and nine children. The connection to the old city was maintained. If he had political ambitions, he could not avoid the old city. The names he gave to his kids even reflected some of his aspirations. I have told you mine, the twins', and that of the son who followed them. As if to invite God to be on his side, his first two children had names of expectation. Olufemi (God loves me) was for his first daughter, an indication that he was doing well early in life. The name of his first son, Adewale (the crown is here), was of a superior order, indicating a preference for a male as well as for honor. Another son connected his present to the past, in the name of Akinlolu, a manifestation of courage and war. Then came his aspirations in another son, Ajibade, "the one who wakes up to see the crown," and Adebayo, "the crown has arrived to add to an existing happiness." Even his second senior daughter was named to affirm his own glory, given the masculine-sounding name of Adeyemi (a crown befits me). As if he knew that his life would end after his last son was born, a new name emerged, Oloruntoyin, just to praise and thank God, perhaps for a flourishing business or for reasons that he carried to his grave.

He kept another leg in the new city. The occupations that gave him a living, making clothes and repairing radios, were not to service those in the old city. No one doubted his genius. He installed the electricity for St. James Cathedral and maintained their communication system, all for free. No one taught him in school how to work with radios and lights. He taught himself, by trial and error, establishing a vast reputation as one of the best in the city. He moved out of the old city, building his house and stores at the edge of the new city, to service the needs of strangers and the new elite, those with cash to buy and repair the objects that defined the new age. He was obviously successful, so successful that he bought a car, which led to a song, actually an insulting one.

Falola ra moto
Ko rale.
Moto ti ko se gbe
Eemo, ki le leyi?

Falola bought a car
Rather than a house
A car that no one can live inside
What a mess?

As the story goes, he was angered by the song condemning his investment strategies, his false sense of priority. To manifest his anger, he built not a house but many houses rolled into one, such that from the front to the back, with an unused lot behind, it was almost the size of a city block. I could not count the number of rooms when I was nine. They were too many, like miniapartments within a complex. The car and the house must have moved him to the front rank in the social and political hierarchies. The car replaced the horse that his ancestors and predecessors had cherished as the most important expression of public status. The car and the horse shared many things in common, not counting the fact that both could move and carry their owners. They were scarce and expensive items that only a few could afford. Whoever could buy a horse or a car had money to buy the most highly valued attire and also had the change to buy and consume liquor, using palm wine or the beer that came later to "wash off the mouth." The horse and car could be parked outside the compound for all to see. They were safe. Whoever dreamed or prayed that the horse or car would die was always reminded that no one else might emerge in the lineage with the money to buy another one. The horse or car did not belong to just one person; all the members of the compound and lineage were entitled to boast that it belonged to them, even if they did not use it. I only saw the carcass of the car, but no one would have expected me to show a member of the lineage the car and the house and say that they belonged to "my father." The only appropriate thing to say was that they belonged to us.

But he built the house where it could also belong to others. Tenants, strangers, and citizens occupied the complex. While he fulfilled the ambition of building a compound instead of a house, as his ancestors must have done, he must have had profit making in mind. Unlike lineage members, who were entitled to live in a compound for free, the new immigrants brought by the trains and roads had to pay. They were no longer the strangers who had to be accommodated in the compound and given free land to farm as Ibadan had done during the nineteenth century. The new ones did not come to the city to farm but to make money, and my father had an eye on collecting some of it from them.

I never knew all the occupants of our house, most of whom were tenants when I was nine years of age. Tenants came from everywhere, and the second language in the house was pidgin. The tenants added to my language and vocabulary. I could speak the Yoruba that I learned in school; the Ibadan dialect, which is very close to the standard one; English; and pidgin, which combines English and Yoruba. I could pick out important words in Itsekiri and Igbo. My palate became eclectic, happy to receive various cuisines from other lands. My worldview was expanding rapidly, becoming a mosaic. I never noticed the change in myself until I got into trouble. When I imitated what I had seen in tenants, I could be tongue-lashed for not being Yoruba or for being disrespectful to elders. The tenants added to my pranks. The pranks I noticed, as I had to cultivate all the bad ones myself. Some boys already knew about nightlife, the clubs with the best singers. The big boys knew about gambling, the favorite being the betting pools played by adults who followed the British soccer league to make some money. Even those who could not read or write knew all the clubs by memory. They could point to the names of clubs on the entry form to mark their winning entries. I began to follow the British league as well, on radio and in the papers that we eagerly awaited every Sunday. I knew the tenants who won and lost. The big boys knew about all the new films, and they could imitate the best actors. Small boys like me were interested in the pranks of the big boys, their endless stories of encounters with magicians or famous musical bands, their travels to Lagos, and their romances with beautiful girls. Some even talked about London and New York, how they were making plans to visit these places in the months ahead. A few actually did, or so I thought, as tenants could break their contracts and the big boys had to follow their parents to places that I never knew. I was born into a cosmopolitan environment, and I lived in a heterogeneous complex. I did not fully understand the consequences until many years later.

My two ears never heard the same messages. With my left, I was being told to read the books that would get me to the Government Reservation Area. Emere was being compelled to take Christianity very seriously. The Bible and the messengers of Christ were everywhere. We did not need an alarm clock to wake up in the morning. Before the cock could crow, the messenger of God, a self-proclaimed prophet wearing a white gown and carrying a Bible and a bell, would go from street to street, from house to house, shouting at the top of his voice.

Wake up,
The Kingdom of God is near,
It is time for you to repent.
The ignorant ones,
Repent your sins,
Change your ways,
Judgment awaits you in heaven.

He was calling us to wake up, to pray and attend the morning service. The messenger was not from the cathedral. Many churches had been created, some even in living rooms. They were smaller than my church, and their sermons were much longer. Anytime I was dragged to one of them, I saw it as a punishment, and I could see other kids falling asleep in protest. These new churches were intrusive, and their pastors would come to the house uninvited to preach, read the Bible, and invite anyone who listened to the next Sunday service. Many of the churches and their leaders, always dressed in white, used the front of our house for open services, without obtaining permission from anyone. One came every evening for five days, each day attracting a bigger crowd. I would weave through the crowd to play with my friends and run errands, without paying much attention to their songs and long prayers. The vacant valleys and hills of Ibadan were being occupied by these churches. The hills and valleys were also being renamed—Oke Anu (The Hill of Mercy), Oke Iyanu (Miracle Hill), Isale Alafia (Peace Valley), and Ode Igbala (the Place of Salvation). They promised miracles and healing, which the cathedral never promised. Some tenants preached to me.

I was not confused about God; I was interested in singing, not in the message of God sent through the tenants and prophets. But I had to hear the message whether I liked it or not. Every day, when the bell rang outside, it was time to wake up. Half asleep and half awake, the morning prayer was offered as a preface to the chores. On getting to school, one must also confront the Bible, not just as a discipline called Bible studies, but as songs, sermons, and prayers. School opened and closed with prayers. I never understood many of the prayers, but I said "Amen" anyway. I do remember one very well.

Thy Kingdom come O Lord
Thy rule O Christ begin
Break with Thine iron rod
The tyranny of sin.

What is sin? To me, it was to covet the *asaro* of the other boys. *Asaro* was my favorite food—porridge made of yam, softened with water and spices; yellowish or pinkish in color, it looked so enticing. The aroma drove me to lose my concentration on all other things. I would want to eat my share along with that of the other boys in the class. To try to steal the *asaro* of a girl was considered mean, and one might lose the friendship of other boys. Coveting *asaro* was my only sin in school, as far as I understood it. Thus, when we were asked to pray silently and confess our sins to God, I would say:

Oh Lord,
Give me more *asaro*
So that I will not like to eat the *asaro* of others.

God never gave me more than my share, but I never stopped asking Him for more so that I wouldn't be a sinner. Now you can understand the cost of paying the big boys to see the Station, the determination to forego *asaro*, many helpings of *asaro*, in order to see something bigger.

With my right ear, I could hear the stories repeated daily by the big boys. When I changed my school, I could see the places they mentioned. On silent nights, we could hear from far away the fading music of live bands. The big boys would sing along. When similar music was played by anyone in the house, the big boys would boast that they knew the artists. Boys came and left, but their stories of Lagos and London were always the same. The small boys could not wait to become big boys, not because they wanted to repent their sins and change their ways but to experience the nightclubs, to see Lagos and London, to smoke cigarettes, and to carry a bottle of beer in their left hand. The small boys wanted to become adults, not to go to the University of Ibadan but to play the pools and make fast money.

Only the adults could balance the messages. Perhaps they too were confused. My father had moved his family to the zone of cosmopolitanism, abandoning many of the ways of old. To make money from his estate, tenants had to be recruited and retained. The tenants who paid did not see my family as theirs. They sought no incorporation into my household. They were attracted to the house by its location and proximity to where they could find jobs and enjoy the amenities of electricity and water. Many wanted to be close to the church or nightclubs. They could walk to both. Elites and indigenes established cultural and political associations to fight for their rights, to seek amenities. The adults understood the process, but they could not control the outcome. In moving out of the older city, living in the new city with strangers, participating in new occupations and a new religion, a family could produce an *emere*.

To dig a well, one must start at the top although the water lies further down. You and I have been digging the well together, and we are about to reach the water. In 1988, I chose to revisit the spot where I was bathed in public, which had marked the beginning of Emere's new life. I parked my car at a distance from the house. Half of it was no more, rebuilt as a one-story building. In a series of floods, the Ogunpa River decided to take some houses as a sacrifice to Yemoja, the goddess of the sea. The kind goddess took half and left the other half of my father's house. I walked closer to the house. The entire frontage was commercial. I stood still. In a moment, I counted about a hundred people coming to the frontage. I stopped counting, saying to myself that the preacher and his mobile church would not have a place to spread the gospel. I moved to the left, and saw more stores, as all the front rooms had been converted to places in which to sell one item or another. No one recognized me. A man approached me, impatiently posing a question.

What are you looking for? If I don't have it, I can show you the store where they sell it.

I thanked him and said that I was not looking for goods but my father's house. He laughed, and he told me that he rented the store from a man who in turn rented it from another person. "No one knows the owner of the house," he assured me. There was no need for me to tell him that no one had sold the house, lest I sow the seed of revolution in him, encouraging him to go to his so-called landlord, who was probably overcharging him. A successful caretaker must be a parasite, collecting money from various tenants and rendering half the accounts to the landlord. The landlord, good in other currencies, may choose to abandon the tenants to the jaws of the caretaker. I moved away, to the site of my bath. It could not be reached, as piles of iron rods and building materials had been placed on top of it, with the manager of the store chasing buyers on the street. I moved inside the house, then to the backyard. No one stopped me, no one wanted to talk to me, no one even cared to greet. The big boys had left, Emere had gone. I walked away, thinking rapidly, making up new lines to sing or recite, refusing to cry.

Isola, do not think deep
It is when people think deep that they cry
Look, do not see too much
Listen, hear only a little
Talk, wait for no answer.

People of the world, see my plight
Baba Isola has gone, the denizen of heaven
Mama Isola is gone, a child of the earth, food for worms.
Isola do not think deep
People who think deep will cry.

The cattle egret thinks deep and its color turns brown
The elephant becomes a philosopher and it shrinks to a cow
The cat thinks too much and allows the rat to play with its forehead
Isola, think a little, close your eyes
People who think deep turn to Emere.

Tell me: should I have cried?

he mamas were so many that I was confused about my real one. Mama One was my father's first wife, and she lived long after the death of her husband, waiting for an amazing forty-two years before finally agreeing to the reunion that she had spoken about for so long. She often spoke as if in denial, talking to herself about her life and her late husband. I never understood most of what she said, and I sometimes ignored what I did understand.

Mama One had a queen mother, Mama Yeosa, who lived in another house, about ten miles away. I did not know whether there was a Baba Yeosa, the father or husband of Mama Yeosa. Mama Yeosa was always there at her house, seated in her room as if she had no job, gradually accumulating fat and looking bigger each time I saw her.

Before you ask me, let me tell you right away that I did not know their real names other than to call them Mama plus an object associated with them. I am sure there were those who knew their names, but I never did until I saw them in the notices announcing their deaths and the printed programs of their funerals. There was nothing unusual about this. A young woman coming to the household as a wife could simply be called *iyawo*. If there were more than two new wives in the household, the woman could be named after the husband, as in Iyawo Babalola (if Babalola was the husband's name). When the *iyawo* produced her first child (whose name, say, was Bisola), she would become Mama Bisola or Iya Bisola. To complicate things at Ibadan, it was considered rude even to say "your mother" when referring to the mother of your friend or relations in the household. The acceptable label was "Iya mi re," which means "our joint mother." The same was true of a father, such that many people might not know the real names of their fathers. They could know the one-word *oriki* name, like Isola, and they would certainly know the compound's name. It was the British who insisted on the use of last names, compelling all of us in my family to add Falola to our first names. But for the British I would simply be known as Oloruntoyin Isola, both of which were my own names. People knew that I did not give birth to myself, and they knew my compound and parents. If there was a need to identify me, they could say "Isola omo Adesina" (Isola, the son of Adesina) or Isola plus my compound's name, rather than Isola Falola. I remember the story of a woman who took her sick husband to the hospital. When it was time to fill in the forms, which others had to do for her as she could not read or write, they asked her for her husband's name, and her answer was as follows.

A ki pe sere.

We never mention the name in vain.

As a mark of respect, she could not casually mention her husband's name, she insisted. The British officials and their agents were impatient with such answers and actually gave people last names if they failed to come up with one. Those who gave their oriki found that these had been converted to their last names. For hundreds of others, the British simply converted their towns and cities into their last names, as in the case of Tafawa Balewa, the country's first prime minister, who was from the town of Balewa. Shehu Shagari, the country's president from 1979 to 1983, was named after the town of Shagari in Northern Nigeria, his place of birth. Titles could be changed into names. In our case, it was clear: the occupation of one of my ancestors, divination, was converted to our last name. Ifa was the craft of divination; for bringing wealth and prosperity, a longer name emerged, Ifalolawa, which was shortened to Falola. One branch of my family, that of my father's immediate younger brother, refused the name, its members choosing instead the first name of their father, Akinola, which connotes courage and wealth.

To return to the mamas, I called them what others called them, names descriptive of objects, occupations, and their children. If the children were older than me, I could not call them mama plus the child's name, as this was also considered rude; it was more polite and less risky to simply say "my mother."

Mama Elemu lived on the first floor, in a two-bedroom unit located at the righthand corner of the complex. The complex had two main entrances. Looking at the two-story house from the outside, there was some deception to it. It had a long face, a very long horizontal face. One could not see the back extensions, a row of three long houses, two stories each, attached to the main buildings. Even when one entered by either of the two doors, the back extensions were disguised, the long, rectangular, two-story buildings attached to the two main ones. A door at the back, close to the community kitchens and fence, linked the complex together, allowing one to move from one unit to the other. Another door led to the bush behind, the jungle in which kids in trouble would hide, the garden in which the husband of Mama Elemu cultivated tobacco for quite a while.

Mama Elemu had a cowife, a junior one called Mama Ayo. Ayo was my childhood friend, but it took me more than twenty years to know that Mama Ayo was not his real mother. I am sure there were those who knew his real mother. I also thought that the husband of Mama Elemu was his real father. It took me another twenty years to discover that the husband of Mama Elemu was not his father. Ayo was the first grandson of Mama Elemu and her husband, adopted at an early age, integrated into the household, and growing along with the kind of knowledge that I, too, had. I do not know how long it took him to discover the truth, but by the time he did we had gone in separate directions, only meeting during a few social events in the 1980s. When the real Baba Ayo married another wife, she was a lioness who cared little about Ayo or his history. Clever Ayo did not know where he was going, but he was smart enough to know where he came from: he treated the lioness exactly as the goat would do, bringing out its head only when the lions were full and sleepy.

No sooner did I recognize Mama One, Mama Elemu, Mama Yeosa, and Mama Ayo than two other mamas appeared, looking much younger. They were called by some other names until they actually became mamas, one Mama Biodun and the other Mama Ade. The two new mamas were married to my brothers, and they produced their sons when I was old enough to recognize pregnant women. Since I was older than Ade and Biodun, I could use Mama plus the child's name for the latest additions to the list of mamas. Mama Ade did not originally speak Yoruba, but she picked it up quickly and became quite proficient; only her accent gave her away as someone from another land.

Other mamas visited from time to time, and I knew their names as Mama Bayo, Mama Pupa, and Mama Yemi. They used to live in the house, as I was told, but left after the death of their husband. I did not know why they were visiting, but they always expected me to greet them properly and treat them with some respect. I did not care about any of them. As soon as I greeted them in the way that they insisted upon, which was for me to allow my chest to touch the ground and punctuate my statements with "ma," I would proceed with my usual business, which was, of course, to play or run errands.

All the mamas often sat together, as if holding a meeting. Once I followed them to the old city, to Ile-Agbo, the compound of the clans. They spoke at the tops of their voices, as if there were a fight. Apparently the conflict was resolved, as they later spoke normally. Ile-Agbo, I would discover, was my father's birthplace, the home of the ancestors. In later years, I would visit this place many times, even taking researchers there to examine social structures and traditional occupations. I later learned that the real power resided not in my father's house in the new city, at Agbokojo, but at Ile-Agbo in an old neighborhood known as Oja Igbo. No matter how hard one tries, one can never grow older than one's parents. My father's house, as old as it appears to me today, is very young compared to Ile-Agbo.

Back to the mamas before we travel to another location. I knew that Mama Biodun and Mama Ade were not my mothers. On the day they arrived in the household, there were parties to welcome them, new wives of my brothers, Adebayo and Ajibade. They were so young that I called them "sisters" until they had their first sons and their names changed to Mama Biodun and Mama Ade. The other mamas often treated them as they treated me, sending them on errands, giving them instructions, asking them to make food or even to go to the market to buy beef and sundry ingredients. Some errands they would pass on to me, like the baton in a relay. As long as I was happy, I would not tell the big mamas that I ran errands in proxy for the small mamas. Only to settle a score would I reveal the truth to the big mamas. Their answer, demonstrating contempt for the small mamas, was always the same: "I sent the monkey on an errand, and the monkey instructed its tail to do the work." They often asked themselves what the "modern wives" were turning into, and no one dared answer.

I longed for the food of Mama Ade and Mama Biodun because their cooking was different: the sauce contained more curry and tomato paste, the pieces of meat were cut bigger, the servings were larger, and more rice and bread was served. They also used spoons more often than the big mamas, who mostly used their fingers, and they often waited for their husbands, preferring to eat at the same time. There were days when they would wait and the husbands would not show up till late. When the husbands finally showed up from nowhere with many male friends, they would finish the entire pot. Then I would hear Mama Ade or Mama Biodun complaining, abusing their husbands behind their backs for not leaving enough money for housekeeping but consuming the entire ration for the week. In protest, they would refuse to cook dinner or whatever the next meal was. This was certainly the beginning of conflict. I only knew of those instances that led to noise.

"Where is my food?" Baba Ade would shout, his eyes red and wild. He was a short man, the shortest of all the sons, looking more like his mother than his father.

"Go help yourself to the food in the pot," the wife would answer, not fearing the man. Many bitter exchanges of words would follow, even curses. The man would walk out; by the time he returned, he would be so dead drunk that he would remember neither the food nor the fight.

I loved to see fights, including the very first one I saw with a woman confronting a man. Sometimes I prayed for the husbands and wives to fight so that I would have stories to tell my friends. Taller than her husband, charming and elegant, Mama Ade was an Itsekiri, from the southwestern part of the country, about five hours away from Ibadan by road. As to why she was tough, the story I heard several times was that she came from a riverine part of the country where they produced ogogoro (gin). For many years until the 1970s, the British and the Nigerian government that followed regarded ogogoro as "illicit gin," dangerous for human consumption. Science says something different—ogogoro is no more dangerous than other forms of hard liquor. The real motive behind the attack on ogogoro was to protect the market for liquor imported from Europe. They sold ogogoro in my area; a tenant was even trading in it, selling it in small quantities that a customer could gulp in a second, getting drunk or pretending to be drunk and knocking me on the head if I stood in his way to show his new power as he walked away. To return to Mama Ade, when she was born, like other Itsekiri babies, the first thing they gave her, according to the story, was not breast milk or water but ogogoro. Drunk from day one, these babies became tigers and hyenas, tough to handle, tough to deal with. I never saw Mama Ade drink ogogoro, but everybody believed she did, and the big mamas always went about saying behind her back that she was an "ogogoro woman" in order to explain her personality, attributing it to the alcohol, which was difficult to control. When her husband was annoyed with her, he would confirm the rumor.

I saw her cry one afternoon, and I told myself that she was not as strong as me as I happened not to have cried that day. On the day she cried in my presence, she asked me to follow her to the market. The young mamas often wanted a small boy or girl to follow them to the market to carry their shopping bags as they moved from one store to another. We never protested, as there was always something for us, like small snacks of popcorn and peanuts on the way back. If the young mama forgot, one found a clever way to remind her. "I smell roasted peanuts," one would say. "Something is wrong with your nose," she might reply to taunt us, "I smell hot pepper." One knew that it was time to shut up so that she would not decide to buy hot pepper and put it in one's eyes, a threat that had been made many times.

On the day she cried, when she could have used *ogogoro* in large quantities, we were on the way to the market. We saw a small crowd to our left, with two men in the middle of a small circle talking. She asked me to stop, and we both moved to the crowd. They were watching "magicians" in action. There were some big wooden boxes in the circle, containing objects wrapped in used newspapers. "Play and win," the head magician would tell the crowd. One person would play and win a radio, another would play and win a wristwatch. The magician would promise the crowd that everybody would win something; they just had to dip into their pockets and bring out the cash to play. As people in the crowd dipped into their pockets and gave the magician money, he would dip into one of the boxes and utter some strange words.

Janito janito musu musa
Janito janito musu musa
Musu musa

He said some other words as well, but these are the ones I remember since I later used the lines myself, pretending to be a magician. After the words, the magician would take out a packet and open it. Behold, it was a clock or something fanciful, a valuable imported object. The magician was a con artist. He knew what was in the box, and those who won were the boys working for him. I believed him, and I enjoyed the show. Mama Ade believed him, and wanted a piece of the action. She moved to the center, leaving me in the crowd. She took out her wallet. The magician probably saw the amount in it or he was able to guess that she had a lot of money. She decided to play, and the magician asked her to spend more money to get a bigger prize. She listened and emptied her entire wallet. Then came the words from the magician, and some additional ones—"the more you look the less you see, abrakadra, braka, dakra . . ." He dipped into one of the boxes, brought out a package, opened it, and it was empty. "It was not your lucky day," the con artist told Mama Ade, as if he himself were caught by surprise. The magician thought that the game was over, and he prepared to make a speech to attract the next customer whose lucky day it might be.

There would be no next victim, at least not on this day. Mama Ade looked for me in the crowd, which couldn't care less whether she won or lost, handed her bag to me, and rapidly removed her head tie, which she used as a belt to keep her wrapper from falling away from her body and exposing her underwear. As she removed her wristwatch and earrings, she began to look more and more like the headmaster in my school when he was angry with a bad student. She started to cry, gripping the magician, demanding her money. A fight ensued, with the magician pushing her away and she refusing, shouting "kuku pa mi" (better kill me) as many times as she could muster the energy. Mama Ade did not have a job; she was dependent on an allowance from her husband, and she was struggling to recover the money. This was not a story I was thinking of telling my friends at school. This was the biggest public fight I ever saw, and I was not prepared for it.

Without waiting for instructions, I ran home as fast as I could. I reported to the husband that his wife was fighting with a magician on the way to the market. Baba Ade had taken after my father. Like his other senior brother, Ajibade, he had learned from their father how to repair radios, and rather than going to college, they chose that business, staying in the house where they were born. They became successful as well, but not as successful as their father. Baba Ade did not wait for me to finish my report. He gathered all his apprentices and walked to the second store to tell his senior brother, who gathered his own boys. More than fifteen men walked behind me, urging me to move faster, as I led them to the magician. They carried all the fighting tools they could lay their hands on—hammers, cables, machetes, sticks. Baba Ade broke a chair in order to take its leg.

When they sighted the magician and Mama Ade, they all ran past me. The unsuspecting magician was overpowered in one second. The boys who had previously won some items revealed their identity, quickly dropping the items into the box and joining in the big fight. The radio repairers and the magicians engaged in a street fight, with the crowd clapping for them, urging the radio repairers to kill the magician and his boys. No one came to the rescue in order to bring peace. The onlookers wanted the fight to be resolved by superior force. One by one, the magician and his boys were overpowered. One wanted to run away with a particular box, perhaps the one with the valuables, but he was prevented from moving an inch. The magician was beaten to a state of unconsciousness. I was enjoying the street fight, the first that I had seen. Now I had a big story to tell. I had never seen so many adults engaged in such a big fight in my life. When I told the story to my friends, it sounded like a movie to them, and one day we decided to act it out, to divide ourselves into groups and engage in a real fight to see who would be overpowered. It was a drama that led to some small injuries.

Baba Ade asked his apprentices to carry the magician's boxes. He took all the money from the magician and his men, even the money that did not belong to his wife. Now publicly humiliated, the magician and his boys probably crawled away like snakes, but I never saw their departure. Baba Ade held his wife by the left hand, not in any public display of affection but like a policeman holding a criminal. We hurried back home, like an army returning from a war. We had hardly arrived home when Baba Ade took an electric wire, rolled it into a flexible stick, and pounced on his wife, delivering without mercy as many strokes as he could unleash before he was overpowered by his apprentices and his brother. Ajibade grabbed him, pushing him onto the well and delivering a heavy blow to his head. The two brothers began to fight and they fought for several minutes until they were separated. I had seen the first fight in my family, but this was not a story I could tell. It was hard to overpower both of them as they exchanged heavy blows, but eventually the fight ended. The two brothers did not speak to one another for a very long time, after many people had intervened to resolve the conflict. After that, I never saw them drink or smoke together, as they had before. When Ajibade died in 1964, his brother Bayo cried the hardest, as if blaming himself for not resolving the conflict. He went into a long mourning, perhaps a depression. Ajibade was the first to join his father, separated by a decade, the father dying of hypertension and the son by an act of self-destruction.

Both brothers were tough, and I believed they were the toughest men I had ever met. Everybody knew they were tough and would never cross their paths. Even their apprentices were afraid of them. If Baba Ade asked his apprentice to bring a screwdriver and he brought pliers, the apprentice should expect to be hit with the pliers. Everyone knew this. The apprentices only spoke behind their masters' backs. The workshop was always silent, like a graveyard, interrupted with instructions and the sounds of radios being tested. One knew when their masters were away or out of the shops, as the apprentices enjoyed their temporary freedom by playing very loud music, smoking, drinking palm wine, talking about women, and, if they got hold of me, asking me to run tough errands and hitting me hard if I refused. Should I report them, they would find out, and my punishment would double or triple, depending on what my brothers did to them. After a while, I learned not to report their misdeeds, preferring to use clever tricks to avoid them or to run errands with the promise of a tip, which might never come.

The two brothers learned the trade from their father when they were in elementary school. By the time they were twelve, they could repair radios. I was not interested in this trade, although I knew all the tools and had an elementary knowledge of how a radio functioned. The machine that spoke without expecting a reply, as the radio was called in words that described both its function and its manners, had a powerful influence in the country. The radio brought news and music, connecting the country to a bigger world. I listened to the radio as soon as my ears were ready to receive words, and even today I still prefer it to a television, which I regard as a selfish object that wants one's entire attention, both eyes and ears, unlike the radio, which allows me to run errands while it talks to me. The television came later, after 1958, with Ibadan actually having the first opportunity in sub-Saharan Africa to see TV programs. Even then, television was not accessible to the majority of the population until after 1970 when Nigeria's oil boom made more money available and improved technology made mass production possible. Many small boys and girls would leave their houses and parents in the evening to congregate in front of our house, waiting for the television to be turned on, peeping through the window, fighting outside for a favorable location from which to see the television in the living room, and often begging to be allowed inside. When my brothers were not home and the kids were allowed inside, one would be lucky to have any room to place two legs. By the early 1960s, the two brothers had taught themselves how to repair televisions and the other new electric gadgets entering the country. I never saw them run out of radios to repair, and I never saw them without money, although they never bought any land or built any house before they died in the very house where they were born.

The big mamas thought that the small mamas were wasteful with money. Behind her back, Mama Ade was accused of spending her husband's money on the best part of the cow—liver, tripe, intestines, and even the legs. The organs and the legs were the delicacies in those days. The lean beef was cheaper than the leg, far cheaper than the liver. To the big mamas, any wife spending her husband's money on cow organs did not mean well, wasting the money they ought to have saved to buy a piece of land and then build a house.

After the episode with the magician, the big mamas concluded that Mama Ade was not just drinking *ogogoro*, she was smoking weed (marijuana) as well. I heard them say so many times. Whether Mama Ade heard it or not, I cannot say. However, I saw a fight between Mama Ade and her husband's mother, Mama Bayo, when she visited one Sunday afternoon. I was running errands for Mama Ade, expecting to be compensated with rice and stew, and I saw everything. It was time to eat. Mama Ade had two separate pots. The pots were there to see, and her mother-in-law saw them. She dished out the rice, using a poor quality bowl for her mother-in-law. Then she went to one pot and dished out the stew and the beef. The beef was all bone, without any flesh. One could not see the bones, as palm oil and the red bell pepper had given them color to disguise the bone and flesh. Mama Ade deliberately gave her mother-in-law all bones. Then I heard a yell.

"When did I become a dog? Tell me now now now! Am I a dog, can I bark?" The big mama was shouting, yelling, looking agitated, angry. A good herbalist need not advertise himself; an angry mother-in-law need not to do more than yell before she receives public attention.

Sympathizers arrived in the room. The mother-in-law picked up the bones one at a time, asking people to see and touch. They did. They shook their heads in disbelief, asking themselves why a woman would give bones to her mother-in-law. As one of the sympathizers walked out, she carelessly uttered words that no one had ever repeated to Mama Ade's face, calling her "Omo ologogoro" (a child given to hard liquor). Mama Ade pounced on the woman from the back, pushing her down, removing her wrapper, and saying that she would show the woman that she was an "ogogoro proper," the person who could consume undiluted drink, hot to swallow. The woman had no underwear. I had to look away; and this was the first time I saw the naked body of an adult. I closed my eyes, and I did not see the small fight that followed. They were quickly separated, and the woman ran to her room, never to repeat the mistake of leaning on a wall that was not near her. Then Mama Ade turned to her mother-in-law, behaving as if she had had enough, ignoring the rules about age and respect, confirming the adage that white teeth do not mean that the mouth will not smell bad.

"Yes, I gave you bones. It is bones you deserve. You have been telling everybody that I do not allow your son to build a house, your son who spends more money on beer and cigarettes than food." She continued abusing her husband, saying how miserly he was and asking why she had married a Yoruba man, as she had been told that he would never take care of her.

The big mama kept quiet. She could not exchange insults with her daughter-in-law, and she could not fight either. A word is enough for the wise, but Mama Ade was using too many words, as if the big mama were a fool, a big fool. Perhaps Mama Ade wanted a fight, and she kept provoking her mother-in-law, but a fight never came. The big mama was probably thinking that she had invited the attack and it would have been better to simply lick the bones than to receive the bad words from the small mama. A bird was now flying over her head, and all she could do was prevent it from nesting there. She kept still, perhaps asking herself why the eyelids and eyeballs had chosen to quarrel. Mama Ade, too, stopped talking, lest she become a radio, realizing that wearing a tall hat does not make one taller for long. The mother-in-law had nowhere to go; no woman has ever been able to get rid of an unwanted pregnancy by coughing too hard. If the case came to the public court, the big mama had all the evidence to win the case; people knew that Mama Ade was wearing a tall hat, but they knew the level of her head inside the hat.

People walked away, allowing the two to resolve their differences in the privacy of their living room. I did not see the end of the fight between the small and the big mama. Nobody spoke about the incident, at least not in my presence. As to Mama Ade and her husband, the small fights became part of their life and everybody got used to them, even ignoring them, as Baba Ade never tried the rod again, only hitting the road to drink and smoke. The marriage lasted forever, and Mama Ade died years after her husband. It was the big mama who refused to die in time, suffering the agony of burying her son and his wife, tormented by the losses that made her fate worse than death. Ade himself moved on in life to become a notable singer, Dizzy K, with many albums that made him the "Michael Jackson of Nigeria," as the Nigerian media was fond of describing him. Like his father, he refused to go to college, preferring the life of a singer. His talents are much greater than his dad's. When he is broke or his albums are not selling well, he works as a carpenter and cabinet maker, and in the 1990s he was able to establish a successful factory in London. Today he walks exactly like his father, but he moves in circles higher in status and wealth.

The small mamas, Mama Ade and Mama Biodun, were sources of fascination for me. The big mamas were dull, authoritarian, and quick with their tongues and whips. The small mamas were balm to rub on the wounds from the strokes delivered on the body by the big mamas. The small mamas wore different clothes, showing off the new outfits, and even asking me whether I liked what they were wearing and how they looked. I could confide in the small mamas without trouble, although my secrets were small. The big ones of truancy and the pranks with the big boys had to be hidden from the small mamas, who, should they know, would behave like their counterparts. When the small mamas wanted to save money from their housekeeping allowance, they sent me to do jobs, like grinding pepper manually with a stone or pounding yam in the wooden mortar. The small mamas never spoke about the big mamas to me, and they, too, were often afraid of the big mamas. Whenever the small mamas got into trouble or had a problem, the case had to go to the big mamas, who acted like a tribunal of foxes trying the chickens. When the big mamas combined, the small mamas became like a cow without a tail, mocked by flies, the wise chicken who became a fool on reaching the cooking pot.

To survive, I needed to understand the big mamas. I came to understand the small mamas very quickly: just run their errands in return for snacks and pennies. The big mamas were different, and they were too difficult for me to understand. Mama Elemu was the quietest, saving her words for anger or praise. She was named after her trade of selling emu (palm wine.) Her bar was a stone's throw away, where palm wine was delivered at noon, waiting for customers who arrived at around 5:00 P.M. and stayed until they were drunk or the palm wine ran out. She sold tobacco as well, working in the morning to take care of the leaves that were already sun dried. Mama Elemu was not too generous with money; one was lucky to receive a penny or so after waiting for weeks.

Mama Ayo never had money to give, and running errands for her was mandatory and without compensation. Her tongue was a horse, and she knew how to ride it. With me, it was a rough ride, not to give her trouble, as I had none to give, but to get her what she wanted—a quick errand. She could not read a clock, but when it came to an errand Mama Ayo knew when I had been gone too long and asked me to account for each minute. With her husband and others, the horse rode gently, taking her to safety. Whenever anybody praised her, I would become upset, annoyed that anyone would say something nice about her. Mama Ayo once sighted me and called my name to ask me to come, but I pretended that I did not hear. Hiding in another part of the house, I told Ayo and some other boys what I had done. As soon as one of the boys made himself visible, he was grabbed by Mama Ayo, accused of conspiracy, and given a few seconds to produce me or face additional wrath. The boy became a rat before the mouse, running not for safety but in pursuit of me, swapping me for himself for the cat to grab. "Mama Ayo wants to see you right away," he shouted loudly enough for Mama Ayo to hear that the message had been delivered. I left my hiding place, to deliver myself to the cat. She grabbed me, squeezed me, heaped on me the usual insults, and gave me a set of instructions with the usual warning, "I am checking my clock." She had no clock, but her sense of time was exact.

Mama One was the commander in chief. She lived on the second floor in a two-bedroom suite. One of the rooms faced the master bedroom, my father's room, which had been left vacant, as if the owner would one day rise from the grave to reclaim his bed. There was another room, a smaller one, next to the master bedroom, which was used as a guest room. The living room was usually vacant except for meetings. It was huge and could accommodate over fifty people. Her choice of place revealed the seniority rules in the household. Mother One was the most senior wife, the *iyale* of the household. In a smoothly functioning polygamous household, the *iyale* would have some power, convening her own meetings of the mamas in the big living room, settling small disputes, distributing the cleaning workload, sending delegates to Ile-Agbo if there were social functions, organizing community cooking, and monitoring the development of all the children. The *iyale* would be accorded respect, even if the other wives were older in age. But Mama One could no longer exercise all the functions and power of an *iyale*, as Mama Bayo, Mama Pupa, and Mama Yemi had already left the household. Whenever they visited, she probably tried to exercise these functions, but I have no idea how the mamas distributed their power.

When people referred to Mrs. Falola, everybody knew that they were referring to Mama One. Even the small mamas with the same name would not contest it. Whenever it was my turn to distribute the mail, I knew to whom to deliver it, although the letters carried no full names. It was the same people who wrote, and one knew their handwriting, and after a while they simply wrote Mama Ade or Mama Bayo and the address. The tenants were afraid of Mama One as she collected the rents and inspected the house, enforcing some order and rules of cleanliness. She could be tough. When I changed schools at the age of nine, my new school was where she worked as a cook. She kept an eye on me. She was a prominent parishioner of the cathedral, where she also kept an eye on me.

My official bed was with Mama One, but I could sleep with any of the mamas. All the mamas needed to do was check to see whose room I was in. The mama knew to wake me up and send me to the prayer session. There was no problem with this, and no one failed to wake me up. Except for the two small mamas, whom I called after their sons, I called the others just Mama. No one asked me to fill out a form to indicate my mother's name, which I did not know. Whenever anyone asked about my mama, I answered in the plural, "they are home." I never acted or behaved as a child with one mother. When a crack appears in a wall, the lizard finds the opportunity to enter. The crack that I was looking for was the mama with generosity at a particular time, one who would give me more food. When the mamas did not coordinate their activities, I could have two dinners by judging when the food would be ready in two places. They had to give me food anyway. If they cooked at different times, all I had to do was run to the second place and sit down, awaiting my portion. As I ate a second dinner, the Mama who had given me food earlier might walk in, joking that my belly would soon burst. When one mama was hesitant to give me food, I knew that the news had been leaked that I had had a previous dinner. Even the best hunter never goes home with game every day; my trick was probably known to all the mamas.

My kitchen and stomach extended to Mama Yeosa. I could go there faking an errand, saying that I had been asked to check her state of health, all in order to eat. The distance was long, the return journey needed energy, and Mama Yeosa knew that she had to give me something, even if it was a banana. The other visiting mamas never came with food, but they had no instructions or errands for me, which was a fair exchange as far as I could tell. Occasionally, they might bring clothes, and Mama Pupa brought more than the others. A crab is aware of only two types of water—where it lives and where it is boiled when it is captured by men. Like the crab, I only knew two types of mama: those who issued commands and offered food or a few pennies after a series of errands, and those who issued commands and showed no generosity. They all complained of one thing or another—"you look dirty," "your hair has grown too much," "your mouth smells," and a legion of others. I would do whatever they instructed before they used the cane to force me to carry out their wishes. Only the visiting mamas complained without the cane, which they forgot to bring along with them. The philosophy of the mamas was clear: the madman walking around was not embarrassing himself, but his children had been put to shame. My bad breath, dirty clothes, and bad manners were bringing shame to them, not me. And Mama One would be furious, as she was the one holding the purse, saying that people would think she did not want to pay for me to visit the barber.

Ile-Agbo was the headquarters of the Falola clan. It was founded in the nineteenth century and emerged as a prominent compound, producing warriors and chiefs. Its influence extended to the twentieth century, even when some of its members, such as my father, moved away to other places. Ile-Agbo kept the register of families whose members the Falola family must never marry to avoid incest or the breaking of the taboos that strengthened the connections with the ancestors. When I married in 1981, there was no need to check the register, since I chose my partner, as Baba Ade did, from another land, the Yoruba hinterland. Ile-Agbo kept the records of genealogies, and I can recite a list spanning five generations. The genealogies were coded in poems and songs, and when I began to recite or sing them I did not know that I was locking into my memory a deep history dating back more than a hundred years. The names of the male leaders, the earliest ancestors and their successors, did not have to be memorized. Everybody knew them, and there were locations to remind everyone of their histories, their achievements. My father was but one unit of the *idile* (patrilineal clan), and he and his brothers, uncles, and cousins were united by the Agbo clan. When the unit was extended, it became *iran ile-agbo*, a historical and sociological characterization that included all those united by one ancestor. They did not all have Falola as their last name, but everybody was regarded as being related by blood. I could never compile a list of all the members of the clan, simply because it is impossible to do so, as no one person can remember all the names. In a manner of speaking, I could talk about my father, my father's father (stated thus instead of grandfather), my father's father's father, and on and on. The possessor walks behind the object, and one can use a sentence in the attempt to describe a relation.

Agbo was the name of the ancestor who founded the family, the migrant to Ibadan in the 1820s. As the poet reminds everyone, Agbo was the beginning, the source, the founder, the *orisun* who gave birth to everyone, to the successors who kept the lineage going. No other compound or lineage bore the same name. The land on which Ile-Agbo was built was sacrosanct, inalienable, permanent. My father's house could contain tenants; Ile-Agbo could not, as all those who lived there had to be related by blood or marriage, and still must be, even now. They spoke the same language, and those who chose to have marks made on their faces received the same signs as those on my father's face. The taboos of Ile-Agbo, the foods they must avoid, defined their identity. Many miles away, they had Agbo village, the extension of the land in the city to the village (Aba Agbo) where members could farm and also live if they chose. The rights to Ile-Agbo and Aba Agbo were defined as rights and privileges that came with membership, excluding strangers. All the members had one clan *oriki* (the *orile agbo*), and we adopted the totemic name of a ram (*agbo*). Yoruba is a tonal language, and *agbo* (the ram) is pronounced differently from *agbo* (the clan) and *agbo ile* (the compound), although they are spelled the same way. One has to learn the tones, and whoever wants to write must learn the symbols above and below letters. The most commonly recited lines of the clan *oriki* reflect the totemic animal and the tone.

Omo Agbo
Alagbo Magbo so.

Children of rams
The ram owners could control the rams.

We could eat a ram, and why we were not prevented from eating our totemic animal, as in the case of other clans, I do not know. What we could not eat was crocodile, and I refused to eat this during visits to South Africa and Australia. At the edge of the compound there was once a big well, which held the family crocodile; it was one of the few crocodile wells in the city. There was a "crocodile priest" who took care of the crocodile, singing its praise, reciting its poem, talking to it as if it were a human being. I loved to see a fowl thrown into the well, to be hunted by the crocodile, which must be fast so as not to allow the fowl to fly away. Since I never saw the crocodile miss the fowl, I used to believe that the crocodile had all the powers attributed to it. As I grew older, I realized that the crocodile must have been fasting for days, and the mere sight of the fowl would bring back all its energy if it wanted to stay alive. The well is gone, the crocodile is no more, as part of the changes that have overtaken the clan. The ram and its attributes remain; even the devout Christian and Muslim members of the clan continue to refer to themselves as "children of rams."

Ile-Agbo was not one big house, like that of my father, but a series of houses in a big compound that was known as an *agbo-ile*. Each house had its own leader, one with a last name different from mine. A house could be huge, actually a minicompound containing a subclan. We had our own house as part of the chain, and I have been asked to contribute to its maintenance. In popular belief, this house was more important than the one my father built, where he could allow tenants and strangers. Without this house, he could not claim membership in the clan and compete for titles and I could not move up socially to become a legitimate adult. This house, still standing, is not about aesthetics but history. It is about the power of tradition to use symbolism for identity.

I never saw a wall around all the houses, but I knew the boundaries, as everyone else did. Other clans accepted the boundaries as well. The social boundaries could not be crossed, since everyone had to be born into a clan. When daughters married, they had to claim the clan of their husbands, while retaining that of their parents, extending the definition of the lineage, the laws prohibiting intermarriage. Should they divorce, they could return to their natal clan, with rights defined by their fathers. As with all clans and their residences, membership did expand beyond the ability of the houses to contain them. I knew members of the clan who lived elsewhere, but this did not exclude them from claiming membership. I never lived at Ile-Agbo, even for one day, but I have remained a member since birth, and now in far away Austin I am called upon to pay dues for social events, to sponsor new members for titles, to pay funeral expenses, and to repair buildings. My connection to the city is ensured by my participation in the maintenance of Ile-Agbo.

Ile-Agbo was also about power. It was the seat of customary justice, with its own laws, with which the state never interfered. The government could not impose a member on the clan. Ile-Agbo had to regulate access to family land, and if the government appropriated some of its land the clan members had to find a peaceful way to share the compensation. Where power was involved, hierarchies had to be established. When I followed the mamas to Ile-Agbo, it was probably because they were resolving a conflict while I played outside.

I was later to learn that the mamas were in turn subordinate in power and status to another person: the *bale*, the clan leader. The mamas who lived long also attained some power, as in the case of Mama One, but they could not become the *bale*. They were certainly more influential than men younger than them, and they had a great deal of power over me. I actually knew the *bale*, but I did not understand his power or status until much later. The one I first knew lived at Ile-Agbo, but some of his successors lived elsewhere, as my father did, traveling between their houses located elsewhere and the clan compound. The *bale* attained his status through gender (male) and seniority (old age). Age was important in the attainment of power. However, as in the case of my father, wealth could bring status in a way that could somewhat supersede age, making the wealthy man more influential than the older men. The elderly man who shouts in the compound without a penny to his name, so warns a proverb, is like a barking dog. My father did not live to any great age, but he attained considerable status and influence in his thirties. Actually, many of his children, including myself, became important in their thirties. When this happened, the expectation was that we would not live long, since we had used status to circumvent age, to cheat the process of aging slowly and acquiring influence in the process. What we are supposed to seek must bring joy and glory. However, there are two problems: first, joy and glory may not be enough, compared to those of others or what one dreams of; second, joy and glory may not last long. My father had joy, and glory, and they were abundant, but he failed the last test: the longevity of life, joy and glory. Thus the catch remains: early joy and glory destroyed by sudden death. The first two successful children of my father were the first to die, confirming the belief that myths and taboos were probably derived from observation and history.

In 1963, when I was ten years old, the big mamas and the Ile-Agbo were united by money and real estate. Their unity marked the beginning of my new history and life. Unknown to me, the big mamas and Ile-Agbo had engaged in a debate that lasted ten years. It was resolved by a peace meeting that created the new me. When my father died in 1953, he left an inheritance, which had to be split. The interested parties were many; the arguments were complicated. Let us blame the man for not leaving a will to put his house in order after his death; after all, he knew that he had enough to generate competing claims, to bring out the greed in the human character. Wait a minute! Those who died after him, smart enough to have written a will, did not escape a similar situation. Written wills in Nigeria may not be worth the paper on which they are written. They can be contested by wives who are annoyed that not enough has been left for them, by children born out of wedlock who show up on the burial day to announce themselves, by brothers, uncles, and cousins who believe that they are entitled to something and demand a share of the inheritance even when a written will has excluded them. In contesting a written will, the process may drag on for years, and I know of a fight that lasted over twenty years. Allegations of signature forgery are rampant, not to mention the common allegation of "state of mind," which is much harder to prove.

If a written will can still leave tough problems, it is tougher still to handle a dead man's assets without a written statement. I have seen many cases in my lifetime. The moment a man dies, his relations accuse the wife of killing him because of the property. As the woman, now weakened and damaged by the allegation, seeks a response, the man's relations appear all of a sudden with a truck to cart away the beds and chairs, the radios, and the fridge, even before the corpse is buried. When I was working at Ife, I saw a house swept clean when the mourning was still going on, with the movers unable to distinguish between private and public goods, moving those items that belonged to the university as well as the man. The ultimate is to take possession of a house, to take the property of the deceased before anyone else. A wife accused of killing her husband may be forced out of a house so that the brothers and uncles of the deceased may move in. While it is public knowledge that a woman who works contributes a large percentage of the money needed to build a house, the man's relatives may claim that the house belonged solely to him.

I did not know about all the conflicts preceding the sharing of my father's inheritance. I did not care about the meetings held to divide and distribute the assets, although I was around to listen to some of the discussions. When my father died, the wives, cousins, brothers, uncles, and others competed for money, farms, and property. Other members of the clan staked a claim as well. Invoking a nineteenth-century tradition, some brothers and cousins wanted to inherit the wives. None of the women agreed. Mama Bayo, Mama Yemi, and Mama Pupa left some years later to remarry. Of the nine children, Mama One produced six and the others one each. The women could exercise their rights to marry anyone they liked, but they had no power to take the children to the households of other clans. The clan was able to take over my father's farmlands, which was easier since the children of the dead man had opted for either radio repairing or a Western education. The huge house and landed property were the problem; it took a decade to resolve the differences, to negotiate the rules and divide up the assets.

As with many people of his generation, my father was caught in the middle of changing rules regarding inheritance and the rights of children, wives, and the clan. Land was the ultimate item of value before my father was born. Inheritance rules had ensured that land, the most important object anyone could desire, could not be sold and was hard to transfer to strangers or even family members. Occupations, on the other hand, could be transferred from one generation to another as children observed their parents. Over time, families within a city could establish a reputation for being the best in a craft or service, like my ancestors with their complex knowledge of divination. As the children learned the trade from their parents, this could become their greatest legacy, just as my two brothers took to the occupation of repairing radios. With Western education, the nature of the legacy was altered. Those who wanted to do well had to invest in the new knowledge, sending their children to school. Those who did so no longer needed to transfer family occupations to their children, since the school system could create new ones. My father was probably doing both, sending his children to school but also looking for those who could become tailors and radio technicians.

Inheritance included items that those who could run fast enough could grab, such as livestock, money, artwork, and various other movable items. These could be stolen by those who knew where they were kept. As with my father's inheritance, families might fight over the number of valuables, the amount of money, and the worth of chairs and clothes. I did not know who accused whom of stealing or hiding items before others could discover them. All I knew was that he who steals and eats a prawn is not satisfied with one and no matter how strong a thief is he cannot carry land or a house.

What always takes a long time to divide is the house and land. To the traditionalists in Ile-Agbo, the law of old must apply: they belong to the man's children and his extended families, the members of the subclan.

To the man's wives and adult children, the law was anachronistic. One issue was resolved: only the representatives of Ile-Agbo could preside over the distribution ceremony and sanction the decisions.

Under the custom of old, the first thing to be inherited was power, the transfer of the rights and privileges of an elder to a new elder, through a process known as *ogun baba*, which elevated the new person. Thus, my father's brother came to occupy the position of elder. In the new world of the 1960s, this turned out to be a useless position, as the adult children of my father were not respectful or close enough to the new elder to obey his commands. A man dashed to the floor by affliction should expect other insults to follow. The wives, too, could not be inherited. The next thing to be inherited, by custom, would be the wives, who could go to the junior brothers of the dead man. In the new age, wives could not be inherited, leaving the junior brothers angry and eager for other items.

My father's brother could fight back a little; the man who falls into a ditch teaches others around him to be careful. The wives who refused to be inherited had to obey the old rule: there would be nothing for them. Even under the old rules, the inheritance of wives was actually a clever way to delegitimize them, to deny them access to the house, land, and movable items of their husbands. Not all was lost because the children were entitled to all of these and they could allow their mothers to enjoy them. This was what Ile-Agbo decided to do, denying the wives assets and sharing what the women wanted among the children. Under the old customs, the eldest child could take more than the others, even acquiring *ogun baba* status in addition to more land and goods. Ile-Agbo decided otherwise, coming up with a new rule. Since the members of the clan were not going to receive as much as they wanted or thought they were entitled to, they modified some rules as they went along. The family members who had been living in the house could not be thrown out; however, once they packed up and left, they had to renegotiate their readmission. The friends in attendance, hoping to get one thing or another, were disappointed. When one person grumbled, he was asked whether the dead man owed him some money. As his reply was "none at all," Ile-Agbo, too, repeated to him his answer. This was a day when there was no advantage to being a friend or enemy of the dead man. The friend became like the coward who suffers many times, first insulted by a strong man, and then as the coward runs he is further pursued, falling down to be trampled upon by animals. After a small feast, some papers were signed, and everybody disappeared.

The outcome of the 1963 inheritance parley was the second most important event that I remember from my childhood, the first being the train ride to Ilorin a year before. It was on this day that the number of mamas was reduced to one and zero. On this day, I learned the identity of my real mother. She was not Mama One, who had been given a large portion of the inheritance because she had produced more children than the others. My real mom was not Mama Yeosa, Mama Ayo, or Mama Elemu, who did not receive any part of the real estate. She was one of the visiting mamas who had been coming to the house, but not Mama Bayo, who had fought over the bones in the soup. It was not Mama Yemi, who came to the meeting without her daughter.

My mother was Mama Pupa. I learned of my real mother at the age of ten! The first time we slept under the same roof was when she visited my wife and me in 1981 to congratulate us on the birth of our first child. Thereafter, she came for temporary visits until her death in the 1980s. We must have lived in the same house when I was a baby, but I do not remember those days, those moments of early bonding. She left Agbokojo to remarry when I was too young to understand her transition. By the time I could see and understand, I saw her only as a visitor to the house, not as a mother but as one of the big mamas.

Pupa in Yoruba means "red," and those with lighter skin are called red or yellow. I have heard some people refer to my mother as Mama Yellow. Were you to find her in a street in Tunisia, you would think she was an Arab. Were it New York, you would think she was an American, a Mexican, or an Italian since she looked Caucasian. At various times, when she used to visit, the tenants in the house had called her Oyinbo, the Yoruba word for white people. She was an albino with a different look from the others in the city, afin, as they were called. The conventional albino would have reddish hair; hers was black. Their eyes were smaller; hers were normal. "The albino cannot see in the afternoon" was a common saying, comparing them to bats, but she could see all day long. Many albinos had spots on their skin, different from the marks that smallpox or chicken pox scars left on the face, but she had none. As the story went, a minute before she became an albino, the gods changed their minds and stopped the decoloration process. Why they stopped it no one knew, making her half normal and half albino.

If we did not know the minds of the gods, we could know those of human beings. I came to know Mama Pupa's parents later on, and they confirmed the story that others had told. Mama Pupa's mother (my maternal grandmother) could not produce a child for years after her marriage. After many visits to herbalists, diviners, charm makers, priests, and priestesses, she eventually stumbled on someone who told her what to do, which was to plead to Sango for a child. Sango was the god of thunder and lightning, the husband of Oya, the goddess of the river. Both Sango and Oya had the power of fertility. When Sango was angry, he could kill with thunder and lightning, even refusing various appeals to Oba Koso (the king does not commit suicide), Sango's nickname. Sango was a god to fear, one of the most dreaded for his uncontrollable anger and the heavy sacrifices needed to appease him. He was known to have destroyed the houses of an entire clan, striking them down with lightning leading to a conflagration. In his gentle moments, when enjoying Oya's company, he could bestow fertility and prosperity on his devotees. Mama Pupa's mother was not one of his devotees, but she had sought Sango's favor for a child. She was lucky, but Sango left a mark, a reminder that the "redness" was his handiwork. As she could not twice go to the unpredictable god, she had only one child, the "red one."

Mama Pupa was betrayed by one sign. If you looked closely, you would change your mind and conclude that she was no Caucasian even if you did not know where she came from. Looking at her from the back, you would have no clue. You had to look at her face. Like my father, she had ila (facial scarification). I do not have such scarification, nor do any of my father's children, a sign of the changes in the second half of the twentieth century. Ila was not a tattoo meant to beautify the face, although it could have that effect. Ila was meant to distinguish one clan from another, and even citizens of one city from others. An Ibadan man could not have the ila of an Ondo man, the one vertical line on each side of the face. Mama Pupa had gombo, a series of engraved lines that look like crooked Ls while standing and Vs when lying down. As the number of marks and their sizes were not limitless, many clans could actually have similar ila, although one who looked closely could recognize small differences in the depth of the cuts or the length of the lines. Those of Mama Pupa were faint enough to be disguised by heavy makeup, but there was no need for this.

Ila was something to be proud of, not hidden. As the Yoruba with marks traveled abroad, the story they spread was that they had had a long fight with a lion who made the marks in the struggle, turning them into heroes who became chiefs. Since their hosts believed that Africans lived only in dense jungles, at the top of trees, they could easily be fooled with such tales of successful encounters with lions, wrestling matches that tough human beings could win with their bare hands and even without the need to run. As the man carried the dead lion on top of his head, the dripping blood sealed the marks on the face, healing the wounds before the man could reach his hut to clean his face with rainwater. Upon hearing this remarkable story, the people in the town concerned would decide to appoint a new chief and prince, choosing the man who had wrestled with the lion. No one at Ibadan would believe such a story!

The second outcome of the events of 1963 was that I left my father's house at Agbokojo a week after the division of the assets and the estate. According to the will, I would share half of the house jointly with the two siblings produced by Mama Yemi and Mama Bayo. Since I was young, the property would be managed by a cousin. For reasons not stated in the agreement, the cousin would also have to take me, to look after me until I was old enough to manage the property myself. The child and the property were merged to march into the future as one. A beautiful set, they both appeared, but he who marries beauty can marry trouble.

Since I left, I have returned as a guest only for a few hours. I was not the only one to leave, but I was the only victim of the execution of an unwritten will. I do not think my brothers and sisters were waiting for the Ile-Agbo to determine their fates and futures. Two brothers and a sister had earlier left for the United Kingdom to study. By the time I saw them in the 1980s, I did not even recognize the two brothers. One has made London a home ever since, and the other returned to Nigeria in the 1980s to retire, when only a few people were still able to remember his name. The sister returned a year after the execution of the will, but she stayed in Lagos with her husband and children. When I left, two brothers stayed behind to continue the family occupation of repairing radios. When they died, they ended the history of the first generation in our father's house. This ended the history not just of the first generation in the house but of my own relations with many of my half brothers and half sisters.

y world was shattered in 1963, or so it appeared to me in the first few weeks of my readjustment. Lizards lie on their stomachs all the time, but no one knows those among them with mild or serious stomach aches. I could guess which lizards had ailments. Mama One was upset that I would be leaving, as I was the only one available to do her small and big errands. My chores were already clearly defined—cleaning her rooms and the big living place, dusting all items, washing pots and plates. I could cook the main Yoruba foods, and I knew those items to heat first thing in the morning in order to preserve them from damage. I was the only one to be trusted with messages when visitors came and she was not at home. I was the only reliable courier to deliver messages to others outside of the house. I was fast with messages, quick with my legs. I wanted to save time in order to use the rest of the time not to rush home but to play, creating detours on the way to see schoolmates, to buy snacks and eat. I was efficient with pranks, knowing those I could do without being caught and those none of the mamas would associate with me. A village cock knows not to crow in the city. I did not confuse Mama One with the other mamas, and I knew whom to answer when two mamas called at the same time. When my brothers' apprentices and the big boys asked me to run unethical errands, like giving a love note to a woman or sneaking outside of the house to watch a movie at the Odeon, the nearest cinema, I knew that stealing a drum was easier than finding a place to beat it. If I failed to hide the drum, nobody needed to tell me that I would be in big trouble. Should I reveal the truth, nothing but the truth, the apprentices and big boys would be put in the way of danger and tongue-lashed for leading me on a path of moral decadence. An apprentice could lose his ladder to success.

I made friends at my second school, after becoming an *emere* at Agbokojo, and I retained many of those from my previous school. The change in metaphysical status and of school did not cost me all of my old friends from my first school, as many of them were neighborhood kids. Those in the new school lived in different areas. Nobody asked me to do my homework or even checked it. The mamas cared about the end of term results, which had to be good if I wanted to escape trouble. A bad grade would come with a note from the teachers. I knew that the consequence would be the imposition of additional errands to encourage me to improve my grade. The belief was that those who did poorly in school had too much time to play. If they wanted to do well, they had to play less and less until work, mental and physical, became the only thing available to them. A friend of mine who failed in school was despatched to one of the small praying bands in the city, the Aladura they called them, to read the Bible and sing for two weeks. He finished reading the Bible from Genesis to Revelations. When he was released, after God had surely entered his head, he was warned that the next punishment would be to memorize an entire chapter if he did poorly in school. Not only did he do well, but he became a noted professor of chemistry later in life.

My own punishment was standard, irrespective of the sin. It was to raise my two hands and stand on one leg, without leaving the spot. One of the mamas would be holding a flexible whip to spank the leg on which I was trying to balance. Sweat followed, with pleas from me, with assurances that I would not repeat the mistakes. Forgiveness came with a morality lesson, even one of those long tortoise stories. As all of the mamas told the story, I already knew the lines and could repeat them, but I had to keep quiet.

The heart is like a plant that grows wherever it wants. I listened to the mamas, but the big boys and apprentices were also great teachers. One group taught me to avoid pranks if I wanted to be successful; the other taught me to break rules if I wanted to be respected by my peers. I had to do both, balancing the wishes of the two sets of mentors. The big boys and apprentices knew not to cross the line: one must not steal, one must not run away from home; and one must confess to a prank when caught. Confession was appropriate as long as one did not release the names of others involved. A prank could lead to trouble when we mocked the adults. One weekend we wanted to find out which adults were "thieves," based on our own definition. We tied small pebbles in a handkerchief to make it appear as if coins were held inside it and had accidentally dropped from a bag. We hid, waiting for someone to pick it up. As soon as an adult did, we would shout ole, ole, ole!—"thief, thief, thief"—to draw attention and ridicule the person. It worked for a while, until we shouted ole, ole, ole at Baba Ayo. He ran in the direction of our shouts and grabbed me. I could not deny that I was involved. Forced to divulge the details of the game and the list of those who participated, we were lined up like real thieves. Baba Ayo asked us to remove our shirts and bend the entire back of our bodies to lean on one finger while raising one leg. It was one long agonizing pain. Baba Ayo and the adults believed that the best way to cure lapses was through severe punishment. The rules were pretty clear. I was not to be told not to touch a hot lamp, since the lamp itself had a mouth. When the adults overlooked transgressions, one must not regard their tolerance as weakness.

The news of my departure was no secret, although only the adults fully understood the reasons for it. My schoolmates believed, as I did, that it was temporary, even advising me to run home as soon as I could. Later, when I tried to follow their advice, there was no one to take me back. To the big boys, it became a good joke, as they mocked me for going to the "interior," a sort of primitive backwater, instead of Lagos or London. Britain they knew inside out. American cities were becoming popular by 1963, and people knew about Chicago, New York, Atlanta, and Houston. As I was later to find out while living in the United States, Nigerians know more about the United States than the average American does. Not far away from the house, close to the Station, the U.S. government was planning a massive propaganda project, a cultural office with a library, which further assisted the big boys. The big boys could draw the map of the United States, complete with vegetation, climate, and resources. They knew the train routes, the popular music, and the rest. Even my immediate senior brother, Idowu, was already dreaming about Chicago. Soon after, he left for Chicago where he became, like Robinson Crusoe, marooned in a land that swallowed him. If Crusoe devised the means to escape, my brother sought the means to entrench himself, carrying with him the lessons of the big boys I knew in those days. I very much doubt that Chicago taught him many things that he did not learn as one of the big boys. To me, his habits have remained consistent.

It was also while I was about to leave that the radio and the big boys began to speak about India, Japan, and the Soviet Union. The radio was bringing information about current events from these and other countries. The big boys were devising their own interpretations of the stories, telling us about opportunities in other lands. They talked about how easy it was to get to those places. One could use *egbe*, Yoruba magic, for the purposes of disappearance. Warriors in trouble during the nineteenth century had escaped using *egbe*, by turning into thin air or simply disappearing into the ground to appear in another place. The big boys told me that the trouble with *egbe* was that one might plan to land in New York and find himself in India. Even those who invented the initial magic had a similar problem, as folklore told the story of a warrior who, on reaching for his *egbe* when an enemy was about to kill him, disappeared, only to land on top of a palm tree amid thorns and insects. He eventually survived, unlike the one who was dumped into an inferno and roasted beyond recognition. *Egbe* works only once within a period of time, and one must learn to survive India before planning to go to New York. The big boys knew those who had used *egbe*, and it had worked very well for them. Indeed, they could mention the names of those then in London and elsewhere who got there without traveling by sea or air. When Biodun, my brother's son, later went to India to become a technician, the belief was that he got there by accident, as his original intention had been to go to MIT in the United States.

One of the big boys suggested that I look for *egbe* and go to the Soviet Union, where I would not have to work. In translating socialism into Yoruba, the radio presented it as *je ki emi na je*, which is "you eat, I eat," expressing a principle of egalitarianism in practice. We all could eat, in a free spirit and from a common bowl. But eating in Yoruba is not just about food; it connotes wealth and power. Wealth and power had to be shared before it would become possible to eat together, to share food. I could understand this. Whenever I had a meal with the big boys in the house, it was a struggle for me to retain my piece of meat. Before I could blink, my piece would be gone, swallowed by one who was engaged in a race with me. Should I complain, I would be kicked with the right foot, and before I regained my balance the rest of my food would be gone. There were times when I devised tricks in dealing with the big boys. I could hide my piece of meat in my left hand, spit saliva on the entire meal, or run with the food to a hidden place. Sometimes I needed the protection of adults and ate in the company of the mamas in order to keep the big boys at bay. No matter the trick, the big boys would find a way to get my fish head, the ultimate delicacy. Chicken legs and big fish were what kids most sought, perhaps because they could eat them slowly and make them double as toys. The big boys, in transition from boyhood to adulthood, did not want to lose the fish heads and chicken legs, and they would do anything to prevent me and the small boys from having them. They might promise to pay for them, reduce errands and punishments, or share small pieces. If dispossession by diplomacy was not possible, force became appropriate. The radio and the big boys were right about socialism, interpreted to mean that there was no need to fight over fish heads and chicken legs. Not only were these items abundant in the Soviet Union, but there would be no need for me to fight over them when *egbe* landed me there. Before the end of the decade, I read *Animal Farm*, which said something else, but at the time I believed the big boys.

The big boys were serious about *egbe*. They even knew the powerful charm makers in the city who could make *egbe*. A man whose mother had been killed by a red animal is scared by an anthill. The big boys scared me when it came to money. I trusted their stories, but their schemes frightened me. They had asked me too many times to pay for services and information that I later realized I could do or find for myself or for which I had paid far too much. I had lost money to the big boys so many times that when they offered to make me *egbe* to escape relocation I no longer trusted them.

The moon might shine bright at night, but it cannot be compared to daylight. I may have grown wiser, but the big boys were still smarter than me. If I was not ready to make *egbe*, they had other suggestions. The big boys knew the stories of many Nigerians who had reached Europe or the United States by means of tricks and perseverance. At a small meeting, and I should call it a secret meeting since it was held in the bedroom of my father, where we were not supposed to go, I was shown a map. The big boys said that one could take the train to Northern Nigeria, to the city of Maiduguri in the far northeast. From there, one could join some traders and walk northward until one reached the North African sea-coast. Unknown to me, they were right, describing the old trans-Saharan trade routes they had learned about in school. They even confirmed that it had been done, and again they were right, as thousands of people had actually traveled by land from Northern Nigeria to Libya, Tunisia, and Saudi Arabia. Still showing me the map, they said that all I needed to do was to find a ship to cross the Mediterranean to Europe. They confessed that they did not know how to do this, but they assured me that one would meet other big boys whom one could pay. To repeat what you already know: this was in 1963, a long time ago. To tell you what is new: I have heard the same story over and over again since then, and people believe it even today. The knowledge has improved; the big boys did not know then that instead of going to Saudi Arabia, Libya, or Tunisia, one had only to go to Morocco and swim a short distance to reach Spain. Today hundreds of people lose their lives each year trying to flee from Africa to Europe, perishing in the water as Cubans and Haitians do when they want to cross to the United States. The big boys were not telling me a story. As with the *egbe*, they did not invent the story but were giving me useful knowledge.

The big boys had watched Indian and Western movies as well. Heroic deeds impressed them a lot, and they had seen stubborn young men who challenged their parents to marry the women of their choice. One of the key achievements of a Yoruba man is to say that he sponsored a wife for his son, that is, he looked for a nice woman and paid all the expenses, including the bride-price. The younger boys wanted their father to change the statement to "my son got married," which means that the boy looked for his own girl, saved for the dowry, and paid for the guests' entertainment. They wanted to become more than free agents who snatched a beautiful woman; like the apprentices to my brothers, they wanted to attain independence quickly, altering the traditional balance of power between adults and teenagers. The movies offered them a path. They loved actions and guns. While they could only use toy guns, actions were easy to fake. The thought of escape from the house and advising me on how to escape made the big boys happy. None asked me to escape within Nigeria or Ibadan, perhaps because they thought I would be discovered. After all, the mailman had delivered me to my home the previous year. Instead, they wanted me to run away to Europe or the United States at the age of ten. It was possible, and they assured me that they, too, were planning on it. All I needed was the courage to hide in the luggage in the cargo bay of a ship or plane or smuggle myself into the toilet of a plane. The details they did not know. When some of the boys learned the details in later years, they actually did escape, but they found themselves in a world far more difficult than the one they had fled.

I could not have escaped. Like the man who knows only the stream in his village, I did not believe that big oceans exist elsewhere. The big boys' stories about other lands impressed me, but I did not believe, as they did, that the other lands were better than mine. I did not have their experience and knowledge. My world was smaller than theirs, dominated by school, play, church, and food. I had all of these. The trouble I was facing was different from those of the big boys: it was that after I had mastered the rules and territory I had been asked to move. I packed my luggage into a small bag, perhaps thinking that I would come back to live where I already understood the rules. I was not planning to spend my allowance on *egbe* or take the train beyond Ilorin. I did not even know how to swim, as one of the big boys suggested I should do when I reached North Africa.

I was carted to Ode Aje, a neighborhood east of the city. It was an older area, very different from my first home. When I first saw it, I told myself that the big boys were right to call it a jungle. I had previously come close to this place, as Ode Aje was about seven miles or so from Ile-Agbo, which I had also regarded as a jungle during the few previous visits I had made with the big mamas. The big boys did not regard it as a jungle in terms of being a forest, as Ode Aje was densely packed. There were some empty lots, but the owners were known, and there were signs of construction projects under way. The big boys meant by a "jungle" the opposite of the notion of "civilization"—areas far away from Lagos and the Station were regarded as "backward" by the big boys, places to be avoided by those dreaming about traveling to London or Chicago. They told me that they would not even date girls from the jungle, as the girls' parents checked on their virginity on a daily basis. Were they to be discovered to have lost their virginity, the big boys told me, their parents would send them away from the house, abandoned, to suffer on the streets like beggars. At first, I thought that the big boys were right. Much later I discovered for myself that my place of birth was the real jungle, located far away from established traditions, enduring customs, and tested habits.

The houses at Ode Aje were much older than in my previous neighborhood. They were mainly single-story structures built of mud and roofed with corrugated iron sheets. The modern houses were clearly visible, as they were the best ones that dotted the area. The motorable streets were few, and the best houses were located along them. To say that a road passed in front of a house was to praise its favorable location. The number of elites was much fewer. Ode Aje, like all older neighborhoods, was densely populated, merging with the other equally crowded areas to create a cobweb of compounds, thousands of houses that one could only reach on foot. Strangers were rare, except for itinerant traders and hawkers, making Ode Aje and its surrounding areas more homogeneous than my former neighborhood. Yoruba was the only language of communication, even in churches. The schools had to force the students to speak in English, penalizing those who used Yoruba. Vendors walked around selling newspapers, with the majority buying those published in Yoruba. Ode Aje was religiously plural, with more Muslims than Christians, and with "pagans" allowed to practice their religions undisturbed.

Ode Aje had no nightclubs, but there were small shops where one could drink palm wine and beer. There were no bands playing popular music in nightclubs, but one could hear the popular albums in private homes with gramophones or on the radio. Radios were everywhere. A government-sponsored information service had spread radios all over the city. All a house needed was a speaker linked to a city electricity pole. There was only one station, and the radio could only be either on or off.

There were no modern restaurants, but small stores known as buka, where only Yoruba food could be bought, were everywhere. It was a common sight to see children and women hawking cooked food all day long. Eko, a solid meal made from maize, was the most common, and most families ate this daily, buying it from hawkers instead of making it on their own. There were small daily markets at several locations, open spaces dominated by women traders. People walked to bigger markets located within a range of ten miles. The most famous was Oje, held twice a month, every sixteen days. Oje was a magnet, a market that drew thousands of people, buyers and sellers. I was to visit Oje many times, notably in the morning when it reached its climax with hundreds of people buying, selling, and talking. At Oje, goods from Europe could be found side by side with Yoruba goods. The same was true of Ojaba, the oldest of the markets, located in the center of the indigenous city. Ojaba became to me a sort of tourist attraction, with visits to the main mosque and the first town hall, Mapo Hall, now a historic monument. There was a rural market a short distance away from Ode Aje, at Agugu, where farmers dropped off their day's harvest for city dwellers who visited daily, both in the morning and the night. I had to go to Agugu many times a week, walking or riding a bicycle. In the afternoon, things slowed down, and one could see empty stores and stools. Vultures and other birds looked for food, competing with domestic animals such as goats, sheep, and hens, which also visited the market in search of food. One or two madmen and madwomen also wandered here. Once a mad person reached the marketplace, the Yoruba believed that the madness could no longer be cured and the family ignored the insane, praying for the person to die as soon as possible. Early signs of depression or madness were addressed immediately, partly to prevent the person from walking to the market. Once the family humiliation became public, when the mad person was found in the market, even curing the illness would no longer remove the shame.

Ode Aje did not thrive on modern industries, and it did not seek any during my stay in the 1960s and 1970s. Rather, it sought fame in its diverse traditional crafts. One could see a man working on a narrow loom to make handwoven cloth, the expensive *aso oke* used for important ceremonies. A short distance away was a carver making wooden toys or items that gods and spirits would later inhabit. I became fascinated with all the crafts. Indeed, Ode Aje introduced me to traditional crafts, notably wood carving and textile making. While my brothers took an interest in modern crafts, Ode Aje got me interested in indigenous ones.

Aje was symbolic of money and market, and there was a Yoruba god to take care of it, known by the same name. Aje could refer to money, the god of money, or prosperity broadly defined. In time, three interlocking neighborhoods emerged around the concept—Ode Aje, Oke Aje, and Isale Aje, names referring to the hills, valleys, and roads of the place.

Ode Aje was established during the nineteenth century, as Ibadan spread from the initial center of Ojaba and Mapo, located on the hills. People moved around the slopes and then to the valleys. As new warriors emerged, they created huge compounds in many areas resembling traditional palaces in older cities. For fifty years, the city grew rapidly, pushing new people out to frontier areas such as Ode Aje. I heard the fascinating history of Ode Aje: it used to be a forest, visited by hunters, and then became farmland. The most powerful male cult of Ibadan—the Ololu—was located there, originally in the jungle but still there today. The cult of the city was at Mapo, and between Mapo and Ode Aje one could plot a zone of cults, homes of gods and goddesses, and celebrated masquerades. At Ode Aje itself, there was the cult of water and sea, dominated by women and a powerful priestess. Along with cults came herbalists and diviners, and Ode Aje and the surrounding areas were home to many of them. My relocation had moved me to a world of cults and masquerades, of magic and witchcraft.

The various clans were fiercely independent, each inhabiting a clearly demarcated compound and land. A compound comprised an agglomeration of houses established with the idea that the extended family that inhabits them will grow to become a clan. When boys became adults and had the resources, they could add new houses on compound land. Unlike the newly populated area I had come from, each clan and compound in Ode Aje had a strong name to identify its origins, crafts, and distinctions. Many did not have street names or zip codes, but their name would get mail to them. My new playmates were identified less with their parents and more with their clans and compounds. These included the Ile-Ololu, Ile-Omi, and Ile-Aje, all clans marked by cults and masquerades. There were clans defined by occupations, such as the one named Ile-Aladie to indicate its interest in poultry, Ile-Elepo to show its interest in palm oil, and so on. Each had its reservoir of history, its long cognomen, and its pride. The new roads did not cross the compounds, which meant that many could not be reached by road. One could travel behind my new house for over ten miles, passing from one house to another, all of them only reachable on foot. Ibadan has posed an enormous problem for urban planning. With the compounds and clans maintaining their autonomy and integrity, disposing of refuse, providing wells and piped water, and extending telephone and electricity services have always caused problems. When extensions were undertaken, electricity cables and telephone poles lacked any rational order or consistency to outside eyes; they could be straight or crooked, long or short, all depending on what the clans and compounds had allowed. To modernize Ode Aje, as modern planners want, one may have to destroy half the houses, half the compounds. History may have to give way to cables and poles, a difficult choice for people to make.

In Ode Aje, history was a zone of contest and conflicts. The deans and chairs of history departments in universities would have the history teacher make the subject more lively. As he does, he may win major teaching awards as I have done. In celebrating the awards with him, the students, in youthful exuberance, may ask what they can do with their degrees after leaving college. At Ode Aje, history was not about amusement and careers. A microcosm of the larger society, Ode Aje comprised clans that used history to establish social and political hierarchies in the neighborhood. Who came first? Whose ancestor was a hunter and blacksmith? Who had a list of warriors who fought to establish the military might of Ibadan during the nineteenth century? Clan leaders knew all the details, and they ensured that the histories did not die with them.

History was about power. Each compound had a *bale*, the head of the clan. In the list of Ibadan titles, the *bale* occupied the lowest rung of the ladder. Also known as the *mogaji*, he entered into a large pool of compound heads who sought promotion to higher titles. At Ibadan, there are distinctions between traditional, established, and honorary titles. Honorary titles are conferred by kings for a variety of reasons. One does not have to be a citizen to obtain an honorary title—successful Indians and Europeans have received them. The names of the honorary titles are creative, reflecting individual accomplishments. An older friend of mine received a funny title—*Oni gege wura*—"one with a golden pen." When I was invited to receive a title in the 1990s, it came with an even more interesting name, *Asoju oba loke okun*, that is, the "representative of the king abroad," a kind of ambassador without defined duties.

To obtain traditional titles, the ones with the real power, one must be a citizen. One has to be sponsored by a compound and clan. The *mogaji*, a junior title, is the one whom a compound and clan chooses to represent it. Within the clans at Ode Aje, seniority rules were pretty much established, if only to stop an ambitious younger person from upsetting the balance. If a clan calculated that it was in its best interest to choose a junior person over an older one, on the basis of wealth and education, it had to hold long meetings to settle internal conflicts. Only a *mogaji* could hope to move up to become a king. Ode Aje allowed new houses to be built, but they could not become new compounds, laying the basis for the formation of a new clan. By the time I arrived there, the number of clans had become fixed, although new houses were added all the time.

Within a major neighborhood, called a ward, the *mogaji* might compete among themselves. Anyone who was afraid of a fight or conflict could not be a chief. I had to grow in age to see the various sources and manifestations of the conflicts. Siblings could fight over titles and land. *Mogajis* could fight over the collection of taxes and the distribution of wages. Those who were privileged to serve as customary judges could benefit from people in trouble. As gifts were part of the routine of administering justice, clan leaders could fight over who got how many gifts from a client. Guilty or not, one was not exempt from offering payment. When one *mogaji* was elevated to a higher rank by the king, it would come with an additional title that could put the *mogajis* of other clans in a subordinate position.

Fights at Ode Aje could also be about the expression of change. While my father had moved to the new city to build his house, many of those who stayed behind in older areas such as Ode Aje also built modern houses, mainly bungalows constructed with bricks and adorned with glass windows. One could see many new two-story buildings with cement plaster and single-coat paint. Clans and compounds boasted about the change. The first to have a two-story building added to its praise song another line, *ile onigareti*—"the compound with a two-story house"—just to tell others that a clan member was successful. The clans that produced educated people like my father would flaunt them, begging them to build and stay within the clan rather than moving elsewhere. In a short while, I came to know who was who at Ode Aje, the men of status and power, the objects of praise and attraction.

My cousin was one of the new men of status. He had a two-story house, built with mud bricks and plastered with cement. It was never painted, a sign that the owner was not rich enough. Smaller than my father's house, it still had twelve rooms, which was big by Ode Aje's standard. A street passed in front of it, a mark of success. There were large lawns in front and back, providing open courtyards for meetings and small gatherings. My new school was opposite the house, so close that I could leave the house when the morning bell rang to start the day. My cousin was not a *bale*—he did not become one until over twenty years later. However, he was extremely influential in Ode Aje and all the adjoining areas, well known and talked about. Not many people knew his real names—S. O. Adediran—but they were familiar with his nickname, Baba Olopa. *Olopa* means "policeman," and they added *baba* (father) to indicate that he was a senior officer. He was a sergeant-major in the Nigerian Police Force, working in the accounts section at the police headquarters, located far away in the new city, on the same road as the Station. Five days a week, he traveled to the new city, at first by motorcycle. Later he bought a used car.

The people in the neighborhood called me Omo Baba Olopa (son of a police officer), and only my schoolmates and friends called me Toyin. My two names were a source of mockery as well as instant recognition. Toyin was generally regarded as a woman's name, and I was the first male many had come across bearing such a feminine name. When pronounced softly by a man, it was a mock seduction, an offensive way to propose to me. When it was shouted, it was to deride me for being a man with the alleged weakness of a woman. One of my new schoolmates asked the number of my ribs, saying that it was two short of his own; this was an invitation to a wrestling match so I could prove that we had the same masculine number of ribs. I never overcame the association of my name with a woman. All my school diplomas, even from the schools where I was known, including my Ph.D. certificate, came with the addition of "Miss." I have had to engage in many small battles to get them changed to "Mr." When I began to give public lectures and seminars, some people invited me thinking that I was a woman. The most astonishing occasion was at Vancouver, where my roommate was a woman. I was already comfortably asleep; my roommate came very late, and so as not to disturb me she did not turn on the light. When she discovered me the next morning, she screamed while I laughed. There is some fun to the confusion. Once in a while I receive advances by mail from men who think that I am a woman.

The mockery surrounding Omo Baba Olopa lasted only about ten years but was much more brutal. The joke had nothing to do with me; it was more about the police force and those associated with it. Whether in the new or old city, the police were ridiculed by the public. Regarded as agents of government and the errand boys of politicians, the police were treated with contempt. Behind their back, no one said anything pleasant about them. "You should not hope to be successful," someone told me in my very first week because I was associated with a policeman. I did not fully understand the comment until others made similar remarks. The popular belief was that as police officers mistreated people their punishment from God was to have bad children who would be worse than the criminals they had arrested and maltreated. Indeed, some people believed that they should not assist the children of police officers, as this would improve their destinies. The police were also associated with corruption, using all kinds of excuses to take money from innocent people.

Before the innocents released their money, they placed a curse on it, bringing down doom on the receiver and his children. When I fully understood the association of the curse with the police and their children, I quickly denied being the son of a policeman. The history of my relocation and the psychology associated with the name made me want to reject fatherhood, to protest against it.

If I was confused about mamas in the first ten years of my life, matters were clarified thereafter and forever. It was at Ode Aje that I learned about polygamy and its practices. Whether Christian or Muslim, worshiper of the god of iron or thunder, educated or noneducated, the majority of adult males at Ode Aje had two or more wives. Only a few had one wife: members of the modern elite working for the government, the schoolteacher, or just the young man limited by resources. All the neighborhoods surrounding Ode Aje were inhabited by polygamists, making polygamy one of the main "tourist attractions" next to the cults.

It was at Ode Aje that I saw polygamy in action, and I was not prepared for the introduction, a life drama in the accumulation of objects. The experience came too soon, too suddenly. Two days after my arrival, a woman walked in, unaccompanied, with two bags. Before the people could ask who she was, whom she was looking for, and where she was traveling to, Baba Olopa came in smiling and jubilant and announced to the others in the house, "She is my new wife." There was no ceremony, no party, no exchange of gifts, no rituals. This was a shock to me. I had witnessed many weddings as a member of the choir, singing and dancing and praying for brides and bridegrooms I did not know. In turn, we would receive generous shares of excellent food and "minerals" to drink. Rich families would even volunteer to wash our gowns and robes, clean the church, donate a fan, buy a pew. When Mama Ade and Mama Biodun were brought to my old house, they were welcomed with a holiday, too much food and drink, and endless prayers in which I had no interest. I had no clue why the wedding at Ode Aje was different. I was too new to ask questions, but I was not prevented from watching the proceedings.

Baba Olopa asked someone to show the woman her room. The person he asked to act as chaperon was a young lady who did so under protest, rolling her eyes and raising her nose in the process. It was then that I knew she was also Baba Olopa's wife. Rolling her eyes and raising her nose, she had scorned the new woman and insulted her husband at the same time. The new wife said nothing, just remained full of smiles as she was led to her new room. Then the husband, now angry, ordered the chaperon to return as soon as the errand was done. There and then he gave his public lecture, the first in a series that I had to get used to.

Arike, I have warned you many times to check your jealousy. You continue to behave like a small child, ignoring what the elders told us, that a small child who knows how to wash his hands will eat with his elders. You are not behaving in a manner becoming to an elder, and I will not let you remain a child in my house. Your hand is now missing the mouth, preventing you from getting water and food.

He spoke much longer than this, but these were the lines in Yoruba that I memorized and later adapted for a small school drama. As he spoke, some adults disappeared, and those who stayed remained quiet. He reminded those who stayed behind that he had already told them that he had not reached the number of wives he intended to marry. He was not about to become a man who eats and dies alone. Then he narrated a brief family history, a fragmented one, saying that his father had possessed fourteen wives. His father and my father's father were brothers. The Yoruba have no words for cousins, uncles, nephews, and the like, and I could only call him Father. Not everyone whom a Yoruba calls father, brother, sister, or uncle is what Americans associate with those words. Even in Austin, Texas, children of Nigerian parents call me Daddy and their parents call me Brother or Uncle, both more respectful than calling me Toyin. As Baba Olopa spoke, I learned that one of my ancestors had had fourteen wives, and I became curious about the family tree, which later led me to Ile-Agbo to request a chart that became so complicated that it generated an essay as well as a research methodology on family history.

As he continued to speak, he bemoaned the fact that he would not be able to match his own father, not because he did not want to try but because of "useless women" like the chaperon, who complained over nothing, who did not like their fellow human beings. An older lady intervened to calm him down, pleading that Baba Olopa should not be fighting with a woman as young as the chaperon. She was too young to understand, to appreciate, and to be grateful, continued the older woman, now on her knees, pleading. She closed by saying that the wisdom of the chaperon was no greater than that of an ant.

The older woman was right on one score—if wisdom were to be judged by size, the ant would be very foolish before the elephant. Baba Olopa was the elephant, the big man in the jungle who made the ants feel not only small but foolish. He was never a man of violence toward his wives. He used words to weaken them, to cut them down to size, to intimidate them into submission. He had more than words. His strategy was effective: he would encourage any wife to divorce him. Divorce carried no payment, no form of compensation. Other men might legitimately request the return of part of the dowry, if only to make separation difficult and punish the parents of their aggrieved wife. Baba Olopa paid dowry only once in the decade in which I saw him in action. Rather, he concentrated on marrying divorced women whom others probably did not want or younger ones from poor families who demanded very little.

Baba Olopa could not have had fourteen wives like his dad because I never saw him either at home or in any photograph with fourteen women. However, when I tried to make an accurate count in 1976, by asking as many people as I could talk to and adding the number of wives I knew, I counted more than ten. In the short span of seven years, he married five. The trouble was that the divorce rate was high, making it impossible to know which ones to include or exclude. Like a revolving door, one would come in to allow another to leave. Only three wives lasted for about ten years, and one was deadwood of no importance. I never learned the number of his children, even when I tried to count, although I should have asked him directly. I never knew or saw all of his children, as more than half never lived with him.

The deadwood of no account in the household was the older woman who intervened in the row on the day of Baba Olopa's glory. Her name was simple: Iya Aladie, derived from her occupation of selling hens. Every morning, except on Sundays when she went to church, she would carry a cage of birds on her head to the Ojaba or Oje market and return in the evening. Everyone knew that this could not be a profitable occupation, but it was honest and hard enough to keep her busy. Iya Aladie always looked malnourished to me. She was the senior wife, but she exercised no influence or power over the cowives other than occasional pleas for pardon. Her cowives knew that although the hair on the head is older than the beard on the chin a well-cultivated beard may attract more respect than the hair. Iya Aladie lacked the authority of a senior wife. By the time I moved to Ode Aje, Iya Aladie had lost her recognition as senior wife but there was no one to move into her shoes. After she had borne a son to Baba Olopa, the only child whom God and other men gave her, she divorced Baba Olopa and married another man. Years later, this marriage broke up. She returned to Ode Aje after many appeals, based on the need to return to be with her son. Baba Olopa was forgiving. When I was there, two other women who had left also returned. By leaving and returning, Iya Aladie had become damaged goods, a prisoner like the very hens she caged to sell. I later learned that she was not allotted any sex ration by Baba Olopa, who needed his time and energy for the other wives.

The other women knew that Iya Aladie needed to beg for sex. One audacious one said so in a fight, boasting that her looks and skin were still so good that Baba Olopa would not discard her as he had Iya Aladie. I think it was common knowledge that Iya Aladie was ignored by her husband. She was seldom invited to the private bedroom, and her husband never went to her room. They kept to the agreement that she would return to the house just to take care of her son. As her son grew older, it was clear to the other women, who had an eye on the property, that they had to fight two enemies, Iya Aladie and her son, who had come to stay for good. Perhaps to cultivate affection, Iya Aladie would cook free lunch for everyone on Sunday. I partook in the meals for a number of years, until one cowife told me that Iya Aladie was putting a magic potion in them to "buy love." All women in a polygamous arrangement knew very well that love could be purchased through either good manners or magic.

I was probably too young in the beginning to understand the politics of sex. But the maturity to understand what was going on came rather early, I think by the time I was eleven. The new wife was the jewel of the bed, the one who had automatic admission to the private bedroom and actually slept there. If she wanted to sleep there for a long period, her prayer was not to become pregnant. As soon as she became pregnant, her status began to decline. She had to move to her own bedroom to allow another wife the privilege. The next person could be an existing member of the harem, one whose child could be weaned in order to prepare for the production of another baby. Or it could be a new addition such as the one who walked in a few days after my arrival. The most ignored could decide to leave.

Polygamy is like government: the forms and goals are not always the same. Baba Olopa followed the authoritarian model, carrying patriarchy to an extreme. He controlled the wallet; he owned his own house, land, and car; and he distributed his resources according to his whims and caprices. The woman whom he loved the most would get the most at a particular time. The children of the woman he loved the most received the most attention. Once a wife was in trouble, her children, too, would be in trouble. Not only did he not prevent his wives from leaving, but he did not stop them from taking their children with them. Many children left, never to come back. Some returned to seek favors, which they probably did not receive.

Ode Aje had many other forms of polygamy. The next-door neighbor to the right was a Muslim, called an Alhaji because he had performed the pilgrimage to Mecca. When I arrived at Ode Aje, he had only three wives. One of them sold cooked food, and we relied on her for breakfast and dinner. The other sold clothes, hawking them around the city. The third had a small kiosk, selling daily domestic goods such as bath soap, detergents, toothpaste, and milk, which people bought in small quantities. He married another wife a year after my arrival, stopping at four.

In the Alhaji's model, he reduced the number of wives to a manageable number, and he did two other things differently from Baba Olopa. He set up small businesses for all the women. The initial capital was his, and everybody knew this. As far as the women were concerned, the marriage gave multiple meanings to their lives: they became wives, childbearers, and traders. There was no need to complain about Alhaji or to divorce him. They were able to occupy their time in a productive manner, interacting with suppliers to negotiate prices, obtain fresh supplies, and monitor economic changes. The traffic of customers kept them talking and busy all day long. So occupied and busy did they become that they worried less and less about Alhaji and more and more about themselves and their investments. As they succeeded, the Alhaji himself benefited, taking more money as gifts and loans from his wives in excess of the initial capital. Since he had his own business, as well as addition of monies from three sources, he would probably remain richer than the women, thus maintaining the initial imbalance in power and money. Should the Alhaji become reckless, pursuing deals that could bankrupt him, the wives would stop aiding him with money. An angry wife could return the entire initial capital and ask him to leave her alone.

The Alhaji's model was one of the most common. As objectionable as polygamy may have become, the model allowed women to assert themselves and pursue their ambitions within a patriarchal structure. The woman who had a problem was Alhaji's fourth and last wife. Young and beautiful, she could sleep with Alhaji for as long as she wanted. Indeed, the three other women may have been happy to be left alone, satisfied with a once a month visitation. Of course, I have no way of knowing the number of times Alhaji made sexual advances. What I know is that the three women were always at work, even praying in their workplaces instead of going to mosques. I also knew that the three women did not do household chores. The fourth wife complained to me and others that she was a slave to Alhaji and his three other wives. She could only complain outside of the house, coming to ours to voice her grievances and returning quietly to her place. Her salvation lay not in fighting polygamy but in encouraging Alhaji to take a fifth wife. Alhaji refused. I know that she pressured Alhaji to marry more wives, even promising to raise the money to pay the necessary dowry. She asked Baba Olopa to appeal to Alhaji, which he did, but the man said that he had attained the maximum allowed by the Prophet Mohammad. Very cleverly, the Alhaji had combined Yoruba practices with Islam to create a small clan, acquiring tremendous power in the process. As far as the three wives were concerned, the junior wife must cook for her husband. After all, she was entitled to more sex, so she should be allotted more chores. If she was wise, and this particular woman was, she could get money and gifts from the other wives. She worshiped them in public, kneeling down to greet them, calling them "mothers" in the language of respect, and running errands.

Alhaji did not combine his wives and their businesses into a conglomerate. Each operated independently, and the fourth wife wanted to create her own business in order to become free, to acquire status and power. As the three women became successful in their businesses, they acquired influence of their own, independent of Alhaji. The one who started out hawking clothes moved up in the business world and became rich, becoming an honorary chief in the process. By the time she became a chief, Alhaji had lost most of his power over her and relied on the woman's character and memory to sustain the relationship. If he asserted himself too vigorously, the woman could move to her own house. Thus, beginning from a position of inequality and small capital, she had moved up by trading and investing and managing people. Alhaji was not stupid; he had to be circumspect if he did not want to lose a woman who had established an extensive network.

There was another Alhaji, who followed a similar model but did things somewhat differently. Rather than allowing his wives to set up independent businesses, he co-opted all of them into his own business. He sold building materials and started with a store. By 1965, he had established six successful stores, each managed by a wife. He himself stayed in the biggest one with his first wife. The man had married wives to train as saleswomen and business managers. I was to see many examples of this and actually to study it in the 1980s. Realizing that men were not to be trusted with money and business, a man expanded his business by marrying additional wives. The belief was that the wife, with vested interests, would be a good manager. Even if she stole money, as Chief M. K. O. Abiola once said, she would recirculate the stolen money within the family. Abiola was Nigeria's richest man in the 1980s and 1990s. No one knew the number of his wives and mistresses until he died, following the bitter politics of his success in a presidential election and the annulment of the result by the military. Abiola and the Ode Aje businessman did exactly the same thing, turning wives into entrepreneurs in consolidated business ventures that allowed the man to expand his opportunities and make a profit. Notable drama groups led by Hubert Ogunde and Moses Olaiya, and even those with less fame, depended on their wives as actors. When they failed to recruit and retain female professional actors, they opted to marry them as a strategy of staff retention.

The men without respect at Ode Aje were those who kept concubines but presented themselves as monogamists. The polygamist men knew them and spoke about them both in private and in public. I used to think in the mid-1960s that those who kept concubines were only men with Western educations. This was how Ode Aje had presented it to me, and the men who did so were the small number of elite members among them. Rather than doing what Baba Olopa and Alhaji did, they would keep only one wife at home. The Christians among them married in the church, a definitive way of affirming and legalizing monogamy. The sole wives at Ode Aje had probably not gone to school or had not gone further than the elementary level. The men, like Alhaji and Baba Olopa, were the breadwinners. It was expected that the wife would have an unimportant part-time job, take care of the children, and help the man to save and build a family house. The house was the ultimate testimony of success. Whether one wanted to listen to their stories or not, they would tell them, narrating their struggles in life, the good fortune of meeting a woman who was not wasteful, and the saving of pennies and pounds in order to build a house. In a system without mortgages, whoever had a house lived in what had been fully paid for. One would save money to buy the land, then save to build the foundation, followed by another long break and more saving to buy bricks and eventually to build. On the day a house was roofed, there was always a small party, and I attended many such. Then came another long period of waiting so the man could save to buy windows and doors, plaster the walls, fill the rooms with dirt, and level and plaster the floor. Many would move in without electricity or water, saving for months or years to complete the building. It was when the house was completed, when the labor of years of joint effort had produced a result, that the man, now with time and some change in his pocket, began to look for mistresses. At least, this is what the betrayed women told me, and they all said much the same thing. The belief of the women at Ode Aje was that a struggling man was devoted to his wife, so as the wife prayed for the husband to succeed she was also asking God to bring sorrow into her life.

The sorrow might come when the woman was powerless to fight back. I heard stories of surprise and sorrow at home, at school, on the street, and at church. The story lines were similar, and I will share a case that I observed in 1965. A man—who regularly attended our church, St. Peter's Anglican, took care of his children and flaunted his one wife—died. Everybody mourned and prepared for the burial. At the burial, they saw a woman with some kids crying bitterly, behaving as if she should be buried with the corpse. When a man cries harder than the husband of a dead woman, the bereaved is advised to stop crying and ask why another person should outcry him if he had not been making love to the late wife. As the strange woman and her children cried harder than the wife of the bereaved, people's attention turned to them. When the strange woman was sure that everybody was paying attention, she told them that her husband was dead, leaving two children for her to look after. Her life was in shambles, she told those in attendance, while the legal wife looked confused. The legal children, standing still, looked at the half brothers and half sisters they had never met, wondering what was going on. As people concentrated their attention on all the children, they began to notice that the children of the strange woman looked every inch like the dead man. When the burial was over, the strange woman and her children joined in the celebration. Together with her team, she had a prominent corner at the social event, entertaining her own guests and urging her children to become the center of attention. The public show was to serve as a preface to the contest over the will. Meanwhile, the agony of the legal wife multiplied; not only did she have to cope with a dead husband, but she had to deal with a betrayal announced so late, with the new woman and her children, who would claim 50 percent of the inheritance in a normal situation. The legal wife became full of hate for the corpse. She eventually agreed that she was a fool, as someone must have told her before: if a man cheats you once, shame on him; if he cheats you twice, shame on you. She could now see the shame all over her body. Before the husband's body began the decomposition process, the legal wife prepared to violate the Christian injunctions she had taught her children—to avoid violence, to turn the other cheek when slapped, to forgive their enemies. The legal wife changed her attitude, telling her children to fight for their birthright, to defend what she had accumulated with her energy and sweat, what she had planned together with her husband. As she cursed her husband, begging God not to let his soul rest in peace, she prepared for great battles with the husband's brothers, who not only wanted their own share but would protect the interests of the concubine and her children.

Most other women would not have had to wait this long to experience their agony. Their monogamous husbands would drop many hints that having one wife was untraditional, that they had been drawn to monogamy by the spread of Western civilization, and that the practice was not working. The elite man who married an uneducated or partially educated woman complained that his legal wife was not presentable in the circles of his successful friends, at clubs and parties. A modern man needed a modern woman. The hints revealed a deeper problem. The man had a mistress around the corner: Iyabo, "the short devil," as the married women called her. With a car or motorcycle, he could move fast, reporting to the rented "flat" of his mistress on a daily basis and running home without getting caught. Ode Aje had some women hidden by their married "husbands" in modern homes. I knew one who lived in a house down the slope, about five houses away from us. Everybody knew the boyfriend and the times when he came, parking his black Morris Minor, which we all admired. As he was enjoying the company of his mistress, we would gather around his car, pretending to drive it. As soon as he showed up, we would run away, like thieves being pursued. The mistress became pregnant, and it was when we noticed her big stomach that she and the car disappeared.

"The short devil" did not disappear into a wilderness of no return. The man took her home. I heard the story, as everybody did. When a mistress became pregnant, a clever woman would seek the means to leak it to the legal wife. The mistress would go to the man's family and friends to announce the pregnancy, to demonstrate her love for the husband. The listeners were always friendly; the woman was talking to adulterers who had probably done a similar thing. I never heard of any case in which the listeners were angry or blamed the woman for befriending a married man. I once heard that *marriage* means *mari-eji*, a play on words in Yoruba that turns an English word into *marry two*. I know of an angry woman who reported her adulterous husband to her own father. She did not expect what she heard from him:

> Your husband is too gentle. He must have been treating you so well that you have time to go prying into his private affairs. Look at me; your mother who produced you was my number five. Your husband has a girlfriend, and you are complaining. Wait till he marries her.

The weakened woman went home to negotiate with her husband, to calm down and devise a strategy to prevent the husband's girlfriend from becoming a legitimate second wife. With no atmosphere of condemnation of the man, a pregnant mistress with sanity and wisdom could become mobile on the marriage ladder, moving out of her closet to the living room. As the friends and relatives of the boyfriend were supportive and saw nothing wrong, they began to pressure the man to accept the pregnancy even if he did not want the woman. No matter what, the source of one's child must not be confused with immorality or criminality. The logic was that no one who did not know the future should be critical of a relationship that was about to produce a child: a mistress could produce a son who would become a general or a state governor, and the legal wife could end up producing the governor's driver. The success of children was not tied to the mothers who produced them. As Baba Olopa once told me, no one knew the good sperm from the bad; the same penis that produced a thug produced a judge. The vagina was a messenger, with no control over what could come out of it. No one even prayed that the vagina should be so generous as to discharge all of its goodwill: if all seeds that fell were to grow, then no one could follow the path under the trees. The vagina's hidden location symbolized its powerlessness to determine its own fate. Men in pursuit of the mysterious location deserve some praise, and when they get into trouble they are entitled to sympathy.

The man with a single wife who had impregnated his mistress deserved praise, so resolved the assembly, which had selected representatives to break the news to the legal wife. Not only did I witness this kind of message being delivered, but I was appointed, against my will and capacity to negotiate, to lead a delegation in 1977 to announce to a legal wife that her husband was expecting a child by a mistress. Let me spare you from listening to my own delegation and tell you instead of my Ode Aje experience. The one I first witnessed was amusing when it happened, cruel when I thought about it, callous when I analyzed it, and brilliant when I put it in context, and it will appear gracious when I reveal the final outcome. The man told his legal wife that it was his turn to host a social meeting of friends and relatives. There was nothing unusual about this, and the three weeks' notice was adequate. Many times the legal wife asked her husband for money with which to prepare the food, leaving the drinks to her husband. When the man said that food would not be necessary, the legal wife's curiosity was aroused. No one had a social gathering without food, at least not in her experience. As far as the wife was concerned, this was a sign that they wanted to break bad news to her, like the death of someone, a serious illness such as madness or cancer that had afflicted a relative, or the confiscation of their land by the government. She began to think of all the possible disasters and was unable to sleep. The husband had not anticipated this. When he sought the advice of his friends, he was told to give the legal wife the money for food so that she would begin to think positively. True to the advice, the woman's mind became at peace, believing that those coming to her house to eat and drink were not bringing bad news. The husband bought beer, palm wine, gin, and other drinks.

The guests arrived. I had been given the task of serving drinks, noticing when people had finished their drinks, and quickly refilling them so that the host would not be accused of meanness. The pregnant woman was quiet, also enjoying the meal and the soft drinks. She was gracious and respectful, using all the right gestures. When they had finished stuffing their large stomachs, the leader of the delegation asked for attention so that he could talk. I sat on the floor in a corner. I had no idea why they were there, the second person in the room without any knowledge. As in this case and others that I witnessed, the leader must be gifted with language, making extensive use of proverbs, idioms, and cross-references. He must be sufficiently respected that when others spoke it could only be in support, as if they were announcing a consensus. No one must have the authority to stop him from talking. The idea was to use words and influence to overpower the legal wife so that by the time the meeting was over her options would have become severely limited.

As I later understood the various steps, there was a formula to this kind of speech. The head of the delegation started by praising the legal wife for the good food. The praise was extensive, mentioning her good looks, her excellent housekeeping, the odor-free house, and the children doing well in school. One or two humorous comments were added about how robust the wife and husband looked. The legal wife was full of happiness, adjusting her head tie and body language to show that her happiness had become a perfume that she could pour on herself for the guests to appreciate.

As the legal wife beamed with smiles, the leader changed tone. A long list of proverbs followed, interspersed with sermons. "No matter how difficult a problem is, we cannot cut it with a knife, we can only use words to present it. May God not let us face a problem that we cannot overcome, a mountain so high that we cannot climb. When we reach the top of the hill, may we not be too tired to descend to the valley of glory." As the leader spoke, an elderly woman joined in, introducing herself with a proverb: "However large one eye is, two eyes are better than one." What she had seen in life complemented the leader's speech.

The legal wife became confused, and she looked at her husband, waiting for him to speak, begging the leader to move straight to the point. She, too, began to use proverbs to hasten the leader to announce the big news. "As long as there are lice in the seams of the garment, there must be bloodstains on the fingernails," she said, pleading that she could wait no longer. She acknowledged that "the frog does not jump in the daytime without reason." The leader was still in no hurry, continuing to talk. The woman, now overanxious, said that there was no news so bad that the mouth could not deliver it.

A latecomer walked in and interrupted the discussion. The legal wife hurried to bring food, and I followed with drinks. His late arrival was deliberate. He knew the wife very well and did not want to be there when the bad news was broken. Unfortunately for him, he came too soon. Looking for the point at which to enter, he asked whether they had prayed, and he was told that they had already passed that stage. Not to be treated as a child, he made a short speech, drawing from the Bible. Everything in life is vanity, and the members of the audience said "vanity of vanities." One thing I remembered very well is the Bible and the key passages in it, and I will never forget that the latecomer ended his speech with "The thing that hath been, it is that which shall be; and that which is done is that which shall be done; and there is no new thing under the sun."

"Yes," the leader said, "there is no new thing under the sun." This was a cue for him to move to the next stage. "We are all here because of family matters," the leader stated, to announce another long speech, and others joined him to pray for the survival of the family. Shouts of "Amen" became louder, changing the atmosphere to one of fellowship. Then, when the leader saw that everybody had become solemn, he began to break the ice.

"We are here to plead with you," the leader spoke, facing the legal wife, who now looked stupefied. "What your husband did was very bad, but the crocodile does not die under the water so that we can call the monkey to celebrate its funeral." The leader admitted that he himself was not a clean man, and the crowd shouted, "We know too well." "Only God is clean," he continued. "If a blind man says let's throw stones, be assured that he has stepped on one." The leader warned the woman not to be the blind person who wanted to fight a war of stones. The leader praised the woman's destiny for being on her side. She was a lucky woman, the leader assured her: "Although the snake does not fly, it has caught the bird whose home is in the sky." She was the smart snake on land, the husband the bird.

The woman became more impatient, seeking to know what the husband had done to impact her so. The leaders and others adjusted their seats, their eyes fixed on the legal wife. "He is not a thief, a criminal," the leader quickly assured the legal wife. He gave another long speech, saying that their family was yet to produce its first criminal. "May God forbid! Her husband would never become the disobedient fowl who obeys in a pot of soup."

"Then what did my husband do?" the legal wife asked, to which someone in the audience replied, "It is a small matter, okay?" Now moving to the real "small matter," the leader asked the legal wife to look at the pregnant woman.

"That is your wife, *iyawo kekere*." The leader did not say the pregnant woman was the wife of the husband, but of the legal wife, who had been promoted to *iyale*, senior wife, without much notice and without her consent. A dead silence followed, in which everyone watched for her reaction. If she did not accept, the tone would change; they would abuse her, and the husband would threaten a divorce. If she accepted, they would praise her. This particular legal wife refused to talk. She cried so loudly that she had to be taken out of the room. When she returned, the pregnant woman knelt down to indicate her readiness to accept a subordinate position as a junior wife. Now the "legal wife" knew she was no longer the one and only and that the competition for the man's pocket and soul had begun. The meeting dispersed, having attained its objective. It was not for the delegation to resolve the new crisis being created but to close the chapter on what had begun as a secret one.

She had become not a "senior wife" but a "legal wife." It was Baba Olopa who had senior and junior wives; the Christian had a legal wife, who went by the name of Mrs. something, and mistresses who could be called *iyawo* (junior wife) or *ale* (concubine). The legal wife began to learn to behave like the "first lady," watching the mistress from afar so she would not be able take everything. Baba Olopa and Alhaji did not like the men with legal wives nor the women who described themselves as such. To Alhaji, they were living in a world of deception, like the man who wanted to befriend a leper yet shunned his handshake, the weak man who thought that he could extract thorns from his foot with just a finger. Western and Christian laws and values had introduced monogamy, and there was actually a law against bigamy in Nigeria. No woman ever went to court to sue her husband for marrying two wives, legally or illegally. That a man took a second wife was not a sufficient reason to send him to jail. The men at Ode Aje turned out to be no different from men elsewhere, although they appeared to me to be so in those years. A strong male conspiracy has ensured that divorce and inheritance laws favor men and reinforce patriarchy.

The adult males and their marriage models affected their children in various ways. One could not grow up at Ode Aje and not believe in male superiority. The men ran their households with full control, in charge of most expenses, paying most of the bills, borrowing money from their wives when they were broke. No young person could say that he had never heard a woman, probably the mother, asking the husband to repay borrowed money. The young boys in school would speak about the number of wives they would have when they grew up, although the idea of monogamy was becoming popular. If Baba Olopa and Alhaji did not like the men with legal wives keeping mistresses, the boys were impressed by it, saying that it was more peaceful to separate two enemies. The differences were also becoming clearer between the children from polygamous and monogamous homes. The man with a legal wife had a smaller number of kids, and he could spend more money to maximize their opportunities. Some of them were even driven to school in their fathers' cars, which impressed those without this kind opportunity.

Polygamy strengthened the ties between mothers and their children. The father was described as Baba General, that is, one minimally obligated to an infinite number of people. The mother was likened to gold, something to be treasured. School songs celebrated motherhood, avoiding mention, as much as possible, of fathers. More than half of my classmates regarded their mothers as their heroes, their fathers as dispensable. The person they could talk to in the household was the mother with the soft side, who was always there. As I would discover at Ode Aje, without a mother to protect the child in a polygamous home one was actually living in a real jungle, rubbing bottoms with a porcupine.

t is not true that one cannot run and hide at the same time. At Ode Aje, I wanted to run and hide, but I became entrenched, like a man caught in quicksand, in the neighborhood and its customs. If the hand does not stop traveling between the food and the mouth, the stomach will become full, even if the morsel is no bigger than what an ant can carry. At the age of twelve, I had come to understand my environment—the home, the school, other wards, and even villages. I had been able to participate in virtually all the cultural festivals and cults, understanding their key elements, although my full understanding of contexts and their meanings had to await my becoming an adult and a scholar. I had added new knowledge of Islam and an increasing knowledge of Christianity. I had become both Yoruba and Ibadan in the process. My interest in Yoruba language and literature had deepened so remarkably that I had read all the published literary works in Yoruba, and I brought honor to the school in various competitions, notably in drama and Yoruba.

Running and hiding I owe to polygamy; becoming Yoruba I owe to Ode Aje. If the big boys in the new city wanted me to think about change and overseas trips, I became a big boy myself at Ode Aje, thinking about Yoruba and old traditions. As I grew to become a big boy, I was becoming different from my predecessors, the thumb whose space is different from those of the other fingers. The lesson at Agbokojo was to gather sufficient knowledge to integrate oneself into city life; the lessons at Ode Aje were to negotiate the complexities of local traditions and adapt to the forces of change. Agbokojo was able to withstand the excesses of newness; Ode Aje panicked when it saw the first evidence of newness. A woman could not carry a bottle of beer or smoke at Ode Aje without sending everyone into panic and condemnation, talking of a society that was about to be destroyed by the activities of those who were changing too fast.

I knew that I had moved back in time from the first week in my new school. I became an instant celebrity. I was the "new boy" from the "city" with stories to tell. Everybody wanted to be my friend, not because I had food or money to give them but because I could supply stories of the places they dreamed about. I had always known that prestige came with stories, but it was Ode Aje that turned stories into power. And each one was like thunder that hit my new mates. A story must be factual, not imagined, and must capture the drama of places and faces. If one attempted to embellish, a boy would yell "don't add onion and tomato" to warn one that a good story does not require spice to make it tasty. Stories were consumed like food, and the students might actually lick their fingers when they were impressed. In the first one month, I did nothing during break time, and before and after school, except tell stories of my city experiences. This was a preface to my last three years at primary school, making me a big boy from day one. Even the prefects in the highest grade wanted to associate with me, to listen to my stories. One of the senior boys, later a successful businessman, became so fascinated that he smuggled me into his compound so that I could describe the Indian movies I had seen.

As the stories circulated, they ran out of power. To retain my status, I had to become part of the established school culture. My predecessors had worked out their rules before I arrived, rules to negotiate power and seniority among students and between the students and their teachers. After school, students from various schools gathered in some location, usually a school playing field, to play soccer and be governed by their own rules. Yusuf and Philip had been masters of those rules at my new Ode Aje school, and clever boys like Alalade, now a university president, were key players in initiating and settling major conflicts.

Disagreements among boys had to be settled after school with a wrestling match when all the teachers had left. Before school closed, word would spread of the two boys at war who must settle the score with a big fight. Camps were formed, usually lined up behind the contestants. A neutral person was appointed as referee, a boy who had won a recent contest. The two contestants did not think about schoolwork, only about strategies to attain victory. Their spokesmen went about during break time conducting psychological warfare with powerful words meant to frighten one another. It was here that I learned the language of battle. Boys likened themselves to wild animals, notably the tiger, lion, elephant, buffalo, and hyena, threatening that they would eat up their opponents, tearing them to pieces as the lion does a deer. Who does not know that when a dog sees a leopard it becomes quiet?

The first time I witnessed a wrestling contest, I knew that this was not the way I would ever win a conflict. It was tough, fast, and hard. One must hold his rival and at the same time seek the opportunity to pin him down, with his back on the floor. One's rival might stumble or fall, but as long as his back was free one still had to struggle. A bout could be long: the winner was the one able to endure and exploit the fatigue of the opponent. It was a fight without a break and with minimal interference by the referee. It was a contest of wits and muscle, bringing bruises to the body, humiliation after defeat. A boy who fell too quickly would be wise to miss school the next day, as the embarrassment would be hard to bear. I practiced at home, behind the house, far away from any of my mates. I was floored three times within seconds. Except with someone much younger than me, I was unable to win any wrestling bout. According to the rules worked out by students, one could only wrestle within one's own age group. With those who were younger, the announcement of a physical threat should be enough to settle a score. If the threat did not work, one had to seek means other than a wrestling match. Also one must not fight a girl, although they, too, had a way of resolving their conflicts. Under no circumstances must one confuse wrestling with boxing, even if one was about to lose a match or had been badly humiliated in one.

The worst offense one could commit, with severe consequences, was to use the teeth to bite an enemy. A fight between boys was not an opportunity for one of them to become a dog. It was legitimate for a girl to bite a boy, and many of them did, since they were not prohibited from fighting with teeth. A boy who won a conflict with the teeth would suffer immediate ostracism, and this was sufficient reason to change schools. As changing a school could only be done by parents, truancy was the only way out. To regain lost friends was very difficult, as no one wanted to be found in the company of a dog who wanted to feast on human blood and flesh.

At school or on the streets, and irrespective of gender, one could conduct a conflict with words, with or without a referee. This I mastered quickly. The techniques were easy enough, but not the content, which must be based on prior research on the enemy. The conflicts with words usually had a simple beginning.

Boy A: See what you did, your head is not correct.
Boy B: What did I do? I know that my head is not correct, but you
    have a mental problem, the visitor who wants to tell the history of
    a house to the landlord.
Boy A: I am the one with the mental problem? Look at yourself,
    dressed like a madman heading for the market.

Now, the contestants needed an audience to enjoy the exchanges and, if possible, decide on the winner. As with the wrestling contest, the rule was not to separate the contestants until one saw blood. It was not just fun to allow two people to fight; it was a way of creating order, of knowing who the winner was so that others could determine their place in the hierarchy. The smallest elephant can be bigger than a buffalo. One needed to compile a list of those who could be defeated by wrestling or words. The wise boy with a good list knew those he should not challenge, when it would be smarter to retreat and surrender, and those who should not be provoked. Once boys A and B had an audience and wanted to fight, they moved to stage two, which was to introduce themselves to the listeners.

> Boy A: You probably don't know me, the one who wears the mask of death. I visited heaven three times while you stayed on earth chasing the vulture feasting on a dead body. Ask about me in your compound; they will give you a list of those who have bowed to me, who see me as their conqueror. I am the tree that does not allow the grass to grow, the big leaf that lives in the sky where no animal can feast. Before you can find an elephant, you have to go to the forest; before you can find a buffalo, you must travel to the grassland; before you can find a bird like an egret you must wait a long time. Who are you anyway?
>
> Boy B: Do you really know yourself? Let the slave realize that he is a slave, let the pawn know that he is a pawn, and let you and I know that man is a slave of the gods. I am what you cannot know, the cloud in the sky that you can see but cannot touch, the steam that you cannot wrap in your big leaf. If you are death, I am illness, the smallpox that will ruin your face, the lice that will damage your head, the bugs that will suck your blood, the leprosy that will cut off your fingers, the gonorrhea that will damage your penis, the boil on your foot that will not let you walk.

The audience might laugh at the last one to indicate that boy B was doing better. A bigger crowd would gather, encircling them and urging them on.

> Boy A: You are illness? Welcome to the doctor. For seven years, I trained with an herbalist, diviner, and charm maker, not at Ibadan but in the underworld. I am the one taken by a tornado to the land beyond to see ghosts and spirits for seventy years and seventy days. My body is magic. I know that you need a cure, and I

will do it for you for free. What is smallpox before Sopona [the god of smallpox]? What is lice before kerosene? An impotent man cannot make fun of the man with syphilis. I who cure madness am not afraid of a wild dog like you.

Boy A had moved to another level, ending the introduction by calling his opponent a dog. The audience wanted to hear the riposte; otherwise they would have clapped, declared a victory, and dispersed. Boy B began to bark like a dog, just to make his opponent stop talking so that he could take over.

> Boy B: I am glad to be compared to a dog. You are a monkey, and from now on I will be carrying a banana with me to give to you. I don't know what you are doing on land when you should be living in a tree, jumping from branch to branch until a hunter shoots you dead. A roasted monkey will be good for my snacks.

Many more innocent animals were drawn into the verbal warfare, generating spontaneous, creative stories of war and escape, death and survival. Why should a cow boast before a horse? When one boy became a goat, the other could turn into a hyena, as each looked for an animal that could overpower the other. A goat was not always powerless before a hyena, and it could run into a hole where the hyena was afraid to enter. Unknown to the goat, the bees were angry at being disturbed and were ready to attack. As the goat headed out, it saw a snake swallowing a frog. Out of sympathy, the goat used its legs to hit the snake, damaging its spinal cord. Because he had saved a life, the goat was free of the hyena, who in turn was being challenged by a tiger. Even if a boy became a lion, his opponent could turn into a small fly to bother the lion, flying from its tail to its nose while the powerful jaws were unable to do anything to this tiny insect. One of the boys had an answer to the fly: he could swallow it just to humiliate the powerful lion. If one boy turned into an animal, the opponent could also make himself the trap, the cat to kill the rat, the mousetrap to destroy cats and rats, the multiple spider webs to tie up an elephant, or the gun to kill a deer. When the cat returns from a trip, the rat goes into a depression. When the cattle agree to unite, there is no food for the lion. One of the boys could decide to close the chapter on the animals by declaring that the other was the hunter who forgot to sharpen his spears and became dinner for the leopard.

Again no victory was declared by the audience, which had been charmed by the stories and the freshness of their delivery. Soon it was time to get personal, to think of something that was true but annoying, words so painful that those still new to such contests might actually cry. At this level, the best device was to start with a list of one's personal weaknesses so as to prevent the other person from listing them first.

> Boy A: You know I am a short boy and everybody can see me. But you are tall, only that you lack the brain to sustain tallness. My eyes are small, but yours that are big are no better than those of the blind. I am the one sun superior to all of your stars.

The rival would not wait for the entire catalog, which would deny him things to say. He gestured the other boys to stop in order to take his turn.

> Boy B: I have no place to sleep, and a dog is yawning. I am tall and handsome, and all the girls are after me. No woman will marry a short man. My big eyes are like the moon and sun; one sees at night and the other during the day. Your eyes are so small that you will never see the good things in life. I know that my toes are not as good as yours, but at least I can cover them with nice shoes. I know that the hair on my head is not long enough, but I can wear nice caps. Look at you. When you walk, it is sideways like a crab, like one whose right leg is longer than the left.

The attentive audience was thinking that this would result in a tie, and a few people began to leave. When two people were equally matched, the intensity declined after some minutes. The skilled masters of words knew what to say to win, demolishing their rivals with a punch line before the audience dispersed. One must never cross the line and abuse the parents of a rival. If one insulted a person's mother, the use of violence became legitimate. The interested crowd would take the side of the person whose innocent mother had been drawn into the small war.

Wrestling and wars of words defined power for young boys. However, power was not the only thing they were after. As if the household was rather restrictive, outdoor activities, irrespective of their form, were the ultimate pleasure. At Ode Aje, observing and participating in the annual masquerade dance, the Ololu, observing the various public activities of cults and occupational groups, and celebrating the city cult of Okebadan were the high points of the year. But most of the religious and cult celebrations occurred once a year, and we had to fill the time in the interval. No boy in school could complain of boredom. There was just too much to do. Everybody followed the religious traditions of his parents, but to the boys there was no difference between Islam and Christianity. I participated in all the Islamic festivals as fully as a Muslim could do. The Muslims, too, participated in all Christian festivals. Merging both, we maximized the opportunities for fun. Muslims followed me to church at Easter and Christmas, and I followed them to the mosques and the yidi (praying ground) for the celebration of the end of Ramadan and the birth of the Prophet Mohammad. If the adults were eager to reach God, we were interested in bonding with human beings.

School had both serious and playful elements. The teachers handled the serious matters and we the play. Although my school was next door to my house, I still chose to walk to it rather slowly, taking the longest route possible. One student would wait for another, and by the time they reached our house they would have become a crowd. There were even days when I would walk away from the school just to join other students. We were all recognizable by the khaki uniforms we wore and the small metal boxes that we carried each day. We were the kings of the walkways, chatting about all subjects under the sun, evaluating the schoolteachers, and talking about the single women among them who the boys would marry if they could grow older faster. Boys and girls mingled along the way, and there was no separation in the school along gender lines. The shortest people sat closest to the teachers and the tallest in the back row. Walking to school was the first fun of the day, as we joked and laughed. We could also fight, really big fights that would break up the group and turn us into latecomers. The big boys and girls could beat the smaller ones, forcing them to cry, but the smaller children knew not to report the incident to anyone if they did not want to suffer more.

School was about rules and breaking the rules as well. Those who arrived in time had an easy entry, and they could play before the bell rang. Late arrival was punished. "Kneel down on that hard surface," one of the school prefects, a student in the last year, would command, pointing to small rocks and pebbles. The instruction had to be obeyed. Even the senior students carried a cane, and one had to be careful not to allow them to use it: only a stupid rat will challenge a cat to a fight. All latecomers were gathered into one big herd and marched to the assembly already in progress so that the obedient could see them. The other students were not impressed, and no one vowed to use the humiliation of the latecomers as a valuable lesson. The students who were not late knew that they were lucky or that their parents had sent them out of the house early enough or that their crowd of the day had nothing interesting to say.

As Ode Aje was a public school with students from all religious backgrounds, the songs were secular in nature. Rather than Christian prayers, people were asked to engage in "silent prayer" so that they could say whatever they wanted. I would close my eyes and open them when I heard "Amen," without having prayed. I prayed only when I was in trouble, to avoid the punishment that would come with it, but I also happened to know that such prayers are useless.

For two years, I was in the school band, playing either *agogo* (bell gong) or *sekere* (a gourd with beads that makes a rattling sound). The band was an all-male affair, the students selected by the schoolteachers. We could swap instruments, and even the absence or lateness of a person would not stop us from playing. We would play the instruments to their loudest capacity, as if using them to assert a temporary freedom. The drums broke from time to time, and we substituted other objects that could produce sounds, including the drum's metal container. The bands chose the songs, and the students sang at the tops of their voices, with the youngest ones simply babbling, unsure of the words. A song could have multiple rhythms, and the band indicated which one to use. In the first three years of school, the teachers introduced the starters to the songs, practicing with them in their smaller groups. Singing lessons, in addition to civics, arts, and crafts allowed the teachers and students to relax after the more grueling subjects of arithmetic and English.

The songs were creative; some were adapted from famous lullabies or even hymnal songs creatively used to assert Yoruba values. The themes were consistent: the value of education, the need to respect parents and schoolteachers, and the need for community service. So much emphasis was placed on hard work, defined mainly in terms of gaining a Western education, that one had to sing about it daily.

> Awon omo alaigboran po nile iwe,
> Won ki i feti sile lati gbo tolukoo won,
> Boluko won ba kowe to ko raitin [writing] fun won,
> Ounje ni ronu won,
> Ka jeun, jeun, jeun, ka ma we.
> Ise, ise, iyen ki i se ti won;
> Ere, ere, iyen ni won fee se.
> Dodo ati raise [rice] ko gbodo koja firi;
> Ounje ni ronu won,
> Ka jeun, jeun, jeun, ka ma we.

> There are too many disobedient students at school
> They hardly listen to their teachers
> When the teachers instruct in reading and writing
> It is then they think about food

Let us eat and study
Work is hard for them
Play is their only passion
Plantain and rice must not pass by
They think only of food
Let us eat and study.

I very much doubt that anyone in my school would have chosen work over food. Our houses were serving traditional foods, which we could freely get, and the schools were experimenting with modern cuisine. Whenever the government was able to receive aid from abroad, they would serve powdered milk, which the students preferred to lick rather than adding water to drink. Many students saved some of the milk to take home to their parents. The premise of the food and milk provided at school was that most of the students were deficient in protein and vitamins and new nutritional habits could bring about improvements. As the food vendors were arriving and setting up their wares, only the mentally retarded could concentrate on schoolwork instead of food. There was nothing wrong with Yoruba food, but the new elites in power were making bread and tea more important than corn and beans, turning the students' taste buds away from local foods and toward imported ones, preparing them for a future that would enslave them in the global economy.

Some songs, rules, and rules communicated in songs were a nuisance to the kids, like the one that condemned students who spoke in Yoruba. There were even "vernacular prefects" who listened to all conversations, like CIA spies, to "catch someone speeeking in vernakulah." I got into trouble so many times, speaking in Yoruba, that my name almost made it into the much-dreaded Black Book, which contained the names of all the most disobedient students, who were raised in status to the level of criminals. As the headmaster warned us many times, one must never be mentioned in the Black Book—no one was sensitive to labels and names that characterized black as negative—as it would mean that there would be no letters of reference with which to proceed to high school. Some rules made perfect sense, but they were useless, like those on hygiene, which required us to wash our hands after using the toilet when no water was provided.

We sang to open the morning assembly, at which we were arranged by school grades and then by height. The songs to open the school day warned us that education was the key to success in a modern age, similar to the kokoka song in my old school. Some were about gratitude to the schoolteachers, the manufacturers of the keys of success. Some songs were for fun, allowing the band to push creativity to its limit and the students to be more expressive.

Bom bom bom
gbo bi ilu ti ndun
bom bom bom
Gbo bi a ti nkorin
Bom bom bom bom bom bo boma

Bom bom bom
Listen to the drum beats
Bom bom bom
Listen to our songs
Bom bom bom bom bom bo boma

The creative songs even enabled the students to move their bodies in the way they liked, creating opportunities for boys to talk about girls later in the afternoon, describing how one was able to move better than the others. A poor dancer could blame the drum, but the students would not complain about the band when it came to songs they loved.

We sang to disperse the assembly, as each grade marched to its classroom. We all gathered again in the same place to close the school for the day. This ceremony was usually brief, with the headmaster making major announcements and threatening punishment to those who failed to bring back their homework the next day. The closing songs were swift, and the band stopped at the earliest opportunity to dump the instruments in the designated place, usually the headmaster's office. The songs would bid farewell and pray for a safe return:

O dowuro
Ki a sun re
Ki angeli Oluwa
Ko so wa po
T ayo tayo la nlo le
La nlo ile la n lo le
K'Oluwa ko so wa po.

Till tomorrow morning
May we have a good night's sleep
May the angels guard us
All together
We depart with joy

To go home
May the Lord protect us all.

A mi rele o baba
Olojo oni o
Ami rele o
Gbogbo eko ti a ko ninu ile iwe wa
Ma se jekeye esu
Ko sa won je lokan wa
Amin o beni ko ri o.

We head home, O God
The Lord who controls the day
We head home
All the day's knowledge
Do not allow the satanic bird to eat it up
Amen, so shall it be.

The "satanic bird" was powerful enough to land on one's head and pick out all the grains of knowledge. This was usually explained as resulting from too many sports such as soccer or other creative activities such as singing and dancing. The people who later distinguished themselves in music or soccer must have been victims of the satanic birds, which destroyed their mental capacity. Those who listened to their schoolteachers and obeyed all of their instructions did not become King Sunny Ade or Hakeem Olajuwon, the bad ones in those days who played too much, allowing the satanic birds to perch on their heads.

There were also songs to thank the teachers for their hard work, as if the students were ready to receive their final diplomas and embark on a long trip.

A ki yin oluko wa
Akoko to lati lo
Obi wa nduro de wa
Aafe l'ole
O digbose la n ki yin
k'Olorun se to ju wa
Ka tun pade pe l'ayo
Odigbose.

We thank you our teachers
It is time for us to leave
Our parents are waiting

We want to go home
We bid you farewell
May God protect us
Until we reunite in peace
Bye bye.

We also sang to introduce lunch, called the midday meal, a sort of second breakfast for the day. As soon as it was time, without waiting for the teachers' permission, the band boys would rush out to play, generating a loud uproar of songs from all the classrooms, as all the students eagerly interrupted their work.

Wa ba wa jeun Oluwa
Je ka maa yin oruko re
Wa bu si ounje wa si
Ka le ba o jeun lorun.

Come with us, Lord
Let us praise thy name
Bless the food
So that we can eat with you in heaven.

We did not care about the content of this prayer, and no one waited for an amen to seal the blessing. As soon as the band stopped, the students rushed outside with their plates to line up to buy food from the vendors. As for the bad students, it was the teacher's turn to take revenge, telling them to stay in their chairs punished by the aroma of the food they could not touch. A wicked teacher would punish a student for the entire period, incurring insults from all of us. As we abused the teacher behind her back, we sympathized with the fellow student who had been denied the opportunity to respect the stomach. Those from homes that gave out breakfast money would now allow themselves to buy big rations at midday, having skipped breakfast in order to enjoy the food served at school. The food was good, better than what I had at home, and varied, with a different dish served each day. Rice, beans, and *asaro* (yam porridge) were my favorites. Beef was cut in small pieces, so tiny that one might not be able to see them. The delight was *isan*, the muscular part that one could chew endlessly, like gum, without swallowing, until the teachers became annoyed. The competition for *isan* was keen, and the food sellers—women from Ode Aje who were contracted by the school—favored the senior boys. Everybody had his own plate. The dirty boys did not wash their plates for days, wiping them with paper or their tongues. Water was the only beverage; only adults had soda, and they drank it slowly so that the students could see them and the bottles. When a boy brought a bottle to my class, we shared it with a teaspoon, as if taking medication.

The headmaster, often wearing a shirt and knickers and carrying a cane, controlled the assembly, with all the teachers standing behind him. The teachers could never be late, as everybody would know. The assembly was like a head count. We recited the first stanza of the national anthem because it was a public school. The headmaster would deliver a series of moral lessons. Thereafter, one of the latecomers would be identified for caning, as well as others who had done something serious. The headmaster and teachers had the authority to cane, supported by the parents. One could never go home to report that one had been caned without expecting the parents to express public gratitude to the teachers. As far as the parents were concerned, the teachers could be fully trusted. Until the oil boom of the 1970s injected a great deal of money into the system and a new middle class emerged, the teachers were the community elite, the ones with knowledge and power. They dressed in Western clothes, had bicycles, spoke the English language to impress people, and popularized the necessity of Western education.

The success of the teachers was clear to see. Within the school itself, debates were integral to education, with students divided into groups to argue over the worth of certain occupations (a farmer is more important than a teacher), gender (what a man can do a woman can do), and skills (to work with the brain is better than working with the hands). No matter what skills the debaters on the opposing side possessed, the teachers affirmed the answers they wanted us to know: that education with modern skills was superior to traditional occupations and crafts. A farmer could not become a member of Parliament, ride in a car, or travel abroad, some would say in their arguments, which the teachers supported. On the other hand, the teachers and those on the side of farmers would argue the need for food. I played both sides, not because I wanted to but because the teachers assigned the roles. As if by coincidence, although it was a coup on the part of the students, the band would select for that day a song to close the school.

Ise agbe nise ile wa
Eni ko sise a maa jale
Iwe kiko laisi oko
Ko i pe o ko i pe o.

Farming is our main occupation
Who ever does not work will steal

Education without a hoe
Is not enough, not enough.

In time, and as if ignoring their own protest song, the students came to believe in the power of education and youths gradually abandoned farming. No one in my school went back to the village to become a full-time farmer. The only one who went into farming, many years later, was a successful bureaucrat who was looking for a fake "occupation" to justify the enormous wealth he had stolen from government coffers. Now that everybody is hungry, perhaps the schools will revisit those debates and arrive at better answers. And when the new generation sees the wealthy bureaucrat turned farmer the song should be queried, as one who works may also steal.

School was about work and more work. All subjects were important. Failure was not tolerated. Many did fail, and not a few had to endure caning at home. We were ranked both by subjects and by overall performance in class. The parents whose boy brought a term report saying that he was number thirty out of thirty were dejected. The boy would be blamed for days. Behind his back, they would talk to his schoolteacher, arrange additional home lessons, and begin to believe that the boy would not proceed beyond primary education. A popular poem, which we were forced to memorize, became the mandatory "code" to read whenever we failed to meet the expectations of students and teachers. Any time I now see my classmates, and irrespective of the location or time, one of the things we do is to recite a poem.

Work while you work and
Play while you play.
To be useful and happy
This is the way.

All that you do
Do with your might.
Things done by halves
Are never done right.

One thing at a time,
And that done well,
Is a very good rule,
As many can tell.

Moments should never
Be trickled away, so

Work while you work and
Play while you play.

This was an English poem by an author whom we did not know. We knew the time to play, though it was far shorter than the time to work. An hour before the final bell and the closing assembly, the boys would be thinking about wrestling or soccer. As soon as the final assembly was over, the students hurried to disperse, except those undergoing punishment, whom the teachers had instructed to stay for additional time. The soccer boys would remove their shirts to play. Soccer was unsupervised, and there were days when we kept playing until it became dark. But it could also end in a fight, a big fight, if a goal was disputed, or if the referee, who was one of us, wanted to favor one group. The fight would bring the game to an end but only for that day.

Anyone who was afraid of getting into trouble at home could not play soccer. All the boys knew the questions waiting for them: "Why are you late again today?" someone would shout when he reached home. "Did I not ask you not to play soccer again?" "When do you have time for your homework?" Some would be spanked, but it would not stop them from playing soccer the next day. Moral lessons and tough words could not conquer the desire to play, just as the river cannot be so full as to cover the eyes of the fish. Most homes did not have a television, and the rest of the day would be spent on homework, playing with other kids outside the house, and running errands.

The weekend was different. Saturday was the time for cleaning the house, cutting grass, washing clothes manually, and fetching water but also for soccer and other play. I had to hurry to do my chores in order to devote more time to play. We had soccer clubs and engaged in competitions that were always hard to conclude because of conflicts and fights over the referee's decision. Bicycle rides also defined Saturdays, but one must have saved some pennies to rent a bicycle. A thirty-minute ride could cost as much as three pence, but, as one did not have a wristwatch, calculating thirty minutes was a problem. All the boys exceeded the thirty minutes and had to pay fines. Usually we had no money, and the "bicycle repairers," as the agents were called, had a list of debtors. Bicycle rides allowed boys to compete, racing in valleys and on hills. There was not a single boy without wounds caused either when one was learning how to ride or when one had become too confident trying to show that it was unnecessary to use brakes to stop or handles to balance. Treating a wound was casual: the first approach was to sprinkle dust on it. As the wound deteriorated and smelled, attracting flies in the process, parents and dispensary personnel would have to intervene. When they came to heal the wounds, their medicine was simple and painful: very hot water and penicillin powder.

Sunday was for church. All the Christians at Ode Aje dressed well for church. For kids like me, dressing well usually meant wearing the same clothes and shoes that had been bought for Christmas or Easter. Most parents bought clothes for their children only three or four times a year: uniforms to start the school year in January and festival clothes. Until one outgrew them, there was no change. I was actually more privileged than those who had only one set of clothes. Those with just one pair of shoes had to go to school barefoot, saving their shoes for Sunday. Some had feet calloused with overuse, and they would even boast that they could walk on broken bottles without injury. The heat was nothing, as their caked feet tolerated it. Dust was the problem, as many carried their dirty legs to bed, victimized by small insects that we nicknamed *jesejese* (foot eaters), which caused itches that no one paid attention to. Many students appeared in school with dirty uniforms, but it was only on Mondays that the teachers got annoyed, asking them to go home to wash their clothes before coming back. Even if they had only one uniform, they could have washed it during the weekend, but the teachers forgot that the students also played in their uniforms. Apart from Sundays, I could wear my uniform for days on end, sleeping in it as well. As our love for the uniforms was passionate, we began to share them with lice, and some students carried bed bugs to school as well. Over time, the uniforms were torn to pieces, starting at the shoulders of the shirt, then slowly extending to the other parts. This would be good news, as the angry teachers now had to leave the students alone and talk to the parents. If a small fight helped a uniform already in distress to become a rag, one was lucky indeed to have a victim to blame for damaging it.

Of all the activities in the church on Sundays, I enjoyed the songs the most. The Bible stories became repetitive, concluding with moral lessons that we had heard at school. While we used hymns from published hymnals, the Bible teachers introduced Yoruba songs that allowed us to drum and clap. In my early years at Ode Aje, I suspended my participation in the choir, aided by the fact that no one had forced me into it in the first place. Rather, I went to the Sunday School, where I also joined the band, listened to Bible stories, and participated in quizzes on the Bible. When I was twelve, I joined the Boy Scouts, mainly to play and participate in camps. There was not much to do in the Scouts other than listening to the older boys talk about their exploits in the jungle. When it was my turn to visit the same camp or jungle they had spoken about, I found neither the lions nor the snakes the boys told us they had fought. "We killed them all," one told us. Saturdays and Sundays were also devoted to playing tricks and pranks. The list of what we did was endless, and all led to severe punishment when we were caught.

There was one thing I enjoyed more than the songs and Bible lessons: iresi, the rice. Yes, rice, rice, rice! Sunday was the only day when we could ever hope to have rice for lunch. Waiting for Sunday was like waiting for rice, but it might not come if Baba Olopa was broke or Iya Aladie did not make some profits during the week. Rice was expensive, and it was a delicacy at Ode Aje. I loved Sunday because it would bring rice.

If many people I have come across loved school and did well in their studies because of pressure from their parents, my experience was different. I loved school and did well not because anybody told me to but because I enjoyed school and the outdoors more than life at home. I was not ashamed of my home or even of Baba Olopa's polygamous arrangements, which I did not fully understand at the time. I was more comfortable with the outside than the home. It took me over twenty years to reverse this trend, and even now I often have to force myself to stay indoors. For the Nigerian landlord who cannot collect rent from his tenant and is struggling to evict him, the trick is always to make the outside more comfortable than the inside. The landlord will consult a medicine man to make a juju to afflict the tenant so that whenever he is home things will be hot and uncomfortable, forcing him to go outside. When the situation has repeated itself many times, the tenant will realize that his salvation lies in vacating the house. If the juju does not work, the landlord will remove the roof, exposing the tenant to rain, heat, and mosquitoes.

I was not a tenant who required a juju or the removal of a roof before I would run away from the house. I preferred my friends in the neighborhood and at school. It was the first time that had I made so many friends, and the list kept increasing until I no longer had the time and politics to handle so many people. It was at Ode Aje that I began to balance the interests of kinship and friendship, but I was more drawn to friends than kin.

It is not necessary to recruit the services of a psychologist to explain my preferences. I fully understood what was happening. I knew that in my old house that I did not have a father. Of the three men in my old house, two were my brothers and the other, Baba Ayo, behaved like an elder rather than a father. As long as I did not get into trouble, Baba Ayo left me alone, limiting his intervention to correction and punishment.

Whether at Agbokojo or Ode Aje, elders did not need to seek the consent of any parent to discipline children, even the ones they did not know well. In taking up this role, the elders were not imposing their personal values on the young but enforcing collective values such as the commandments to be polite to all those senior to one in age, not to steal, and not to run away from school or errands. Thus, I saw Baba Ayo as performing a role that society had created for him. By the time I got to Ode Aje, however, I had to accept Baba Olopa not as an elder but as a father.

Baba Olopa was clear about his own role, and he did not make any distinction between me and his own children. Indeed, there was never a complaint I made against him with which his own children disagreed. Other than instilling the basic values of obeying his instructions and those of other elders and schoolteachers and running errands when asked to, he never insisted on anything. He had no objection to sending someone to school, but he would not give himself any stress if they did not do well. He never pressured his children to do well in school, to proceed beyond the elementary level, or to return to school if they dropped out of high school. As soon as he thought they were mature enough, he would be hands off, giving advice only when asked or warning them about the consequences of failure. When his sister's son was caught stealing, he assisted the police with the evidence that sent him to jail. Many family members, including his sister, expected him to do otherwise, to use his influence to prevent the thief from going to jail and being destroyed. When he was told that the imprisonment would bring shame to the family, he disagreed, saying that the thief had brought the shame only on his own head. He said many times that those of his children who did not do well deserved to suffer.

There was nothing wicked or evil about Baba Olopa. In his own worldview, people failed or succeeded in accordance with their own destinies. A person could not become a professor or a writer because he wished to—no matter how hard he tried—for his ori (destiny) might make it impossible. Baba Olopa never said that one must not work—he himself did for many years, and five days a week—and he never said that one must not learn a craft or go to school, waiting for his ori to create a living for him.

To say that he did not love his children would be missing the point. The concept of love and its manifestations have changed considerably. As more and more Nigerians went to school and became monogamists, they began to adopt the Western notion of love, building smaller nuclear families and seeking opportunities to empower their small number of children mainly through Western education. I think that Baba Olopa and

Alhaji recognized this trend but were not comfortable with it. I once heard Alhaji remark that the testicles of one of these monogamists were no bigger than his brain and his penis was shorter than his pen, just to ridicule him as a fool. What impressed me and my other friends when we saw a few kids being driven to private schools in their fathers' cars did not impress Alhaji, who saw those kids as already ending their lives, starting where they should have ended: "If the lifetime dream of a man is to own a car and employ a driver, why put a small kid in the back of a car and drive him to school?"

In the world of Alhaji and Baba Olopa, love and raising kids involved duties and responsibility: the children should obey instructions, and their parents should cater for their needs until they were able to take care of themselves. In the villages, independence came when parents gave land to their children to farm on their own. The parents would struggle to find a woman for their son and pay the bride-price. If the boy was a bad son, the father would spend his savings to marry an additional wife himself instead of helping a son whose character was unsatisfactory. As Alhaji and Baba Olopa were not farmers, they promised their sons support if they chose to go to school or learn a craft. Should the sons refuse to do either, they warned that at some point the sons must obtain their independence by leaving their father's household. Ibadan and Lagos grew rapidly due to the in-migration of men and women who wanted to break loose from their parents or had been asked to achieve early independence.

The rules were even tougher for a girl; once she was old enough, she must seek an occupation or a husband or both. Many parents at Ode Aje did not believe that they should invest in the education of their daughters. Aside from those with excess money, they did not see the need to send girls to school beyond the primary level, arguing that it was like investing money so that their husbands would garner the profits. Of the girls who finished primary school with me, only one made it to secondary school. It was not that they were dull or incapable, but their fathers believed that they should learn a craft within two years of leaving primary school and then look for husbands. Many of Alhaji's daughters later went to high school, but they owed it to their mothers, who insisted on and paid for their educations.

As if to reinforce their definition of love, the fathers at Ode Aje made themselves tough. Whether in the household of Baba Olopa or that of Alhaji, children had to hide or stay calm whenever they heard the voices of their fathers. They could not look their fathers in the eye while being spoken to, and their two hands had to remain behind their bodies to indicate respect. As soon as Baba Olopa was seen parking his cycle or car, everyone knew to pretend to be busy or hide in their rooms. Many children treated their fathers' living rooms with respect, using the chairs only when they were not home. Many objects were associated with the father—Baba's chair, Baba's cup, Baba's plate, Baba's bucket, Baba's comb, and one could neither use nor touch them without permission. The most dreaded object was Baba's whip. At Ode Aje, the whip was made of animal leather. I experienced its toughness, since I had many whippings. One had to fetch it, as part of the punishment, and return it to its location when the pain was in progress. For Baba Olopa and Alhaji, children who did not fear their fathers were bad. As the children grew older and became more responsible, they earned the respect and trust of their fathers, and the fear disappeared.

If a bad child was doomed to failure, almost without a second chance, nothing guaranteed that a good child would do well. This fatalism underlined the moral lessons and warnings from Baba Olopa and other men at Ode Aje. While they could be tough, mean, or even careless, they were moralists who told stories and life experiences to their children to urge them to succeed. They did not have an exaggerated notion of success, as they drew mainly from ideas of contentment: what one attained should fit into one's dream, so that the individual could maintain an emotional balance. Alhaji did not see the educated schoolteacher or police officer as superior to him, only different in the ways they made a living.

What united all the male elders, including the Muslims and Christians among them, was their very strong belief in the concept of ori. As fathers, they could only try their best, and the destiny of the child would be the sole determinant of success. The belief was a stress reliever: if a child became successful, the father could take limited credit, boasting occasionally that it was his ability to discipline the child that had made it possible. If the child became a failure, the father could create distance, saying that in spite of what he did the child had been ruined by a negative destiny. Most statements about individuals were punctuated with words that placed emphasis on destiny—ayanmo, ori, kadara—indicating the powerlessness of human beings to shape their future in the way they chose. The yet unborn had a connection to God and other supernatural agencies who negotiated with its destiny. While one chose to be a king, the other could decide to be a king's messenger. At birth, the destiny was locked, and the person was unable to change most aspects of it. The trouble, as Alhaji and Baba Olopa always warned their children, was that a good destiny could change to bad, not because the gods were angry but because the children were bad. To ensure the actualization of one's ori, one must not only work, one must also have a good character. The endless stories and morality lessons all revolved around achieving iwa (a good character) so that one could keep one's good destiny intact. A bad fate could be swapped for a good one, as one used a good character to compensate for a bad destiny. Similarly, a good destiny could go sour as one damaged oneself with pranks and tricks. Neither Baba Olopa nor Alhaji was able to know when the good ori would turn bad and when the bad one would move in the direction of goodness. I was so fascinated by this concept that I was made one of the lead actors in a play on destiny staged to entertain the parents at the end of the 1964 school year. As if to support Baba Olopa and Alhaji, who were in the audience, the boy with the destiny to become a king ended as a slave, punished for his excesses and disobedience to his elders.

The mamas at Ode Aje were different from those I had known before. The difference was apparent from the very first day. I knew they were not my mothers, and they knew I was not their adopted son. However, age was a factor in social relations: as they were all older than me, they were entitled to automatic respect. I also had to run errands for them, such as buying household supplies, although they knew to be nice to me if they did not want me to refuse. I learned at Ode Aje that only Baba Olopa's elderly wives could call me by my first name. The younger ones and all the junior wives who arrived after me were not allowed by custom to call me Toyin. As a sign of respect to the "children of the household," the wives had to invent nicknames. A childhood friend of mine, Tinwo Fatoki, was nicknamed Elegbo by his brother's wife, a name that signified someone with wounds befriended by flies. Tinwo and I had had multiple injuries and wounds from soccer and falling from bicycles, and the woman used this fact to nickname him. The young wives were full of creative names, in part to buy goodwill, calling some people Adumaradan (black beauty), Ibadiaran (velvet bottom), Idileke (bottom of beads), Eyinafe (beautiful teeth), Opelenge (slim) and other imaginative names. I was named Akowe (scholar), and the name stuck forever. When I was in high school and a classmate came to check on me, asking one of the junior wives for Toyin, she replied that there was no one living in the house by that name! Nicknames are different from oriki, however, and they do not generate new poems.

The mamas at Ode Aje were not as attractive to me as Mama Ade and Mama Biodun, and they only cared about their attire and looks on Sundays and when they had social engagements. They were not protective of their breasts, as Mama Ade and Mama Biodun were, and most of the other women at Ode Aje did not pay much attention to their breasts either. It was not that they wanted to exhibit them, only that they did not consider them as objects to be hidden from sight or protected from sagging with brassieres. When they were breast-feeding or changing their tops, they couldn't care less, and the three older women in the house often walked around bare chested. After a while, I overcame the initial shock of seeing so many breasts. The big boys at Agbokojo had told me stories about breasts and their exploits in trying to see them. But at Ode Aje there was no need for courage and no stories to tell when I saw a breast, as they were everywhere, even on the streets, as older women walked by unconcerned with the obsession of the big boys at Agbokojo. While Mama Ade and Mama Biodun had spent long hours in the morning applying their makeup, the women at Ode Aje did not bother. After their morning bath, they would rub their bodies with *epo* (palm kernel oil) to prevent dryness and use *tiro* (galena) on their eyelashes, all within a minute or so. Heavy makeup was associated with elite women, and many women at Ode Aje did not understand why someone who was not a prostitute would want to turn the face and body into a statue to be admired by men. It was not that they avoided all body adornments, but they depended on local ones such as the reddish *osun* (camwood) powder for their feet. The younger women among them painted their nails. All paid attention to their hair, braiding it regularly in various stripes, designs with names, which reflected the seasons or their moods. Those with tattoos and facial marks believed that these made them more beautiful, and some women had their teeth chipped to improve their looks.

A wise man not only admires another man's wife; he needs to dress his own and feed her very well. When Alhaji and Baba Olopa fed a wife and bought her new clothes, everybody knew that it was the woman's turn to move to the man's bedroom. When the woman created new braids, those with seductive names, she, too, was announcing that the short person hangs her bag where her hands can reach it, using head adornment to move closer to the private bedroom. Attraction became a useful way to improve one's memory, like lending people money, about the last time one had become the favorite bride and when it was necessary to add to the number of children.

Within days, I also knew that Baba Olopa's wives were not as powerful as those with whom I was familiar, and I was not at all afraid of them. Except for Iya Aladie, they all reminded me of Mama Ade and Mama Biodun, but only in age. I was to discover that there were minigovernments within the household and that I did not belong to any of them. A wife lived in the same room with her children, creating an effective social and political unit. The number of units was never fixed, but there were always units. A woman formed a formidable alliance with her children, strategizing with them on a daily basis, giving them civics lessons, and warning them about what not to say, where not to eat, and whom to avoid. The children became pillars of strength for the mother—and to get at the mother one had to seek ways to neutralize the children. Whether a mother was at fault was irrelevant, as her children moved fast to defend her. The songs that celebrated motherhood began to acquire greater meaning to me. At school, the justification was the pain of pregnancy and the bond passed through breast milk. At home, I saw that the justification differed from statements of the schoolteachers, incorporating elements of competition and conflict in which the role of the mother was to defend her children. The fate of the mother and the children was bound by politics, the need for them to protect themselves against other cowives and their children.

When I fully understood the politics of the social units, thanks to other young children in the household, who told me many things, I was able to operate as an outsider and manipulate the units for specific reasons. My first lesson in politics came within the household, the negotiations of power among women and their children on the one hand and between all of them and Baba Olopa on the other. There were even days and moments when I was the most trusted, best ally for many women and children. Gradually, I began to understand the difference between useless and sensitive pieces of information, between secrets and statements for general circulation. I knew when one wife wanted to use me to pass information to another, who would place the blame on me if I were stupid enough to relay it. I could read gestures, and I understood perfectly the meanings of smiles and laughter and how laughter could communicate disagreement.

What I noticed at Ode Aje was that the man was the center of the household. It was Baba Olopa's house that had brought all the women together, although they were living in different rooms. They had a roster for taking care of the house, and each did her share of the cleaning and cooking. The rules of seniority were very clear, with the junior wife doing more than the others and Iya Aladie only having to take care of her own room. I had my chores as well. Twice a day I went to fetch water. Although the house was piped for water, the city dam could not supply all the houses that needed it. To apportion the available supply, areas in the old city had public taps. One had to wake up very early in the morning to go to the public tap and line up with one's bucket. The water only ran for about two hours each day, and on some days the pipe had gone dry by the time it was one's turn. Families with severe shortages would send someone to stay at the public tap all night, waiting for the water to run. As daylight appeared and people knew that the water would soon stop running, the lines would break, physical might would replace orderliness, and those who could fight the hardest would take control. When the fighting was fierce, they might break the faucet or damage the entire system. In the evening, I traveled not to a public tap but to a stream. The stream was reliable, as there was always water available to fill a bucket for washing clothes and even for play. Going to the stream was fun, as half the time was actually spent speaking with friends on the way, playing soccer, or just chatting. A trip that should have taken thirty minutes could last until darkness. As one headed home, the prayer was always that no one would remember when one had left. Whenever they did, there was trouble. For two years, I fetched so much water that the crown of my head became bald, resembling a small island in an ocean of hair. As my friends would joke, a bird could perch on it to sing and nest.

Baba Olopa did not interfere with the chores since the rules were defined. I was given my own jobs as soon as I arrived. I think the wives must have worked things out on their own. I saw at Ode Aje examples of communal cooking and eating. Some families would cook big meals, and they would all eat at the same time. My friends often invited me, without obtaining the permission of their parents but only telling me the right time to come. Anyone who arrived when meals were being served was entitled to food, unless he declined. Where a family engaged in communal cooking, the wives had to agree to a roster. With us, it was only the Sunday lunch that united everybody. Under the Baba Olopa model, the wives had separate pots, which meant that he was giving each of them money. He had a pot, and the junior wife was the one who prepared all his food. It was from this that I had my share, since I was not a member of any of the units. Even then, cooking was limited to lunch, reducing the chores in the household. Breakfast and dinner were supplied by Alhaji's wife next door. Even when I did not go to her with money, she knew what to give me and I had no idea how this was arranged with Baba Olopa. On school days, I collected money for midday meals. If I had to save to ride a bicycle on the weekend, I had to forgo meals or run errands that led to tips.

No one had to tell a wife at Ode Aje to maintain solid relations with her parents' household. They all did, visiting their mothers and fathers at intervals and going to their old houses for all social and religious functions. Only a foolish woman would love her husband to the extent of abandoning her own father and mother, spending so much time and money to buy a monkey that lived in a treetop. My mother did not inherit any assets from my father, but she obtained one-third of an extensive farm and half of a plot of commercial land when her own father died. Not only was inheritance assured through one's parents and clans, but other forms of support were also expected. Until a woman's children became old enough to fight for their mother, the young wife knew that her compound and clan were safe and protective. If she believed the story of the husband who presented himself as a saint, she would have turned herself into an angel.

When a divorce occurred, the woman's original compound was the first port of call, so she could reclaim the room she had vacated when she got married. At Ode Aje itself, there were divorced women, many of them in transit. To distinguish them from other women, there was a name for them, *dalemosu*. Always ready to provide marriage counseling, the *dalemosu* were the antimale women who coached girls and young wives on the politics of marriage. The bitter ones were so antipatriarchy that they presented all men as useless, telling young wives to take money from their husbands when the love was still "hot" to start small businesses and telling young girls to pursue careers rather than husbands. As much as Alhaji and Baba Olopa resented this category of women, the *dalemosu* could not just be thrown out of the compounds, since they had a stake in the inheritance and were members of the clan. When I later read literature on women that assumed men had all the power, I knew for certain that the researchers had not spoken with the large number of *dalemosu* who had anticipated all the feminist ideas about liberation and self-empowerment. The cunning *dalemosu* aged gracefully, perfecting the means to be free of men and patriarchy and using their bodies and sex for power. Indeed, they could be counted among the first to build their own bungalows in the city, including one at Ode Aje owned by my teacher.

Ode Aje was a laboratory of cultures, at home, at school, in compounds and streets. From the evening to night and at every moment, Yoruba culture was being displayed in ways that were different from what occurs today. As I have enjoyed the lived culture, embodying many aspects of it, I have also grown to become the narrator of a past that is no more. The real shock to me is that what I saw at Ode Aje, whether it was a marriage or death ceremony, money raising or debt repayment, has disappeared or been modified so substantially within a period of thirty years. I have read about profound cultural changes in centuries long gone, but I never knew that a similar process could occur within a life span, within my own generation, which is a project in the making. I have never fully recovered from the shock of change and the agony of revisiting a past that has been violently reshaped.

Unlike my first home, Ode Aje was interlocked with other neighborhoods in the city and with hundreds of small villages outside the city. People traveled between wards and between the city and the village on a continual basis. As I was heading for school, a lorry might stop in front of the house to drop a visitor from the village and pick up someone heading to the village. There was no telephone to announce the movements, and people simply showed up to attend social events or announce good or bad news. There must always be food at home, or the ingredients to prepare a quick meal, since no one knew who would show up. Fascinated by lorry trips and the village, I, too, joined in the trips, showing up in villages unannounced and returning to the city when no one expected me.

Compounds, neighborhoods, and villages were united in many social events. All religious ceremonies attracted people from various places and families. People came to the city for cult and masquerade events. Tragedy united everybody, as many suspended their activities when people died. Even when a relation died elsewhere, people flooded our house to sympathize, some staying for days if they had traveled from a distance, and we had to feed them. Marriages and births were unifiers, social events used to determine the geography of influence. "It is when someone dies or gets married that you know the extent of your relations," is a saying that could be heard over and again to welcome someone coming from faraway Kano in Northern Nigeria. Long notices had to be given to celebrate any major event, to allow letters, some of which I wrote for people, to reach various destinations. People at Ode Aje would walk the distance to the Station to give letters to strangers to deliver for them in northern cities. I participated in this mode of communication, and it worked. One simply went around looking for passengers traveling to the city where a letter was to be sent, even shouting, "Please, who is heading for Maiduguri?" An address did not have to be complete, merely stating the name and the area, and the letter would manage to reach it. Lorry drivers delivered messages free of charge, dropping letters or words as they moved from place to place. There was trust, with words and money. Strangers gave me money to deliver to others, and it never crossed my mind to steal. Living in a "moral community," if one could call it that, the expectation was that younger people like me must help the adults, carrying their loads for them, relieving them of difficult assignments, and showing respect. The big boys in the new city knew that they had to do these things, but many of them would dodge their responsibilities. At Ode Aje, not many avoided their responsibilities to the elders.

The household at Ode Aje was Yoruba in culture, although Baba Olopa had a formal job and the young people were in school. No one denied the relevance of education, although at Ode Aje many parents did not think that Western education was the only route to success. Old age, rather than education or income, was the rule that guided relations. The most respected person in the household was the eldest woman, the mother of Baba Olopa, called by everybody Iya Agba (elderly mother), the only name by which she was known. She moved to Ode Aje after the death of her husband; in general, mothers could relocate to their sons' houses even if they had divorced their fathers. No matter how angry one was, one must stop when instructed to do so by Iya Agba. Her errands were top priority, even if one was running a different one when she gave you hers. All of Baba Olopa's wives, including Iya Aladie, were afraid of her. Whether it was true or not, they all believed that she could instruct Baba Olopa to divorce them. The children and youths believed that a report from Iya Agba to Baba Olopa was an invitation to a whipping. He would not listen to the evidence, simply reaching for his dreaded koboko, the tough leather whip. Iya Agba had her own pot, and she preferred to cook in her room, sometimes even refusing to open the window. We all joked behind her back that she would one day die of fire or smoke, although neither of these was the eventual cause of her death.

Iya Agba understood only Yoruba culture. Yoruba was the only language she knew. Every sentence she spoke combined idioms with proverbs. When she spoke, one had to listen, even if the subject was of no interest. She could not be interrupted, so she could take all the time she needed to narrate stories, pass judgments, and condemn bad behavior. She expected to be greeted properly in the morning. In turn, she took the time to recite the praise poem of each person, a difficult task that she did very well. "Did you wake up well, my son?" Iya Agba would ask every morning. And without waiting for me to answer she would recite a short version of my oriki (praise name).

Isola
Isola, the scion of Agbo
He who dreams daily of wealth
He who thinks daily of the good things of life
Isola, the scion of Agbo
Isola, spring to your feet

The guinea fowl flies up as free as the air
The woodpecker taps the tree with a rattling sound
Isola, heights never make the monkey lose his breath
Isola, the scion of Agbo.

On days when she woke up earlier than me, she would come to the room to ask me to get up. I would crawl out of bed, yawning, asking why the night could not be longer than the day so that I could sleep more. "Have you cleaned your mouth?" Iya Agba would yell. "Have you had your bath?" she would yell. Feeling like a goat pursued by a tiger, I would rush to wash my mouth, pick up the bucket, and head for the public tap. Sometimes, by the time I came back, it would be too late to have a bath, but I knew that I would play in the stream later in the day.

In Iya Agba's opinion, no one in the household should break any Yoruba taboo, even those that science had disproved. She was the taboo police, and one way to annoy her was to break a taboo or even query her. She repeated taboos before scolding or administering any punishment. Within twenty-four hours of my arrival, I received a long list of taboos from the others, and the list kept getting longer with time. A rough list that I compiled in 1966 contained over a hundred of them. Each taboo is a statement of what one must never do and the consequences of doing it. Known as *eewo*, these taboos cover the entire spectrum of human activities, including occupations, behavior, and interpersonal relations. While Iya Agba did not explain the reason behind each *eewo*, I later did, and some of them became part of my school exercises. I memorized all the interesting ones, and I, too, insisted that some of them be observed within the house and with friends. What follows are just a few examples to educate you in the ways of my people:

(i) A pregnant woman must never cross a long line of walking insects.
The expected result was that the baby would have no hair on the back of his or her head. When a baby was born without such hair, it could be attributed to the woman, who had violated the taboo. What Iya Agba did was tell us the taboo and the sanction. I later understood that it was meant to prevent a pregnant woman from falling in the process of avoiding deadly insects.

(ii) A child must not narrate stories in the afternoon.
The outcome of violation of this taboo was that the child would become lost on the way home from the farm or some other place. The rationale was that children love to hear and tell stories and if

they are absorbed by them they will lose focus and fail to reach home in time or perform errands as instructed. As one teacher told us, it was also meant to prevent a child from being kidnapped.

(iii) A king must never see a dead body.
The consequence was grim: the king would die shortly afterward. The *eewo* was to affirm the link between a king and life, forcing him to pay all his attention to the reality of life itself.

(iv) A man must not sit on a mortar used to pound yam.
Well, who ever did so would forfeit his manhood to impotency. This was a taboo intended to enforce elementary rules of hygiene, to prevent one from spreading dirt and disease on the main domestic implement used to make all kinds of food.

(v) One must not eat an orange in the bedroom.
This is yet another way to insist on good sanitation and to keep insects at bay. Most people slept on mats, and the smell of oranges would surely attract insects, which might bite them. The sanction for violating this was that all one's medicine, both charms and herbal potions, would lose their potency.

Eewo were not political but moral sanctions. Nothing was more effective or efficient in teaching children than *eewo*, simple, practical comments backed with threats of punishment for breaking simple rules. As Iya Agba repeated many of them daily, one had to either believe in them or simply obey them to avoid trouble. Even strangers outside the house would affirm them. Many of them focused on the sanctions, to drive home the point, rather than the explanation, which curious minds would contest. Rather than seeing them as jokes, we regarded them as facts to be memorized. When one reviews the *eewo* in their totality, there is no doubt that the intention was to prevent common accidents, enforce basic rules of hygiene, ensure respect for elders and customs, prevent waste, promote spirituality, and provide an understanding of elementary science. Iya Agba effectively used *eewo* to teach moral lessons and enforce the authority of elders. In using *eewe*, Iya Agba did not discriminate between others and myself on the basis of age or gender. Other members of the household were expected to respect *eewo*, as many applied to them as well: the pregnant wives of Baba Olopa should not eat from the cooking pot if they did not want to produce very dark babies; people should not cut their nails and leave them on the floor if they did not want to attract the hostility of those who stepped on them; unless a goat could talk, one should never curse it to escape a more powerful curse that the goat could make in silence; and an angry wife should not fight to the extent of burning her husband's clothes if she did not want the man to die in poverty.

If Iya Agba was teaching values and morality to sustain established hierarchies and social orders, I learned at the same time that there were others to show me the ways to subvert them. Iya Agba was like the horse who carried the warrior to the battlefield but could not fight the battle for him. The horse, like Iya Agba, could see but it refused to talk.

 was terribly scared when I first saw her in the early hours of the first morning at Ode Aje. She was short, about my height at over four feet but less than five. She had tied a wrapper around her waist, exposing her upper body. Her breasts were flat and so unnoticeable. The smell from her tobacco pipe was very strong, stronger than the cigarette smoke that I associated with the big boys who smoked in hideouts, afraid of being caught by parents or other adults. I greeted her, half prostrated, but she returned a casual greeting and went to the backyard where the bathroom and toilet were located.

She was different from any woman I had ever seen. Right away I told myself that I had seen an *iwin*, a spirit in human skin. She fit perfectly well into the many descriptions of an *iwin* that I had heard or read about. The schoolbooks were full of stories of spirits and ghosts. Not only did I know many of the stories, but I was living among those who believed that the stories were true. Adults presented *iwin* as living beings with powers greater than theirs. *Iwin* could appear all of a sudden, from nowhere. The woman walked in my direction on that morning, but I had no idea where she had come from. She was definitely not a ghost. I had had an encounter with a ghost some four years earlier. That was also in the early hours of the day. I saw a man wearing a white gown. I told Mama One and others that I had seen my father, since that's who I thought the man was. I was bombarded with many questions, each person urging me to describe what I had seen and heard. I must have told them what they themselves had told me about my father. I was probably using the photograph in my head to answer the questions they posed. As I spoke, they all concluded that I must have seen the ghost of my father. It was not I who reached this conclusion, but adults said that the man I saw was a ghost and I accepted it as true. I confirmed the story of Mama One that she, too, had seen the ghost a few times, in the same spot. It was another confirmation that the dead man was not far from the house and could appear at any time to those he loved. They wanted to be sure that the ghost had not given me a message to relay to them or even an instruction they must obey.

But what I saw on that morning at Ode Aje was no ghost. All moonlight stories portrayed an *iwin* as smallish and pipe smoking. I had seen one. An *iwin* could look ragged, naked, half-dressed. This woman was scantily dressed, with just a small wrapper tied around her body. There was not enough light for me to see her fully, to describe all her features. An *iwin* revealed only small parts of itself and only in a short appearance so that no one would be able to capture the full picture. The woman spoke little; actually, she mumbled her response, as spirits did in their world. As she had appeared from nowhere, and the main door had been locked (I checked the door twice), I told myself that the woman was one of those *iwin* that came from the underworld. In moonlight stories and schoolbooks, spirits inhabit the forest, caves, tree hollows, the sky, and the underworld. I was fascinated by spirit stories, and the narrators, whether schoolteachers or adults, always made them sound believable.

In Ode Aje and many other parts of the city, many people, including the educated ones, did not see spirit stories as fantasies, the imaginative creations of fertile minds, but as events, episodes, histories, and reality. Adults and children used objects to seal oaths, asking ghosts, spirits, and the underworld to punish them if they betrayed anyone. *Iwin* were among those unseen forces that overwhelmed the living, but they were not included in the list of beings and spirits to be worshiped. *Iwin* were not like ghosts who could be venerated or the dead who appeared once a year as masquerades. *Iwin* were not part of the invisible essence of self, like the spirit that dominated the *emere* or *abiku*. No one worshiped an *iwin*, as one did a god or goddess, but they were dreaded beings. An *iwin* could be so evil that to see it could mean the end of one's life. One *iwin* in a popular storybook was after one's blood, the food she relied upon for survival. Not all *iwin* were evil: many actually led one onto the path of success and wealth; others simply gave advice or wisdom. The one I saw did nothing; she simply walked away, not even removing the pipe from her mouth.

I chose to keep the discovery of the *iwin* to myself. When I had seen a ghost, I had been bombarded with too many questions, many of which I could not answer. I could only describe what I saw. I did not know whether this *iwin* was evil or good, and she did nothing to me. In the stories, while many *iwin* walked away as this one had done, others engaged in a short conversation, even giving instructions. What I saw was big; what I had to say was small. Then again, I was new; I was yet to meet my new friends at school. I knew only a few folk in the household, and my friendship with Kola, my age mate, was only beginning. The discovery of an *iwin* was my second research project in life, the first being the pursuit of rail lines and trains. The search for the train ended in my insertion into a mythical worldview, with the train turning me into an *emere*. The search for an *iwin* moved me far deeper into cosmology, the internalization of ideas bigger than the self, and an eye-opener to the world beyond. My wings began to grow, but my legs were too big to allow me to fly.

The next day I woke up early. I cannot say that I woke up at the same time since I was not using a clock to determine when to go to bed and wake up. No *iwin* showed up. Another two days passed, and nothing showed up. I was right: what I had seen was an *iwin*. This was true to type; like ghosts, *iwin* revealed themselves in their own time, without notice. Then I told Kola, with whom I had developed a close friendship in less than a week. Kola said that I had made a big mistake in not asking the *iwin* for a wish. As far as he was concerned, he needed only a one-minute encounter with an *iwin*. We began to draw up a request list. Kola wanted the gift of invisibility, to be able to move around without being seen. With this power, he would turn into thin air to fight, take the best clothes from the Indian stores in the new city, watch the movies that I had told him about for free, and even perch on people's heads and release his faeces on those who had offended him. He would become a hawk and use his beak to pluck an eye or two from his enemies. When I told Kola about my wish, which was for the *iwin* to return me to Agbokojo, he heaped a series of insults on me, saying that the *iwin* already knew that I had nothing tangible to say, which was why she refused to speak to me. He himself could deliver me to Agbokojo, he assured me, adding that if I paid him a small fee he would carry me on his shoulders so that the whole world could see me. I was convinced, and I revised my wish list: I needed the ability to fly, like birds and airplanes. Airplanes fascinated me, and no one had been able to explain the science of planes to me. My father's first son, Adewale, had become a hero due to his decision to travel to the United Kingdom and become a pilot. Kola was not convinced that the ability to fly was enough. "What would happen if you were trapped in a net?" he asked. I was preoccupied with revising my wish list, as I did other things at home and school.

She appeared again, like before, with the pipe and the smoke following her in the morning. Rather than even tying her wrapper around her waist she had simply thrown it over her shoulders, covering only half of her body. This time around, she did not even speak to me or reply to my customary greetings. She walked away, toward the backyard. I was curious, and I hid behind a door waiting for her to walk back. As she did, still smoking her pipe, she entered a room. From the inside courtyard, facing the front entrance, the room was to the right. I felt sorry for the occupant of the room, receiving a guest from the underworld so suddenly. Perhaps there was trouble. I hurried to wake up Kola and told him what I had seen. Half awake, he followed me so that I could show him the room. Kola hissed, pushing me so hard that I hit a wall, and said, "You did not see an *iwin*; you saw Leku, Iya Lekuleja."

I had seen a human being, not a spirit! It was the word *Iya* (elderly woman) in his sentence that gave me an instant clue. I must have confused the knowledge in the books and stories with the reality of life, moving too fast between the realm of the underworld and the living, confusing the shells of peanuts with coffins. Even then, I had no immediate idea what he meant by *Leku*. As Kola and I went about our ways and chores, I had to wait till after school to talk more. Had I jumped into a river without knowing how to swim?

As far as Kola was concerned, everyone knew that the woman was mysterious, but I was the first to associate her with the underworld. I had not noticed her room, the first to the left on entering the house, as it was always locked. Her room was well located, with windows opening onto the front veranda and the side yard. I never saw the windows open, and until the woman entered the room that morning I never saw the room open either.

The full discovery of Leku led me to the mysterious world of herbs and magic, secrecy and healing. She actually was an *iwin* but not of the kind described in the literature. Indeed, no literature, then or now, has been able to record, capture, and analyze the women in Leku's category. And half of what I later found out I cannot reveal. By the time I could seek her permission to reveal her essence and quote her, she was long dead. And each time I feel like revealing the full essence I am tormented by an overpowering feeling of awe and danger. The first time I mentioned a small part of her secret at a seminar at the Institute of African Studies at the University of Ibadan, I had a nightmare in which I was pursued by a tiger that would have killed me if I had not awakened in time. Most of my misfortunes, all my negative feelings, and my anticipation of troubles I attribute to a part of me that desires to unlock what I know about Leku. Perhaps I will, but not today, not even tomorrow. Nobody tells all he knows.

Let me start with what Kola told me. The reason I did not see Leku in my first days at Ode Aje was that she left home early in the morning and returned late at night, seven days a week, twelve months a year, in rain or sunshine. According to Kola, she took the same route, and she always looked down, such that over time her back and body were reshaped. He was right, but he did not know that the reason she looked down was to avoid eye contact and conversation with people. By traveling early and late, she also minimized contact. In a culture in which dialogue was intensely important, this was rather strange behavior.

Her destination was no secret. She had a successful store on a street corner about six miles from the house. This was the most famous store for herbs, ingredients for all diseases and ailments, and mixtures and materials for all kinds of charms, both for good and for evil. Kola took me to the store, and we did not have to disguise ourselves. We walked in and sat down, and she continued to smoke her pipe and attend to customers. I would visit this store many times in seven years, in part because I became fascinated with her and also because of the knowledge offered by Leku and her store. I doubt if Leku herself could have known the number of items in the store. Arranged in a way known only to her, they comprised an assortment of all known herbs, dried leaves, roots of many kinds of trees and shrubs, fresh and dead plants, bones of various animals (including tigers, leopards, and hyenas), skulls of various animals, dried rats, rodents, other animals, dry and living insects such as millipedes and centipedes, reptiles (including parts of snakes, lizards, and alligators), rocks and soils, and ritual lamps and pots. Tortoises, snails, and small cats walked around, and they, too, were for sale. Dangerous scorpions in bottles, as well as snakes in cages, were waiting for food and ready to bite. It was from these various objects, as I came to learn from Kola and others, that she got her name of Iya Lekuleja (the seller of assorted charms and medicine). Leku was just an abbreviation, used mainly behind her back; it is shorter, but it cuts off the dignified word, *Iya* (elderly mother).

There was nothing unusual in naming a person after her occupation. But in Leku's case, there was no other choice. She had no children of her own: many women were named after their children. Indeed, she had no husband. She had married once, but nobody remembered who the husband had been or how long the marriage had lasted. According to Kola, citing a rumor he had picked up from an adult, the marriage lasted only a few weeks, as the husband realized that he had married a very powerful woman: should he provoke Leku, he would lose his manhood. A second rumor from a schoolmate was a variation on this theme. When the husband wanted to take another wife because Leku could not become pregnant, she left in anger but threatened serious consequences. The disobedient man took a second wife but died during his first sexual encounter, and his penis had to be sawn off the body of the woman. No one knew what the truth was.

In any case, the truth is that no one can say much about Leku, either rumors or facts. She was an elder, but one with a difference. At home, she never got involved in anything, never showed up for any celebration, never commented on any issue, and she would never give advice, rebuke, complain, or even talk. I was the only one privileged to enter her room, but even this was after many months of interaction, and even I could not enter as often as I wished. Leku spoke in her store with her customers who wanted to buy or sell. Most of the items she dealt in were sold to her at her store, and she also had contacts to whom she could send for supplies. Unlike the majority of traders, she never advertised or begged anyone to buy from her. Most business was conducted by haggling, with the trader and buyer arriving at a price after a series of negotiations. With Leku, it was on a basis of buy or leave. She allowed no room for negotiation, an unusual trading strategy.

The clue to her strategy might have been in her room. It contained no objects other than those that could be found in her store. Her room looked exactly like her store, only with a space to spread a sleeping mat. She acquired no property, bought few clothes and shoes. In other words, there was no evidence that she was channeling profits from her trade into other forms of investment or savings. When Yoruba women engaged in trade, and they actually dominated trade, their purpose was to accumulate, to become independent of their husbands, and to acquire money to help their children. Leku was not motivated by any of these desires: she was free anyway and had no children to train. She was recirculating her profits to buy more items for the store rather than for herself. Her only passion was the store, not as a space in which to make money but one in which to make herbs and medicine available to whoever wanted them. She was certainly not counting on riches.

Leku was not a *babalawo* (father of mysteries), a diviner who had esoteric knowledge and could predict the future. So deep was the belief in this capacity to know about the future and to prevent failure that many consulted a *babalawo*, even those who had accepted Islam and Christianity. The *babalawo* relied on *ifa*, a geomantic divination system based on the ability to interpret over 256 ancient verses. The *babalawo* lived in their private homes all over the city, and I knew quite a few. They relied on Leku to obtain the necessary materials for sacrifices and charms. *Babalawo* were among the clients who visited Leku's store. They also referred their customers to her to purchase items for sacrifices or to cure diseases. Leku was not one of the known charm makers, the specialists with the knowledge of powerful medicine against all forms of witchcraft, sorcery, and serious trouble. But, like the *babalawo*, the charm makers relied on her to supply their needs. Leku knew three things, two of which were public knowledge and the third a secret known to only a few.

To start with what was obvious, she was knowledgeable about all items used to cure diseases, that is, she was a trader in herbs and all ingredients for charms and medicine. Her knowledge of traditional pharmacology was deep. She had not gone to school and had memorized all the items. Even the smaller items, the visible dried leaves, and the wrapped ground leaves ran to over a thousand types. The bone pieces ran to another thousand. Even the various types of clay lamps were many. Leku could produce an object in a split second, pointing to where a customer should go and get it when she was not in the mood to get up. The knowledge impressed even the most talented person. My headmaster once used her in a school sermon, saying that what the teachers wanted us to learn was nothing compared to what Leku knew. This was true, although we were dealing with different kinds of knowledge.

Because she knew so much, she became an object of discussions on knowledge. As the story goes, a powerful tornado had occurred many years before, and she was a victim of it. Carried by the tornado to a distant land, she was suspended in air for over seven years. It was there that she was able to observe the earth and all of its contents, knowing not just the name but the purpose of each item. Suspended without food or water, she could endure hardship, and her body was tiny so she would not need much food to survive. Other than her nonstop smoking, not many saw Leku when she cooked or ate. Even when I saw her cooking pot, it was so small that I could have eaten the entire contents as an appetizer. The lessons on what to do with all plants, insects, animals, and other objects were given to Leku by heavenly bodies. As the story goes, she signed a pact with the heavenly bodies not to reveal the sources of her knowledge but to constantly renew her vow. As Leku did not transmit this knowledge directly to others, people believed the story. She had no apprentice, no one interested in inheriting the store or learning the herbs. Indeed, when she died her death meant the end of the store and her knowledge, the loss of an entire laboratory and library.

Leku's second strength was a source of mystery: she knew the combinations of plants and other objects needed to cure all common diseases, and she could provide advice for the more complicated ailments. Kola told me that she could interpret dreams. I never knew before Kola told me that dreams required any interpretation. Thereafter, together with other students, we would narrate our dreams and interpret them. We put stress on signs showing us how to overcome tough parents and schoolteachers and signs that bad grades were imminent. When Kola washed his body with a medicated local soap, he told me that his mother had obtained it from Leku after he complained of bad dreams.

Leku operated in a less than commercial manner. If the babalawo and herbalists charged for consultations, Leku did not, charging only token fees for her herbs and charms. If the babalawo and herbalists explained the illnesses and diseases and how they wanted to cure them, Leku offered no explanation. I witnessed her method many times. A woman would walk in complaining that her son was suffering from prolonged stomach pain. Leku would listen to the story. As she picked one herb from one part of the store, she would pose a question, and the answer would prompt her to drop one leaf and take another. When she was done, she would simply instruct, "Grind them together, cook in a boiling pot, and give to your son for two days." No more questions, no more explanation. She mentioned her price; the woman paid and left. Leku would not even check the money or touch it, only pointing the client in the direction of a bowl in which to drop it and from which to take the change, which she also never checked. If the woman had no money, Leku would still give her the medicine and refused to reply or respond to the long statement of gratitude. It was not that the gratitude was wasted or the beneficiary should not thank her; it was as if she were saying that her help was rendered on behalf of some higher forces. When Leku had no answer to a medical problem, she referred the client to another herbalist or babalawo. One day when she saw a very deep wound on my right leg, which left a scar that remains noticeable even today, she advised me to go to Adeoyo, which was a facility for Western medicine. She gave no explanation, just a single sentence.

It was Leku's third type of knowledge that bound us in secrecy and actually made me the most informed about her. A simple act led to some bonding, which in turn led to greater interaction. It started casually, without any thought on my part. As Leku appeared late one evening, she was carrying a basket on her head. It could not have been heavy, and she was over a quarter of a mile away from the house. I just saw her ahead of me, a total coincidence. I ran to her to take the luggage, actually snatching it from her head without giving her the option to decline. It was customary practice for younger people to relieve elders and seniors of such luggage. However, no one helped Leku with this kind of task anymore. From what Kola told me, she had refused the offer of assistance so many times that people had simply given up. But there was also a belief that coming too close to Leku might carry some risk. Kola mentioned hearing the story of a woman who touched her and became a leper. The contents of her baskets and luggage were believed to be potent and danger-ous. Kola once saw a tortoise walk out of her room, putting everyone in a panic, worried by the meaning of the event. Since Leku did not talk, explain herself, or apologize to anyone, the sight of the tortoise had to be interpreted and they attributed magical significance to it. Carrying a bas-ket of charms and magic on one's head without the power to neutralize them was risky. Leku's persona, too, contributed to this kind of belief. There were times when, on reaching the house, she would stop and say some words to herself, as if uttering powerful prayers, before entering. Even mysterious were the days when she would enter the house back-ward, as if she must not see certain people or objects. She left home at different times early in the morning, which was why I did not see her when I thought she was an *iwin*. As Kola and others believed, she must not see the same person in the morning twice a week.

I did not contract leprosy from Leku's basket. For reasons best known to her, she allowed me to carry the basket into her room. I saw chaos. It was the first time I had entered her room, and I was surprised not to see a bed or table. It was no more than a place of storage, an extension of her store. Her bag was for moving items between the room and the store. Her few possessions were in a medium-sized basket. Although the house had electricity, Leku preferred the clay lamp that burned with red oil. It was a hot room. As she entered, she knew where she had put her box of matches. The lamp she lit was not the usual one with one wick; it had five. I did not understand the symbolism of the number five or of the pedestal on which the lamp was placed. Behind the lamp was a wooden statue, a representation of a god or goddess. I had seen similar statues in other houses, and I knew that they were objects of worship. Leku was not a Muslim, and she never went to church. This was her religion, I told myself. She placed different food objects in front of the statue. This was all I saw, and I left before I could be dismissed. Leku said nothing, not even thank-you.

Thereafter, I stopped by her store several times, some days in the company of Kola and other friends. Some classmates recognized a few of the objects and could name about five of the plants. Like sheep, we guessed at random what the objects were used for. There were some whose mothers had visited Leku to obtain herbs and who remembered drinking some of her mixtures for minor ailments. And there were some who had been given a list of items to purchase, viewing them as either curious or useless. The smell in the store was never pleasant, which was probably why Leku was always smoking, using tobacco to neutralize the powerful odor. Young girls and boys sent on an errand to the store hardly wanted to enter, preferring to stay outside, collect the objects, and hurry back home. The kids did not want to walk into a snake pit with their eyes open.

I would just sit inside the store, looking at the objects, associating those that I recognized with the stories I had heard or read. When I saw the live tortoise, I was surprised that what appeared to be an ugly and harmless animal could be associated with evil, wisdom, and knowledge. Many great Yoruba stories revolved around the tortoise, each with a theme to teach morality and hard work. Some stories contained riddles and puzzles, such as why the tortoise's shell is crooked, why its tiny head has to be hidden, and why many tortoises live so long. There was a huge tortoise in Leku's store, big enough for a baby to sit on.

I did not count the number of times I went to Leku's store, but there was no consistent pattern to my visits. Sometimes I just followed friends who were sent there on errands. At other times, I stopped there on the way to other places. Kola was always passing through the area on the way to his mother's compound, and many times we went together. All my friends were annoyed that I would take a moment to leave them and go inside the store to look around. Leku knew all of us, but she did not say much, only conveying with her facial expression that she was not hostile to us. One day, again without thinking, I asked whether she could teach me about the herbs and magic. She removed the pipe from her mouth, smiled, and said nothing. I forgot about my request.

Sali was the first schoolmate and neighborhood friend of mine interested in having a girlfriend. He was also the first to marry. By the time my third and last child was born, Sali's first son was already in college, registered for one of my history courses. Sali did not go to high school or college, but he has successfully used his children to overtake all of his classmates who did, some of whom are still struggling with their teenagers. Sali did not anticipate the life story I just told you, and I am quite sure it was not intended. I cannot say that he was obsessed with women. What I know for sure is that he wanted to have a girlfriend at the age of eleven. Risi, the girl he was interested in, was a year older, in the final grade. It was unusual for girls and boys of the same age to date. Men tended to be much older than their wives, and a boy who wanted to date sought a girl much younger than himself. Sali wanted to break the rules. Then he added another complication: the girl he wanted was the school prefect for girls. She was not particularly attractive; the qualification for her office was not beauty but sternness. To be a prefect, one must be bright and mean, eager to punish the junior ones for the slightest offense, ready to fight peers who broke the rules, and willing to defend the headmaster and the schoolteachers at the expense of the students. No one liked school prefects, and the clever boys sought by all means to avoid being appointed as prefects. Indeed, there were those who deliberately cultivated bad manners in order to prevent the schoolteachers from recommending them. Prefects must obey all the school rules, including arriving early and ensuring that they were in the headmaster's good book.

Sali set up an advisory board on how to approach Risi and embark upon a relationship. I was a member, actually an active one; it was my first such experience, and Sali's boldness was impressive. Our first strategy was a direct approach, which was for Sali to approach Risi and speak his mind. We crafted a dialogue, anticipating all the answers that Risi would come up with. From the "big boys," we knew some of the possible lines, although the first one, "It seems as if I know you from somewhere," would definitely not apply in this case. They already knew one another. If Sali made an error, Risi could use her power as a prefect to impose an instant punishment. Like the teachers and the headmaster, a prefect could ask students to kneel down and raise their hands, order them to close their eyes for five minutes, and impose other forms of punishment. For Sali to speak with Risi, there must be an opportunity, like a five-minute period when they would be left alone. For days on end, the opportunity did not arise. We set up small teams to check when Risi was by herself, including the times when she was on her way to school. Most of the time she was not alone. On the few occasions when word came that she was alone, Sali was not free to talk, either because adults and teachers were around or because he was running errands.

We moved to the next stage. The advisory board decided to choose an intermediary, who would arrange a meeting. This was to be a younger person on whom Risi would have mercy if she got angry. The boy's task was simply to ask Risi for a time and venue when Sali could speak to her. The answer came immediately. Risi wanted to know the reason for a meeting and asked the messenger to relay a riddle: in what ways and under what circumstances can a goat and a tiger meet for a conference? We understood the riddle to mean that Risi would tear Sali apart, and we sent an immediate response: when the tiger is full and dealing with serious constipation. Risi dismissed the boy and asked him never to show his face.

The advisory board opted for a third approach. We would send a love letter. We debated about the type of letter, the language and style, the paper, and the person who would deliver it. The choice of words and tone became something of a competition. One person suggested the "Yanibo style." Yanibo is the Yoruba name for the tortoise, whose wisdom could manifest love, kindness, and evil genius. The Yanibo style was to offer love and threats simultaneously, listing the various acts of kindness and support that Risi would receive for saying yes as well as the consequences of saying no. Sali, now the "wise tortoise," would promise full protection: if the world became uncomfortable, he would take her with him to heaven; if the earth was drowned in a flood, Sali and Risi could live on top of a tree for as long as they wanted; if it became overpoweringly hot, they could move to a cold cave. Risi need not fear drought or famine, as Yanibo had a store whose contents would last till the second coming of Christ. The ultimate promise was that Sali would not take a second wife without Risi's permission. The advisory board agreed that this promise should interrupt each sentence, just to underscore its sincerity. In the Yanibo style, one must also issue some veiled threats. Risi's refusal could mean a life of misery with an unsuccessful man who would be so poor that the family would never have enough money for food, medicine, and other needs. A threat must not be a curse, as this would cause offense: no one said that Risi would be poor, only that the unfortunate man who chose her would be. But she had to be frightened to take Yanibo seriously. Thus, we decided to add that if Risi did not date and marry Sali her husband would have over forty wives and she would be ignored for the rest of her life.

The Yanibo style fell through. We had not even finished composing the letter when we opted against it. I think it was my fault, as I mentioned that Risi was not Yoruba enough. On the school drama team of which I was a member, she could never get a major role and had to play the part of a silent crowd member. For the Yanibo style to work, the person must understand the context, since the name of the tortoise would not be invoked, just its method. The Yanibo style used idioms and codes to communicate, so the reader should not read the letter at the surface level. Everybody was persuaded. We also dropped the "poetry style," which was to compose an elegant love letter in a traditional oriki form.

We opted for a "modern love letter." This is the real name—modern for its newness and association with literacy, letter for its formal structure, and love for its directness. There were so many samples for us to use, many of which had been circulated by peers and seniors and some of which we spent endless hours improving on in practice sessions. Small love pamphlets had also been printed and were sold by hawkers at various locations. I cannot locate the original letter to Risi, and no one can, since the only copy was handwritten and sent to her. As to the words, I can actually be exact, since I have on numerous occasions sent modified versions to friends and colleagues just to entertain them. Here is this sample of a collaborative effort, with words drawn from soft-sell pamphlets and what the big boys, some of them in secondary schools, had told or shown us:

At school, July 10, 1964

Dearest Queen Risi:

I am one hundred percent certain that this letter meets you in a fabulous state of anatomy and metabolism. If so, eternal gratitude to our Creator. If not, I am the only doctor in town for the Queen.

Oh beautiful Queen! The geography of your body is perfect. Your body is full of milk and honey, your fingers are richer than gold, your eyes see better than the moon and sun, your head contains more wisdom than the sea can hold water. Queen Risi is the model of perfection, accepted by all the angels, created by God on a Sunday when He had no time for other duties. You are the last Queen created by God. Other women that came after you are servants of the Queen.

Risi, I know that you are always busy, the Queen that has a kingdom to rule. Without a King, a Queen is useless. My principal aim of writing this letter to you is to gravitate your mind towards a matter of importance which has bothered my soul. This matter is so important. Even as I am writing, my soul is shaking, my temperature is rising, the wind vane of my mind and body is pointing everywhere at the same time. Queen Risi, you need a King.

Queen Risi, you are the only one I see at school, at home, and on the road. The mirror in my eyes has only your divine image, your majesty, your throne. I see you in my dream everyday. When I sleep, you are the one in my medulla oblongata, the only mosquito in my net, the only sugar in my tea, the only fly in my ointment.

To go straight to the point. I want to be your King. I want to wake up in the morning and see only the Queen. You should be the only grey matter of my system, the wall clock of my room, the only oxygen in my head, the only rock in my universe, the only river whose water I can drink. My sweetest, dearest, talented, fantastic, fondest, extraordinary paragon of beauty, be mine today, be mine tomorrow, be mine for ever. Let us live and die together, buried in the Garden of Eden with our love.

Say Yes, Queen Risi. Only a weak Queen says No. Listen to what the Lord says. He says we should ask and we shall be given, we should seek and we will find, and that we should knock and it will be open unto us. I am this 10th day of the seventh month in the year of our Lord, one thousand, nineteen hundred and sixty-four, asking, seeking and knocking at the door of the only Queen. Open the door so that thy servant may enter. Queen Risi means love itself; the noun, pronoun, metaphor, oxymoron, thesis, antithesis, irony, conjunction and the adverb of love. Life has no meaning to me if I cannot wake up in the morning and behold your beautiful face, your long legs, your angelic eyes, your majestic lips, your fantabulous head, your smile.

You are a wise Queen. You realize the mountain that I want to climb, the ocean I want to swim, the desert I want to cross. If you say no, there will be no King for the Queen. My life will be like tea without sugar, like a snail without shell, a cow without horns, a car without a driver, a cup without tea, a town without people. Queen Risi, I am Adam, you are Eve. If you say no, I will not be alive to finish reading your reply. In fact I will kill myself. What is life without Queen Risi? A man without love is like a fish out of water.

Queen Risi, reply today through the bearer. God's time is the best. This is the time for the Queen to meet the King. God has united us in the Garden of Eden. What God has put together let no man put asunder. A woman without a man is like a field without seed.

From one and only,
Sali Kasali
Your beloved, faithful, loyal, loving king

I must let you know that the advisory committee did not complete the process of the "modern love letter." As the big boys and the pamphlets instructed, we should have asked Risi to fill out a form that accompanied the letter. The standard form contained the following questions.

What is your name?
Age?
Do you have a boyfriend? If yes, please state why? If no, please explain?
Do you love me? If no, state why. If yes, doxology.
What is your favorite food?
What is your hobby?
Mother's occupation?
Father's occupation?
Are you from a polygamous home?
Is your father rich and handsome?

Is your mummy a paragon of beauty like you?

What do your parents want their son-in-law to become in life?

The Sali advisory board decided that we should write two letters, the first one as above and the second to congratulate her on saying yes, adding this set of questions as part of the reply. The king should exercise his power gradually so that the queen will not be frightened of a man with so much power.

We selected a boy to deliver the letter. The middleman had to be a trusted person. We had heard of cases in which the middleman rewrote the letter, inserting his name and taking the girl. The middleman had to be paid a token fee for his aggressiveness in delivering the message and insisting on a reply. There were cases in which a girl would pounce on the middleman, tear his shirt, kick him, and insult him with unprintable words. The middleman could not fight back, as this would hurt the chances of his sponsor. One must first cross the river before saying that the crocodile has a lump on his snout. He could not just drop the letter and walk back without being scolded for his carelessness, ineffectiveness, even irresponsibility. Problems with the girl would be blamed on the middleman. We went back to the boy who had delivered the first message, as he was too young to compete for Risi and had demonstrated competence. Although the pamphlets and the big boys had assured us that all such letters were read, this was not the case with Risi. According to the boy, she received the letter, opened it, read two sentences, and shredded it to pieces in his presence. Risi herself had lost the original, which could have become a valuable treasure!

The boy was either naive or too honest. He started with the last part, Risi's angry reaction and letter shredding. Everybody felt humiliated and enraged. A big rock can mangle a lizard; he who is strong can hurt the weak. Sali had become the lizard and Risi the rock sitting on its entire body, mangling it until it broke into small pieces. Sali vowed not to give up, and the task of the advisory board was broadened to include the search for another strategy. It did not take many days for someone to come up with the best strategy: the use of a love potion.

The hunt for a love potion took me back to Leku's world, but only after various detours. Everybody of my age knew that there were love potions. The use of charms and magic to win love was a popular theme in many stories and books. The morality was always ambiguous; no one emphatically said that it should not be used. The efficacy was trusted and fully assured if one knew the best *babalawo*, charm makers or herbalists such as Leku. As with all charms, the trouble was always deception by many mediocre charm makers, who did not know the right herbs and their combinations. For the person in search of a love potion, it could be a process of trial and error, buying a series of fake charms before buying the correct one. A love potion could take the form of a powder to be sprinkled on the food and drink of one's target. If one was close enough, it could be a small object that could be smuggled under the bed or pillow. A powerful charm maker could even instruct the targets in their dreams to love only a particular person. Or the person chasing love could rub his or her body with magical perfume that worked on the target.

When a man with many wives had a favorite, the standard allegation was that the favorite wife had used the right love potion. When the favorite wife fell out of favor, the explanation was that the efficacy of the love potion had reached its end. Women in conflict accused one another of visiting charm makers. It must have been lucrative to be a male charm maker, visited by hundreds of women. Some male charm makers were known to have increased the size of their harem by giving the wrong charms to their clients: rather than the client winning the love of the man she desired, she would end up with the charm maker. A woman could also be unlucky enough to have paid for bad medicine. Rather than receiving a love potion, she could end up with a death potion, accidentally killing her husband. Or she might just be unlucky, getting caught with the love potion before it was administered, thus creating a crisis that could lead to a divorce. Everyone knew that being discovered in possession of a love potion could lead to serious problems, as the thought of it might be regarded as evil. If the medicine worked well, the man became converted to the woman, behaving meekly and weakly, granting all the requests of his wife, and even running useless errands. To fall victim to a love potion was to lose part of the essence of masculinity.

I hope I have not misled you into thinking that only women hunted for charm makers. Far from it. Men did the same thing, and one could see them wearing magical bracelets, chains, and amulets or rubbing their bodies with magical oil. The charms were intended to buy "general love," not targeted at a specific person. If the aye (seen and unseen forces) were sufficiently placated, I was told by Alhaji when I asked him to explain the need for his various amulets, one would do well in all interactions with human beings. As he explained it to me, failure occurred when one had too many enemies. In Alhaji's case, he had only to visit the Islamic teachers and charm makers, who were everywhere. The babalawo could sell the same medicine.

"Only a wicked man can marry two wives," pronounced an influential visitor to the house as I was serving palm wine to Baba Olopa and his guests. It was the wickedness part that aroused my attention and encouraged me to stay longer to hear the rest of the juicy story, which I needed to share with my friends. The adults paid no attention to me: when the cock is drunk, he can forget about the hawk. As the guests drank and laughed, he said in a serious tone that one must be able to plant conflicts in both wives. The other men agreed. If the two wives were friendly, he continued his thesis, the man would be in trouble: they could demand equal allowances, request gifts and sex at the same time, and generally create trouble. However, the rivalry and fighting could get out of hand, as I saw with Baba Olopa's wives and the many other cases requiring conflict resolution. Indeed, many men, unable to resolve such conflicts, would seek the intervention of the *babalawo* to end a conflict and ensure that the two women would love the husband even if they hated each other. Baba Olopa's visitor, still drinking but not drunk, blamed men who were unable to manage their many wives, calling them weaklings. He dipped into his pocket to bring out an amulet, wrapped in leather.

"This is *ajipanupo*, the real *ajipanupo*, the original." He shouted this four times to the applause of his friends. As I later heard, from one of Baba Olopa's wives, *ajipanupo* was a potent love charm used by men to prevent two wives from fighting to the point of leaving their husband. Even if one of them did leave, the husband could use *ajipanupo* to order her body and soul to return to his house. As Baba Olopa's wife told me, a woman contemplating divorce should set money aside to buy the magic to neutralize the man's *ajipanupo*. The way I understood it, a love medicine could be countered with a hate potion. Indeed, I saw many hate potions as well, charms that worked in an indirect way. One was not seeking love but a medicine to ensure that one's enemy would not receive love. A man could use such a potent hate potion on his wife that no other men would ever want to be near her. In the most potent form of the potion, if another man had sex with his wife he would have a heart attack, crow three times like a cock, and die on top of her. It was known as *magun*, and the fame of this potent charm was well known by all. A woman who believed that her husband had a powerful *magun* remained in check unless she had a charm to counter it. A few times, when young men died suddenly, I was told that the cause was nothing but the deadly impact of *magun*. As they cried and mourned, the most outspoken would say that the man was warned many times to avoid other people's wives.

What Sali wanted was the affirmation of his manhood, a magic potion to obtain Risi's consent, making him a king. Sali had indicated his power, appointing Risi a queen and himself a king. But he was powerless, indeed impotent; not only was he unable to reach Rìsí and talk, but the queen had no need of him. The love potion would change the situation: if the charm worked, Rìsí would not only talk, she would say only what would please Sali. We had heard stories of men who used powerful charms to win love. We even compiled a list of men with hunchbacks, crippled legs, single eyes, and humble occupations who had beautiful women as wives. "If they did not use love magic," Sali concluded, "who would have married them?" We all agreed with him, with one boy reminding us of a line in one of the stories: a bad woman does not return a man's love; a good woman is easier to woo. One can dance or fight to acquire a beautiful woman but should not begrudge the man who has other means. A big fish can only be caught with big bait.

To assist Sali, we needed to expand the membership of the advisory board. Its original members did not include anyone knowledgeable about obtaining love potions. We all knew about charms and love potions, but we had no understanding of how to obtain them or approach the makers. It was easy to find out, as the school had students from compounds of diviners and charm makers; some were even alleged to come from homes with powerful witches. We all agreed to solicit the help of a schoolmate, Omo Baba Olosanyin (the son of an Osanyin priest). Osanyin was a Yoruba god with power over plants who could also reveal one's future. The Osanyin priest was known in the school, as many had visited him to discover who had stolen their books or pens. His fee was moderate. In the corner of his cluttered room was a doll representing Osanyin, which could speak in a whistling manner. As I later learned, the priest used a form of ventriloquism to communicate. He posed a question to Osanyin, and the doll would answer. The priest would supply an interpretation that was clear and could not be contested, such as "I was certainly not ready to stop the woodpecker from pecking; the bird may wish to speak frankly with a tree."

We wasted no time in recruiting the schoolmate, who led us to his compound to see his father, the priest of Osanyin. The boy believed in the power of his father and had used it to protect himself from excessive punishment by the senior boys. I, too, had warned a few people not to get into trouble with him as his father had the magic to produce madness. The priest was receptive, behaving like a door with two options: if it does not open inward, it has to open outward; if it does not close inward, it should close outward. The priest could either dismiss us or ask us to stay. The priest asked Sali to present his case, which he did in a few seconds. The priest told him that there was no problem, and he praised his Osanyin: "The slender, one-legged god more powerful than the gods with two legs, the *okooroo dugbe dugbe* who saves all those in trouble." He even spoke with the Osanyin doll, which whistled the response that there was no problem. Sali paid the equivalent of his breakfast money for three weeks and received a powder medication. He could use the powder once, look Risi in the eye, and the love would begin. We were delighted. This was faster than all the meetings, the letter writing, and the search for a middleman to deliver messages. We were happy, and we only had to wait for the result and disband the advisory board.

The next day, Sali used the powder, walked around the school in the company of his friends, and saw Risi a few times. We expected the love to begin. For days, nothing happened. We forgot to ask the Osanyin priest about the clues, how Sali would know when Risi was in love. We had to go back to the priest. Sali had to pay again, just to ask for the clues. The Osanyin priest said that at that very moment Risi was frantically searching for Sali to start the love affair. We wanted to rush back so as not to miss the opportunity, but the priest said we were too late and the medicine would work only once. The mission had failed, caused by our impatience; we had set the trap after the rat had passed. Sali had lost money, a huge sum, which he needed for his breakfast for a whole month. We all had to contribute part of our food ration to sustain our friend.

Our losses had multiplied. As we mourned the loss of Risi, money, and the food ration of members of the advisory board, one of us brought a small book on charms and medicine to class. Just as there were pamphlets on love, there were many others on a variety of other subjects. Usually short and self-printed, many pamphlets appeared in the 1950s and 1960s containing short stories, poems, historical narratives, and information on love, magic, and charms. There were many on religion, printed by various religious organizations, advising how to pray, avoid sin, talk to God, befriend Allah, see Jesus Christ, and cross the dangerous line from paganism to salvation. Hawkers moved about the city selling the pamphlets. A parent of one member of our group had bought the pamphlet on charms and magic, and his son had stolen it to show it to us. We had wasted our time and money visiting the Osanyin priest. If the Osanyin priest and Risi had wished us ill luck, they simply forgot that those who expected another man's failure ignored the reality of providence. The pamphlet contained many examples of charms used to win the love of a woman, the necessary herbs, and all their combinations. We selected the one with the simplest instructions: Sali was to mix all the herbs, rub them on his hand, recite an incantation, hold Risi, ask her to be his love, and she could only say yes. The instructions repeated in bold type, "The woman can only say yes." We were happy.

The difficult part, according to the pamphlet, was that one must not miss a line of the incantation or the charm would not work. Sali and all the members of his board decided to memorize the lines, written in Yoruba, before we combined the plants and roots. Here is a poor rendition in English, with all the untranslatable lines excluded:

The command to Ogbo is final
The command to Ogba is final
The command to Risi is final
Risi, you are for Sali.

I, Sali, am a bag of good luck
Good things follow me
Risi, follow me.

Whenever the eluluu invokes rain, rain must fall
If a frog invokes rain, the rain must fall on him
I, Sali, invoke Risi, she must fall on me.

I am reborn, reborn into good luck
Let all fortunes follow me
If a child sees honey, it throws away the bean cake
Today, new things must follow me
Risi must follow me.

I never expected that the preparation of the herbs would involve me until Sali himself said that the rest of the job was now mine. "How?" I asked. I had to go to Leku to procure all the items. Men make plans, God acts! Sali and the rest had become only men, turning me into the God who would deliver.

"Why can't you go?" I asked a simple question.

Sali looked surprised that I would ask that question. "Me, go to Iya Lekuleja at the junction?" It was then that I learned that everybody was afraid of Leku for various reasons. Sali told me that he had heard a rumor that Leku could turn a client into a snake and that the skulls in the store were not those of animals but of human beings. According to Sali, several small boys had gone there to buy herbs and never returned, as Leku had converted them into ingredients to make powerful charms. According to Sali, Leku only ate one meal a year, usually around June, and she needed only small snacks for the next twelve months.

"Sali, why are you telling me all this for the first time?" I asked.

"You have touched Iya Lekuleja at the junction. You have carried her loads. Kola said that you have been to her room." Sali recited a long list of my interactions with Leku.

"Yes, I did, what does it mean?" I asked impatiently.

"Death!" Sali concluded. "You will die suddenly, any time now." Sali mentioned a number, over fifty, of those who had touched Leku and not lived long thereafter. He confessed that everyone at school had been expecting my death for some time.

"I am alive, Sali," I assured him.

"You are alive because Iya Lekuleja's stomach is full." Sali explained that her annual big meal comprised human flesh and blood. In any case, I needed to help him.

"We all have to go to Leku to buy the ingredients," I said in a commanding tone. I was not afraid of dying, I said, but I would not visit the store by myself. I had been to Leku's many times, not to buy but to look. Sali agreed that I had to come up with a reason why I needed the roots and leaves before Leku would sell them to me. Sali believed that Leku was the most honest of all the herbal dealers in the city, as she would not substitute the leaves of camwood for those of locust bean. Sali also wanted to ensure that each item mentioned in the pamphlet was the right one, since we could not identify them all.

Sali spent days and used all his negotiation skills to persuade the members of the advisory board to go with us to Leku's store. He must have used even greater diplomacy to convince the three boys that he had to obtain Risi's love. He was the same person who had told all the horror stories about Leku, all of a sudden becoming an emaciated child who wanted to be fattened in a day. Even then, they all looked scared as we hurried to Leku's store after school, avoiding others, not even telling them about our secret mission. Others had noted our meetings and isolation, but they had no clue as to our motive.

As we approached the store, all of us developed cold feet, and one boy wanted to change his mind. Sali had to beg all over again, assuring them that they did not have to say anything. They did not even have to enter the store, as only Toyin would do so.

"If you enter the store and touch her," one of the boys threatened, "I will never speak with you again."

We inched forward, Sali pleading that they should not abandon him. Leku was smoking her pipe as we arrived. There was a customer ahead of us. When the customer left, I entered the store. The rest of the boys stood outside, but they could see us and hear everything. Leku used a finger to signal that I should sit. I refused, saying that I was there to obtain some items. She signaled that I should read the list. I took out the pamphlet from my pocket, now rumpled, and read the eleven items. Leku stood up to get about three and asked me to get about two from other parts of the store. Then she asked me to read the list again. I did so.

"I am confused; do you mean *ape* or *apepe*, *ayan* or *iyin*, *botuje* or *buje*?" asked Leku.

The other boys and I had confused the names of the items. The pamphlet did not indicate the accent on the words to indicate the tones, and we had settled for the easy pronunciations. In later years, I realized that of the eleven items mentioned we missed almost nine. By mispronouncing them, we had confused a vine (*ape*) with mahogany (*apepe*), wood (*ayan*) with roots (*iyin*), and a plant (*buje*) with nuts (*botuje*). I looked at Sali and the others, and we were lost. Wanting to be helpful, Leku asked:

"What is the school project about?" She was probably thinking that we had an experiment in mind.

"It is not for our homework," I said. "My friend needs to make a small charm." The unexpected had happened. We could not retreat to restrategize. We had not expected an interrogation. We had no time to appoint a leader to think of answers.

"Who is your friend?" Leku asked. Wanting to protect me and his friends, Sali stepped forward, but not close enough to be touched by Leku.

"My son, what part of your body is aching?" asked Leku.

"I am fine, Iya Lekuleja, I just needed the medicine for Risi's problem."

"What part of Risi has a sore?" Sali was now confused. He looked to the other boys, and one of them whispered that he should tell her about Risi, perhaps because he knew how desperate Sali was, or he was merely respecting the adage that one falsehood spoils a thousand truths. Sali admitted:

"I wanted to make the potion for Risi to agree."

Leku understood what he meant. She said that it was easy and I should come back on Saturday afternoon to collect everything. She even told us to come at the Islamic praying hour, a way of being precise as to when we should arrive. It was common in Ibadan, even among "pagans" and Christians, to divide the day into five parts based on the times when Muslims prayed. It was convenient to do so, and was as reliable as using a wristwatch, but it allowed greater flexibility. While the clock simply said 2:00 P.M., the use of the praying time allowed one to be early or late by about thirty minutes. She told Sali and the other boys that they did not have to come with me, that she understood all the items and needed a few days to put things together. She betrayed no emotion, she did not waste her words, and she sounded as professional as she had always been.

Our victory party was immediate, as we walked back, singing, dancing, and looking for the nearest soccer field to join others in playing. The pamphlet and Leku had delivered Ṛisi to Sali. None of the boys complained that the herbs and charms would come from the mystery woman who allegedly ate human flesh and drank human blood once a year.

I walked into a deadly trap, like the restless feet walking into a snake pit. Nothing had prepared my mind for it. No warning came in a dream. No clue was visible. Saturday came quickly, and all the boys gathered at school. We had decided to ignore Leku's instruction that not all of us should come to the store. We all decided to go, but the rest would stay out of Leku's reach and sight. One boy said that Leku could not see beyond five feet, which was why people did not move closer to her, so that she could not put them on her list of whom to kill or roast for medication. I was to grab the medication and rush out. In contrast to visiting other places and people, one did not have to rehearse what to say, what words and sentences to avoid, and how long to speak. Leku would not speak anyway. I had nothing to fear. She had always welcomed me to her store, gesturing for me to sit down, and removing her pipe to signal "bye bye" when I decided to leave. I even took fruits from the store without seeking permission to do so. I would peel bananas and oranges and leave the skins on the ground. Leku would pick them up, sun dry them, and store them for reasons that I did not know. She had in store dried skins of many nuts and fruits, including those that did not even grow in Western Nigeria where the Yoruba are located. Sali and the rest of his advisory board walked jubilantly toward the store. As we approached the site, the boys stopped, leaving me to cross the street while they looked on from a distance.

As I walked in, I was grabbed by two fierce-looking adults and pushed to the back of the store. Two women quickly held up a long piece of blue cloth to create a curtain so that no one could see the inside of the store. Without the curtain, the entire store could be seen from the roadside by onlookers. Then I saw my mother, my mother's mother, my mother's father, and some other faces, about twelve or so. I could not count. Events were moving too fast for me. They must have been hiding and suddenly appeared when I showed up.

I was held on the ground, so firmly that I could hardly breathe. Within two minutes, my entire head was shaved with a sharp knife. I protested once, but when I saw blood I gave up. Then Leku came with a new blade and made over a hundred incisions on my head. She opened a small container and rubbed a dark-looking powder on the small cuts, speaking in tongues as she did. The words and lines were archaic, too fast for me to grasp. I know the chorus, which was a prayer to cast evil out of my brain.

Then a more frightening part followed, too much for me to bear then and even now as I write. Leku took a dried rat, mixed it with some ingredients in a bowl and stirred it many times. As she prepared my mind for the fact that I would drink the mixture, she removed her cloth, and stood naked for all to see. She moved in circles many times, uttering archaic words in rapid succession. Then she knelt over the bowl and washed her breasts and vagina into its contents. I very much doubt that anyone paid attention to her nakedness, only to her performance. No one but me was shocked about the short and dirty bath that I witnessed. When she said something they would reply "*ase*" (amen). Only Leku could ever repeat what she said. For someone who was always quiet, the rapidity of her speech and its esotericism were astounding. One line was repeated many times: "May he not die at the hands of a woman." When she finished, she lifted the bowl and asked me to drink. I refused. I was probably telling myself that this could not have been intended for a human being; even if thrown to the ground as a waste product, one should take care not to step in it. I was hit by the two men who had originally grabbed me, ordering me to drink. I did, remembering the saying that we had used in reference to the schoolteachers several times: an oppressor that one cannot stand up to should be committed to God. I became like an accused man who proclaimed his guilt quickly in order to avoid staying too long on his knees. As I drank the medication slowly, I wanted to throw up.

"If you vomit, you will lick all of it with your tongue," said Leku. I looked around for sympathy, but I realized that I was a cockroach in a court of fowls. It was only my will that kept the dangerous liquid inside me. The experience stayed with me for a long time; I had to close my eyes before I could swallow any medication. The ceremony was over within a few minutes. Leku returned to her chair; now dressed, she lit her pipe, ordered that the temporary screen be removed, and pretended nothing had happened. She was so calm that no one would ever associate her with the leadership of the ritual that had just occurred. I was asked to sit down. Everybody departed, saying nothing other than thanking Leku for "removing evil from his head" and "saving his life." No one was ready to challenge Leku, but they probably knew what they were doing—even one who is feebleminded knows the location of his house.

I stayed in the store for the rest of the day, speechless. I did not even think of the boys who had followed me. I am sure they took to their heels when they saw the screen held up. When the store closed, as darkness came, Leku closed the door. I noticed that she did not lock it, only putting an assortment of charms in three pots outside it. Neither did she bother to take the money from the bowl. Kola had told me that even if Leku's money fell on the ground, no one would pick it up for fear of contracting smallpox. On that evening, everybody I knew was bad. I had committed no offense to deserve their punishment. Even if I had, I told myself that there must be guilt in innocence, just as there is innocence in guilt. I did not understand their willingness to collaborate with Leku if they departed so quickly. To me, all the adults were like the cane that was used to kill a snake but was not invited to share the meal when the animal was roasted.

I carried Leku's loads, walking side by side for the entire journey. She walked too slowly for me, like the moon that travels slowly as he crosses the city. I could not push her, shout, or walk faster, as I would have done with Sali and my other friends. I was the termite in Leku's rock: a termite can do nothing to a rock but lick it. I had already licked too much. If the heart is sad, tears will flow like a stream, but I knew that Leku had no eyes to see, and if she did she would say that my eyes smelled. I could do nothing, not even talk or yawn: for the mouse to laugh in the presence of a cat, there must be a hole close by.

I dropped her loads without even caring to look at her room. I went into my own room, without even asking for food. I noticed that no one wanted to speak with me, including Kola, who had gone into hiding: well, he who derided the unfortunate person should carry no blame; it was the fate of the ridiculed that was at fault. Friends and relatives had become detractors, so I believed, and I had to make sure that they did not damage my destiny. I had become a broken chain that could not regain its wholeness. I told myself that they were all talking about me, reminding myself of many famous lines in which the disreputable person thinks that people are speaking of him; the wicked are full of suspicion. As I lay down, I was plotting revenge in my head, thinking of how I would obtain the power to make them eat cow dung. I agreed with what I had heard, that it is better to spend the night in anger than in repentance. I fell asleep, but my sleep must have been short.

Early the next morning, Baba Olopa instructed me to wake up. Since he only woke me up when I was in trouble, I immediately knew that he was calling a dog with a whip in his hand. Leku was ready for me. On Sunday and Monday, I repeated the journey with Leku, staying with her for three days in her store, and eating only minimally, notably fruits and bean cake. I missed school on Monday and was disconnected from all my friends. I was not allowed to bathe or clean my head or face so that the concoction would not be washed off. I ate and drank little so that the medicine would stay in my body for some time. I understood Leku a little bit more. When she was not smoking her pipe, she was talking to unseen strangers, appealing to gods, cursing witches, praising herbs, and begging the gods. Too strange for me to understand, she was obsessed with appealing to the gods and all universal forces not to make impotent the plants, roots, bones, and other items in her store. The Yoruba she used to communicate, to talk to herself, and to say all these strange things was not the language we used at home or school. Leku was so strange that I began to believe Sali, who claimed that the woman had twenty-four eyes. When I thought she was dozing off, she was quick to welcome a customer to her store. I paid attention to what the customers wanted, much of which sounded curious and strange. Some needed medicine to ward off bad dreams, and Leku would give them powders to apply to their eyelashes or to drink dissolved in water. The regular customers said nothing, just collecting their routine medication. A few men came for mixtures to treat sexually transmitted diseases, and Leku asked one of them to show her his penis, using a short stick to examine it.

I did not understand the purpose of the magic involved in incising my head and forcing a powerful concoction down my throat. I could not have understood it. I knew that they had performed elaborate magic on me, casting out some spell but returning some forces to create a balance. They believed that I was evil, based on only one piece of evidence: I wanted to procure the medicine to help a friend. Could they have had other evidence unknown to me? I was not the one who was after Risi. It had never occurred to me to have a girlfriend. I had had a wife or even several in dramas in which I acted the role of a successful man or a chief, but I did not turn these dramas into dreams. No one had ever discussed sex with me. It was not one of those topics that came up in any discussions among us: talking about soccer and bicycle rides had greater priority. The big boys used to talk of girls, but not of sex. Sali wanted Risi, but he never fully explained to us what he wanted her for.

I was further confused about their fear that I would be destroyed by a woman, necessitating the use of magic to prevent it. I could not understand Leku's intent since I was not Sali. Were they saying that I should stay away from all women or some women? Was the magic about overcoming the power of the naked body, fully revealed in the aging nakedness of Leku? Could it be that the love of a woman would not undermine my masculinity, sap my energy, damage my brain? Would I be saved from the influence of men like Sali and the members of his advisory board? Could it be that evil and women were associated and had to be disconnected? Did I drink enough of the hidden contents of breast and vagina that I would no longer desire them? Did I drink the breast and vagina juice to make me scared of their excesses? Or was the medication to assert manliness over femininity or to prevent a possible perpetual subordination to a woman? To one who is ignorant, a small garden is a forest.

By the time I could seriously demand answers, Leku had completely overwhelmed me, showing me her other side, which was more secretive, more frightening, more threatening, and more powerful. I became like a person who, because he is bored to death at a meeting with the king and his chiefs, decides to put a lot of salt in his mouth: it is impossible to spit out the salt and also impossible to swallow the saliva. I couldn't learn but not talk, see but not admit. As I learned more about Leku, without all the details of what she did, I worried no more about my own rituals and experience. Eventually, I was able to claim, and even then only privately, that I fully understood her essence, her representation in the realm of the living and the underworld. I never said that I understood her power or its sources. I could only know bits and pieces: but for the reality of death, even diviners and herbalists could claim to be God. Whenever I read the literature or listen to speeches claiming that African women lack power, I repeat quietly "Leku, Leku, Leku," to remind myself that the picture has never been fully revealed. A mouth that turns into a knife will cut its own lips. The full picture will not be revealed until many more people discover an *iwin* who will either grant their requests or torment them. Even then, the experience of the last person to die will be hard to imagine.

f you lived in Agbokojo and the new parts of the city, you would think that a village was no better than the biblical hell. It represented an abode of suffering: no electricity, no water delivered to the houses by hidden pipes, no cinema at which to see cowboys running and shooting without ever being killed or Indian lovers about to kiss, only that their lips must be separated, and no nightclubs with live bands and young men smoking and drinking in the company of beautiful girls. As my brothers' apprentices told me, in the village there were not even any hiding places for criminals and truants. One of the big boys said that even spiders had a great deal of difficulty spinning their webs in the village, as the careful women would stop them from their honest work; that village people had so much time that they could talk all day long; and that little girls and boys played with cockroaches and termites, since they had no other toys.

In the very first fascinating story that I heard of an encounter between man and beast, the setting was a village. The narrator was none other than one of the apprentices. When their masters were not around, they were fun to watch—they spoke, played, abused one another, and even fought when necessary. The boy who told the story was born in a village, where he lived for the first thirteen years of his life before running away to Ibadan. As he told us, he felt restless in the middle of the night during one of the most memorable days of his life. As he turned on his side, he discovered that he had made contact with a live object. Perhaps, he thought, it was another boy sleeping by his side, until he saw that it was a crawling object. Mocking the village, he said that there was no portable torch light by his side and no button to press to bring electric light, as he would do in the radio shop. To impress us, he said that he was not frightened by the object—the big boys always hid their fear and would use handkerchiefs to wipe off sweat as soon as a drop appeared so that no one would notice any sign of fear or fatigue. Very casually, he moved to stand up on that fateful night. As he tried to move, he discovered that the object was so heavy that he could not lift either of his legs. Now, it was time for him to worry. When people shouted for help, everyone knew there was trouble that they could not handle on their own. When this big boy shouted, it was not because he needed any help, since, as he told us, he could stay in one spot for three days, but to warn others that their legs might stick to the floor should they try to stand up. In any case, his scream alerted the adults. As they appeared with their kerosene lamps, what they saw, according to the big boy, was unbelievable: a boa constrictor, "as long as two Goliaths," had wrapped itself around his body. An ox and an elephant had been paired by accident.

A huge, long snake had entered the sleeping room to devour the big boy. Everybody knew who Goliath was, from reading the biblical story of his encounter with David. We did not know how tall Goliath was, but the standard idea was that he was as tall as a two-story house. The snake must have been acting rather slowly, enjoying the look of its delicate meal before consuming it. Perhaps, the boa was not hungry or it was hungry and realized that the boy was too small to fill its Goliath length. In any case, why wait for the adults to come with their lamps? Before the boa could make its final dart, it was overpowered by the adults. The boy's mom, according to this story, even ignored the timeless warning never to touch the tail of a snake to avoid provoking it to anger. By the time it was over, the boy had escaped and the boa was dead. So rural were these people, continued the big boy with his fascinating story, that their jubilation was not because they had saved his life but because they had killed a boa. They sang around the snake before it was roasted. In the evening, they made a big meal of pounded yam with vegetable soup, and the boa was the delicacy. This became his "sendoff" dinner. The next day, he ran away to the city. As he boasted, one might think that he would actually have stayed in the village to wait for another encounter with a boa so that he could fight.

His mates applauded his story and his decision. "They are mainly fools," one of the other boys said of the "ruralites." At Agbokojo, a "rural" person was one with the characteristics of a village person. They were described as dirt, as though they had to scratch their disease-invested bodies with knives and machetes. The textile dealers and traders in imported items were always praying to see *ara oko* (villagers) in the hope that they could cheat them, overcharging them for their purchases. In the new parts of the city, they recognized *ara oko* by their mannerisms, their simplicity of look and speech, and, according to them, their naïveté, believing anything they were told. They mocked *ara oko* for their inability to speak English. Their rich Yoruba, laden with idioms, spiced with proverbs, and seasoned with epigrams, became a source of ridicule. To use pidgin, a bastardized combination of Yoruba and English, was even regarded as more respectable in the new city. After all, the population was mixed, and whoever wanted to participate in life and communication must move away from the rich, pure Yoruba that was harder to understand.

All forms of negativity were associated with the *ara oko* by the "civilized" elements in the new city. If you woke up in the morning and you did not clean your mouth, you were called an *ara oko*. If you chose to use the chewing stick instead of the brush and paste imported from England, you were an *ara oko*. I even heard a question posed to a man using a chewing stick as to why he was cleaning his teeth with a tree. The chewing stick was about three times the size of my finger, and it was being compared to a giant tree growing outside the house. The clever man responded that it was because each of his teeth was as big as an elephant tusk.

A tree is a code word for an *ara oko*. Just as the nineteenth-century European visitors to Africa had sent reports home, with horror stories of meeting despicable characters no better than dogs, the new elements in the city used similar words for those based in the village. "They are like monkeys on a tree," was one way to describe them. Like monkeys, all that the *ara oko* was presented as doing was playing, looking for food, and having sex. The play was not necessarily creative, just hopping from one tree branch to another, glancing at insects. This was not the play associated with "high-life" music and cold beer. Rather than smoking real cigarettes produced by the British Tobacco Company, the *ara oko* were derided for rolling raw tobacco and using fire from any dirty source to light it. They would even substitute paw paw leaves if tobacco was not available. Rather than drinking beer, the *ara oko* relied on palm wine. They had none of those "mineral" beverages, the tantalizing "Fanta" with its yellowish look. Even when they managed to smuggle "modern drinks" into their villages, the *ara oko* had no refrigerators to make them cold. Even their water was not cold, drawn from the big pot in the corridor.

The "civilized" folks in the new city believed that they would live longer than the *ara oko*, who had no access to hospitals or Western medicine. Sanitary inspectors who traveled round the city in their khaki uniforms warned that whoever went to the village must "cook" the water before drinking it in order to avoid over a hundred diseases. Their lectures warned that water from the village stream could give me a deadly disease, "guinea worm," that would take off my toes and fingers. Water became so dangerous that not a few would ask for the source when they were offered some. The people in the city would even complain that the water container was that of an *ara oko* and that a small boy like me who offered it in a bowl they disliked behaved like an *ara oko*.

The racist Europeans and the "civilized Yoruba" began to behave alike. The racist Europeans had used all sorts of offensive words to describe Africans. In turn, the civilized Yoruba were using their advantages—access to jobs, city life, and Western education—to turn others, because of their location outside the cities, into primitives, comparing them with monkeys, infantilizing their ideas, marginalizing their abodes. The racist Europeans used their ideology of superiority to justify the spread of Christianity, the colonial conquest, and the expansion of the market. The civilized Yoruba, too, had gains to make from splitting society into urban and rural, civilized and noncivilized. For one thing, the *ara oko* made them look good. When people bought radios, clocks, and other gadgets in the stores at Agbokojo, their plea for quick service was usually that they should not be turned into an *ara oko*, who could not listen to the news or the "latest music." Since I had taken news and music for granted, it took a long time for me to understand what they were really saying. Neither did I understand for a long time that "proper dressing" for church on Sundays was a mark of status, a way to mark one as different from an *ara oko*.

The big boys at Agbokojo knew what they wanted: the greater the distance they created from an *ara oko*, the more successful they thought they had become. Western education, the knowledge of Western crafts, and traveling abroad would move them away from the villages. The sympathy they had for me when I had to move to Ode Aje was not for losing a friend or relation but for my journey of regression, one that would move me closer to the *ara oko*. Rather than taking the train to Lagos to build the credentials of civilization, I was taking a trip in the opposite direction, a route from which the big boys had sought escape.

The big boys at Agbokojo were justified in their fear. Ode Aje was linked to the rural areas. One could actually walk to several farms and villages. Farmlands, huts, and small settlements known as *oko etile* (nearby farms or countryside) were within two hours' walking distance. Everybody in my school had to walk to these farms and villages at least three times a year. The teachers would always order us to fetch palm fronds, sticks, tree branches, shrubs, and related materials to build tents for plays, parent-staff meetings, food vendors' kiosks, and other uses. The school fence had to be constantly maintained, and it was the responsibility of the students to fetch the materials and make the repairs.

In my old schools in the new city, the fences were made of permanent materials and did not require the use of student labor to repair them. In these schools, the only connection to the land was the creation of school gardens, with each class having to take care of a small plot. The teachers harvested the corn, tomatoes, various types of peppers, and "garden eggs" (eggplants). The students were always unhappy when the teachers took the whole harvest, and the big boys used this as an excuse to steal from the gardens. If the purpose of the gardens was to encourage participation in farming, the schools achieved the very opposite. The parents who sent their children to city schools did so with the unqualified desire and expectation that their children would never have anything to do with the land. The teachers, too, were not committed to the gardens, inserting them into the school curricula as a way to take occasional breaks from the rigors of teaching. As the students worked on the farms, the teachers gathered in small groups to talk, only complaining when a student was lazy or disturbing others.

At Ode Aje, the *oko etile* enabled those in the city and its immediate countryside to interact on a daily basis. The students were not the only ones who walked to *oko etile*. Hundreds of adults also did so daily, turning the farms into their workplace and the city into their place of abode. Even those with other occupations, the modern ones such as teaching, joined in farming so that they did not have to rely on the market for many of their regular needs. The easy linkage between the farms and the city enabled most families to obtain fresh products on a daily basis, enough to cook for the day without having to bother about long preservation and storage.

If new city residents regarded gardens and farms as backward workplaces, Ode Aje residents did not see it that way. Not only did they have access to cheap food; they also had a way to engage young people in productive enterprises. Girls and boys would follow their mothers to the farms, carrying fruits, vegetables, corn, and yams in baskets back to the city. In the process, mothers and their children engaged in bonding as they spoke on a variety of subjects and issues. The girls and boys were not being prepared for jobs on farms, as the big boys in the new city believed, but were being socialized into the ethics of work, into the habits of good behavior.

The threat to *oko etile* was not the condemnation of farmers and farming practices by the new elite, but the expansion of the city and land commercialization. Within a period of twenty years, all the farms and villages near Ode Aje and other neighborhoods were gone, swallowed up by the city. The establishment of schools, churches, and mosques encouraged the acquisition of large areas of land. Even cemeteries that used to be at a distance have become part of the city, with the dead and the living interacting regularly within the same space. It became lucrative for landowners to sell their land rather than use it for farming. The fight over the land and the distribution of income from sales became intense from the 1970s onward. Those fights were not anticipated in the 1960s, and attention was focused on the food resources that *oke etile* provided for city dwellers.

Cheaper food made it possible for adults to use their money, as meager as it was, for other things. Again, the big boys in the old city missed the relevance of the countryside. As food traveled to the new city and onward to Lagos, it became more expensive, since a large number of middlemen made their profits by buying cheaply at Ode Aje and other areas and transporting the food to those who lived away from the farms. At Ode Aje, cheap food was taken for granted, and it was easy to be generous to others because there was always something to give. People shared food more generously, more openly, than today.

I went to *oko etile* not to obtain foodstuffs, as my household bought them in the local market, but to collect materials for school and to play with friends. A small group of us would also visit a friend whose parents had instructed him to work on a farm. As we approached the farm, we had to shout at the tops of our voices to locate our friend. Sometimes we wandered in a completely different direction, so far away that we had to head back home after a series of unsuccessful attempts. Directions were never precise: "After the second palm tree on your right, look for a mound—a red bird often perches on it—then turn left, take about *idaji buso* [roughly half a mile] and call my name." One could have counted the wrong palm tree, the termites could have made another mound, and the older one could have been leveled by those in search of a queen to roast as a snack.

New knowledge was acquired in the process of traveling to *oko etile*. The most striking information, which I will elaborate upon in another setting, was rich data on birds, plants, and land that those in the new city would never know. In the new city, my attention was concentrated on buildings, on people and what they did. In *oko etile*, my focus shifted to nature. If I saw birds and other animals in textbooks in the new city, I began to see many real ones in Ode Aje and its countryside. The most common birds, *adaba* (brown dove) and *lekeleke* (cattle egret), visited schools and homes. There were those that stayed on the farms, refusing to venture to the city, such as *elulu* (cuckoo) and *olongo* (red-billed firefinch). Some lived between the city and the farms, looking for food on the streets, notably the *awodi* (kite) and *igun* (vulture). The only pet bird was the parrot, which was found in a few homes, where kids teased them endlessly to repeat their statements.

Bird hunting became part of the game of youth, with many boys purchasing rubber slings (known as catapults) that could hit birds with rocks. There were more slingshots and lost rocks than dead birds. Some of the birds prized as delicacies, such as *aparo* (bush fowl), were too smart to be killed by young boys. The bush fowl knew our intentions, daring us to come closer before they escaped. The smaller birds, although edible, were too fast to kill. I never had a single bit of luck aiming at the *tiotio* (brown shrike) or the *kolekole* (plantain eater). And many chose to live permanently high in the sky where we could not reach them. The birds must be having a good laugh, turning me into a fool who learned the game only after the players had dispersed. When I became wiser, I opted for rat hunting, since the rats left many clues about their homes and travels.

"Don't touch it!" shouted Yusuf, as I moved near the wooden dolls, snail shells, and painted cow horn hanging on a stick at the entrance to his father's farm. Yusuf was agitated that I was even moving toward the objects and contemplating touching them. They were *ale*, he warned, magic meant to destroy thieves. Because of the accessibility of *oko etile* to the city, they attracted thieves, who would come in the early hours of the morning or the late evening to steal fruits, vegetables, and corn, taking them home as if they were coming from the market. It was risky to be a thief in Ode Aje and the old city neighborhoods. The thief relied on his speed to escape, but it was difficult to run faster than the mob in pursuit. When he was caught, the mob would beat the thief into unconsciousness before asking the police to remove his body. Only strangers would risk this public disgrace and permanent injury. In a period of ten years, I witnessed two cases of pursuit of a thief that ended in a serious physical assault, to the point that both men died before they reached hospital.

There was no one watching the farm thief. Even if the farmer was there, this was a case when the legs were reliable in ensuring an escape, either because the farmer could not run just as fast as the thief or, having recovered the goods that the thief had abandoned, he felt no need to waste his energy and time. A thief could not run too fast with a basket of yams on his head. Since the farm was immobile, unlike the clothes and goats that the city thief was after, the farm thief could try again.

Here is where *ale* came into the picture, the powerful magic intended to keep the thief permanently at bay. *Ale* prevented the thief from coming, both by day and at night. It also prevented the farmer from worrying, leaving him time to concentrate on his farm-related jobs. After Yusuf told me about *ale*, I began to notice that many farms used them, composed of various objects such as red peppers, snail shells, rags, tins, and rotten animals. The objects communicated a message between the farm owner and the thief. All *ale* required to be effective was for the thief and the farm owner to share the same worldview. A rag would tell the thief that stealing would make him a pauper for the rest of his life; a red pepper told him that his life would be full of misery. The empty shell showed that the thief's pocket and household would forever be in want. All *ale* objects invoked powerful curses to frighten the thief. Why should one steal a handful of red peppers and end up in misery for a lifetime?

It was the fascination with *oko etile* that drew me into the real village. Irrespective of where one lived, whether it was Lagos or London, everyone knew there were villages, where a large percentage of Africans lived. The difference with regard to the Yoruba is that, due to the intensity of their urbanization process, they have many more cities than other groups on the continent. Cities tend to undermine villages, turning them into suppliers of food without promoting the infrastructure of change. Only the roads that link them to the cities are necessary, and these are mainly dirt roads. In the case of the Yoruba, the traffic between the cities and villages was constant and the volume of goods was huge. Villages and cities were connected in more ways than one. Most people in the villages had reasons to travel to the cities, for social events, religious activities, and interaction with friends and relatives. All successful farmers with money built houses in the city, better houses than those in the village, where they spent more time. "The trousers that make the purchase of the velvet possible reside in the village," is a popular saying that captures the relationship between the village and the city. The village was a zone of work, where one wore dirty pants and behaved like a dirty pig. The city was a zone of pleasure, where one wore clean clothes and flaunted wealth. One did not buy a car and put it in a village, limiting the number of people who could see it.

My access to a village was assured. Baba Olopa's sister lived in a village, and I went there many times, even on overnight trips. My father's lineage had a village named after it, and I went there twice, once to see my father's extensive holdings. Of all the villages I loved to visit, Elepo was the one I enjoyed the most, and this was where I spent many vacation weeks. My mother's father lived at Elepo most of the time, only coming to the city about twice a month unless there were ceremonies and events in which he had to participate. He had a house in the city, as part of his own lineage's complex in a neighborhood called Gbenla, named after a war chief. His houses in the city and the village looked alike, except that the one in the village was bigger. Both were one-story buildings, built of mud. There was no cement plastering. Inside only his sitting room had a cement floor, which reduced the dust. Other floors had to be occasionally coated with dye, made locally from various plants, not only to make them look nicer but to reduce dust and kill insects. Taking care of the floor was essentially a woman's job, with kids joining in. Either because they were poor or because they were not materialistic, the houses had very limited furnishings. The living rooms contained only a few folding chairs and a bench, made by local carpenters, plus a small table on which were placed the Bible and a few other books, together with a kerosene lamp.

My grandfather was called Pasitor. He was a licensed preacher in the Anglican Church, but he occupied a low position in the ministerial ladder. He was a pastor, but not many seemed able to pronounce the word, changing it to Paitor or Pasitor, which became the most common. Pasitor was a respectable name and occupation. My grandfather could read and write, but he did not use his skills in a formal-sector job. He managed the church in the village, but he drew little or no salary, relying mainly on the proceeds from his farms.

Elepo was like other villages. It had no electricity, piped water, tarred roads, hospitals, or places of recreation. The majority of people at Elepo spoke Yoruba. Rarely did I hear anyone use English. No newspapers reached the village, and only a few people had radio sets. My grandfather had a small radio, but he used it sparingly in order to cut down on the cost of batteries. The only people who were different were the *alagbaro*, hired farm workers who came from other parts of Nigeria. What distinguished the hired workers was not their residence, attire, or physical looks but their language. Since neither English nor pidgin were used by their hosts, the workers had to learn Yoruba in order to interact and understand instructions. Their Yoruba had a peculiar sound, lacking the correct tones that distinguished words and sentences. Behind their backs, jokes were regularly made about their pronunciation of words in ways that altered their meanings.

Elepo was a model of the primitive Christianity that we had read about. There was a small church, with the only school behind it. The congregation was small, and everybody knew one another. If anyone missed service without informing the clergyman in charge, the entire congregation would visit the missing church member to see if there was illness or misfortune. The students were from the same social background, and they were expected to both go to school and assist their parents in their various occupations. A student could, at the same time, be an accomplished drummer. I never saw the school in session, or even any of the schoolteachers. Since I was at Elepo during vacations, I saw only the classrooms and benches. It was a much poorer building than my own school, with termites having destroyed most of the windows. I knew only a few of the students, as the large majority came from other villages or had gone to the city on vacation.

Elepo was diverse in its religious practices. There was an Islamic population there as well as a Christian population. However, the village was not segregated on the basis of religion. Christians and Muslims lived within the same households. The Muslims had a mosque in the center of the village, unlike the church, which stood on the outskirts. Built of mud like the rest of the houses, the mosque was an ordinary building without many visible assets. Dirty kettles littered its frontage, and worshipers could take one to fetch water from the pot at the corner and perform their ablutions. I saw women and children constantly pouring water in the pot, which was never empty. A small gate kept goats, sheep, and dogs from entering the mosque. The inside was not impressive either, containing only folded mats used for prayer. The Muslims there did not impress me too much, and the Muslim boys were different from Yusuf and Sali in the city. They did not have a smooth-talking imam, and their call to prayer was not as loud as what I was used to. The boys were not as good at reciting the Quran as Yusuf, and I could successfully compete with them in basic Quranic recitation. While the boys in my city school were talking about future occupations such as medicine and engineering, those at Elepo were thinking in terms of finishing primary school and becoming apprenticed to a craftsman. One of them told me that he would be a carver, making replicas of gods and other objects. I did not know what I wanted to do in the future, but I was surprised that someone would mention carving. Thereafter, I called him *gbegi lere*, a Yoruba word meaning "wood carving."

Farming dominated village life. Of course, there were artisans and craft workers, but these were few. There was always a blacksmith ready to make tools and sharpen others. Kids tended to gather around the blacksmiths, if only to see the fire and hear the noise emanating from the heavy hammer. I became an amateur in farm work: I could make heaps and sow and harvest yam, cassava, and corn. We also had to harvest kola nuts and cocoa, although this was seasonal. No aspect of the farm work was mechanized. As we headed back home, I had to carry in a basket the foodstuffs needed for dinner. If the farmer was late, dinner, too, would be late. As soon as I delivered the basket, I would return to the farm or river, together with a small group of boys, to check the trap for small rats and fish before it was dark.

I became an amateur hunter, perfecting the art of rat catching. Those the same age as me often went fishing, and we always caught something small to take back home. Adults did not share the rats and fish, which we would roast by the fireplace and share with one another. No one could receive more than a tiny piece, and there were days when even the small tail of a rat would look like a big ration. My knowledge of birds improved. So also did my knowledge of insects. Crickets were good for food, and we hunted them. We were all clever enough to know which insects had deadly tongues and quick tempers.

My fascination was with the small group of hunters and a few of their followers who generated a different kind of excitement. At the entrance to the village was a small spot dedicated to Ogun, the god of iron. An old machete, coins, some food items, and palm oil were placed around a small rock. Each time I passed the place, I saw that the items were fresh, especially the oil. I had read about the Yoruba gods in the literature and had seen many of their priests and priestesses at Ode Aje. I already knew a great deal about the cults of women, fertility, Sango, and a few others. It was at Elepo that I saw firsthand the cult of Ogun and some activities associated with hunters. Deer, snakes, and big rats were their common game. Once in a while, the hunters would go away on long trips, to areas far away, and return home with warthogs, bush pigs, monkeys, and porcupines. At the minimum, the hunters would kill squirrels and giant rats. Contrary to the stories of previous achievements, I never saw anyone with the heads or skins of lions, elephants, or hyenas. They were all saluted as ode aperin—"killers of elephants"—to denote courage, but none did anything close to what we read about in the storybooks and the image of hunters we presented in school dramas.

I never followed any of the hunters on their expeditions, but I noticed various things. Their uniforms, which resembled the uniforms of the warriors of the nineteenth century, and their hunting materials were visible. Many kids would touch or play with the uniform when the hunter was not there, wondering why anyone would wear something so dirty. Hunters very rarely changed their uniforms, and the pockets were full of charms. They used long guns, which had to be reloaded every time they wanted to fire them. Anyone could help a hunter grind the bullets into powder, not for any fee but to listen to stories of animals. Hunters believed that animals talk, though humans do not understand the language. Night hunting was common, especially when the moon was not bright enough for the animals to see clearly. Hunters also told stories about night and darkness, usually to terrify us.

All farmers, whether young or old, knew to look out for the signs made by hunters on farms, along the paths to the farms, and at the entrances to the village. This was the first lecture I received. Rather than killing a game animal, a hunter might kill a human being, especially a kid of my age and size, who might be mistaken for an animal. One must be able to read the clues the hunters provided to indicate their presence. One must look out for traps, as not a few had been injured by powerful noose traps and iron traps.

I also noticed the connection between hunting and religion and magic. A few hunters doubled as herbalists, curing minor illnesses and offering advice on the medicinal importance of roots, plants, and animals. Twice the hunters gathered their colleagues from other villages and towns and held a meeting at Elepo. I was told that they rotated such meetings in different villages and towns. Wearing their uniforms, they provided a spectacle. Only their members attended the meeting. However, at the end of it their songs and performances drew the entire village. I thought that they were all very boastful. Like clergymen in churches, they praised their own god, only theirs was Ogun. As if directing the message to the Christians and Muslims, they even said that they did not need Allah and Jesu Kiristi (Jesus Christ) to survive life. All they needed was Ogun.

> The pathfinder
> The master of iron
> The lord of the universe
> The lord of the grassland and forest
> The controller of mountains and valleys.

They promised full protection from motor accidents and injuries caused by metal objects on the condition that one obeyed Ogun's wishes. Without expecting an answer, they asked Muslims and Christians in the crowd whether they knew those who would receive salvation in heaven: "Only heaven knows the answer."

But they also boasted about themselves. Singing songs known as ijala, each person would take a turn, then be stopped by another, as if in a competition. They themselves asserted that they were talkative, garrulous, brilliant, and clever. I could compete in Christian and Islamic songs, but theirs sounded too hard for me. The lines of Christian songs were fixed, but the hunters were making up the words and lines as they went along, without the equivalent of a hymn book. With the Islamic songs with which I was familiar, we could notice the contexts and adapt various previous songs. The hunters applied different rules of singing, storytelling, praying, warning, and boasting all simultaneously and in shifting verses. I tried to practice the songs without any luck, and I failed to adapt Islamic and Christian songs to the *ijala* genre. It took me many years to discover that it was much easier to accomplish the reverse: adapt *ijala* to Christian songs, using the words in praise of Yoruba gods for the prophets of the Middle East!

Two houses away from us, an entire family decided all of a sudden to announce that they wanted to leave the village. As we prepared for breakfast on that Sunday morning, the man entered the house to break the news to my grandfather. Crying and talking simultaneously, he said that he could take it no more and had to leave the village for another place. Sympathizers gathered around him, asking questions about his motives, his new place, his alternative plans. The man had none, simply saying that "no one could satisfy the chief." The discussion moved to the chief and how my grandfather should step in to help the man, to prevent the calamity about to befall him. The man continued to say that people should leave the chief to God and the day of resurrection. "No one can satisfy the chief, not even God," the man said over and over again. People continued to plead, begging him to reconsider a move that would destroy his children and put his only wife in trouble.

The man's wife, too, came, carrying a young baby on her back. In her haste to join her husband, she had loosely tied the baby to her back, necessitating a temporary change of topic, as those around begged her to carry the baby properly. "Leave my house is not the same as leave the world," a young woman warned her, not seeing their problem as sufficient reason to lose a child. Others joined in, and a series of moral admonitions followed. "Anyone who is not dead has hope," said a man, who finally broke his silence. He himself had been considered a failure by others, but, as he reminded them, he now had a large cocoa farm and had completed the construction of his bungalow in the city. "If grace belongs to God, I will even become a chief." People shouted "Amen," and one person said that "grace belongs to no one other than God." The assembly asked the wife to pressure her husband not to take any rash decisions. Now lost for words, the man thanked them and promised to calm down and stay in the village. Facing my grandfather, he prostrated himself for a long time and asked him to speak with the chief.

I knew that they had asked the man to stay in the village and that the chief had been mentioned as the cause of the family wanting to leave, but I did not understand what the chief had done. There was no one to turn to in those early hours to explain anything to me. Not that I didn't know those who would talk. My grandfather's second wife was a talker who opened up quite easily. My grandfather was reticent, but he never ignored a question, even if he would plead for time to answer it or use his busy schedule to postpone the answer. Meanwhile, I and the others were told to go to some other households and tell people that Pasitor wanted them in church. "Pasitor wants you in church" was the statement that I delivered in three places without understanding its full meaning.

The church was full, with nonmembers outnumbering regular churchgoers. As I learned later, people also came from the neighboring village, which constituted a cluster within a radius of about ten miles. A man on a bicycle could reach about two villages within an hour. Unknown to me, Pasitor had sent messages to many other villages, asking people to show up in church. Muslims were there, too, as well as some hunters and craftsmen who worshiped their own gods. The service became truly nondenominational.

Pasitor changed the order of the service, moving the sermon forward. He gave the longest sermon that I will ever associate with him. He spoke about death. I had listened to sermons on death before, in the context of funeral ceremonies at St. Peter's and St. James'. In those sermons, the theme was the conquest of death and the celebration of life. The man to be buried, the minister in my two big city churches would assure us, was not dead—he had successful children, and he would soon be resurrected to be close to Jesus, specifically on his right side. Everybody who died was presented as a good person, and we were all urged not to worry. Indeed, the ministers spoke in such a way that one might believe that they could follow the body to the grave and to heaven and report on their satisfactory condition.

Pasitor's sermon on death took a different course, with a threatening tone that aroused my curiosity. Pasitor was angry. Indeed, he started his sermon with a command:

"The wicked people around us today, please show yourself, stand up." A dead silence followed.

"I said that I want the wicked people to raise their hands." No one did.

"I know that you will not stand up, you wicked people." He looked around, as if he could identify the wicked people or had a particular person in mind.

"Wicked people who cover themselves with beautiful robes, elegant shoes, embroidered caps, all to hide their wicked souls and naked bodies." As if cursing, he said that "God will remove the shoes of the wicked, the attire of the wicked, the cap of the wicked. All will become the wood for the fire to burn the wicked person."

Unlike the ministers in my church, who delayed mentioning the day of judgment and hell, Pasitor told his listeners that the wicked would burn for all to see. Punishment for evil and the wicked would begin on earth, even around the village for "you and I" to see, and the suffering would move to the world beyond. The innocent would suffer as well, as all those associated with the wicked would have a share in the suffering. "Their sons will perish before our eyes; their daughters will be barren, even if they change ten husbands." He piled more curses on the wicked.

"We will all die, but our deaths will be different, our destinations will not be the same." He confessed that he was no God who knew three things: when a person would die, the cause of the death, and the location of death. Only God knew the answers to questions of timing, venue, and cause. Some would drown, others might be killed by animals or accidents, some might not even last another week. One thing he knew was that the wicked would die in shame, not restfully in their sleep, but publicly in shame. He narrated various stories of the wicked that he had known: those clubbed to death by their own children, those killed by charms bought by their wives, and those killed and roasted for food by their witch mothers.

"Who wants to die peacefully?" he asked, and everybody shouted, "Me, me, it is me."

"Well, do not be wicked. If you are wicked, you will die in this village in our presence, with your son clubbing you to death. Yes, your own son. And after your son has killed you, the government will kill your son so that both of you can burn together in hellfire." I did not understand what he was driving at. He never quoted passages from the Bible, as ministers often did to support their statements. He was preaching a sermon without reference to "Our Lord," to Jesus Christ.

"Let me tell you about the wicked person. A wicked man can prosper, acquire wealth and fortune, but what matters the most is the last day, the day of death." He warned all of us not to envy the wicked. They have a lot to envy: large farms, a house in the city, a house in the village, seventy-five children, eighteen wives, and six concubines. Some people laughed, but Pasitor was in no mood to allow them to laugh for long, as he continued his speech. The wicked had good clothes, so many that ten lorries could not contain them. They could use the thigh of a chicken as a toothbrush, and eat the leg of a goat for breakfast, turkey for lunch, and the best fish for dinner.

The poor, and that included himself and some members of the congregation, were powerless before the wicked. Then he digressed, talking about the poor and the excesses of the rich. Pasitor admitted that no one wanted to be poor, although he knew that hard work was no cure for poverty. "Only God bestows wealth; one may work like a termite and still be poor; one's work could be as big as an elephant, but one's reward could be as small as a mouse." In the first apparent reference to the family that visited us in the morning to announce that it was moving away, I heard Pasitor refer to a neighbor in the village who worked twelve hours a day. He had seen him coming from the farm to the village with a torch. "Who stays at a farm till dark except a slave?" His neighbor was not the only poor person; there were too many of them around without help. The rich and the government, Pasitor explained, were the same: "agents of darkness, messengers of evil." He quickly apologized for the statement, perhaps so as not to offend some members of his congregation, revising the statement to allow that there were "good rich people and some good governments."

Then he moved to the main theme on which he had promised to dwell: death. He started with a poem on death. It was long, and it has forever aroused my interest. Indeed, no sooner did I return to the city than I began to recite part of it to my friends. The theme fascinated a friend of mine, Tinwo Fatoki, who later wrote a poem on death in high school that won a major award, one that propelled him to take a university degree in Yoruba. Since I heard the poem and the sermon, the theme of death has forever remained in my consciousness, not as a fear that is incapacitating but as a redundant phenomenon that is liberating. I have internalized the marginality of death but without the consciousness of reincarnation. To return to Pasitor's poem and his sermon, I can only reconstruct some memorable lines with the additions that I made some years later.

> The poor, the rich, and the powerful
> All are six feet under, no more no less
> One does not because of excess wealth
> Consume more salt than others
> A grave cannot be shallow because one is poor
> The gate of heaven does not close because one is rich.

> God keeps five secrets
> God, the mighty, the Being without boundaries
> The Almighty keeps four secrets to Himself
> He reveals only one to powerless humans: we will all die
> Of the four no one knows
> What will kill you?
> Where will death get you?

When will you die?
Who is next that death will take?

Call the corpse
Curse the corpse
Salute the corpse
Praise the corpse
Thou shall get no answer
He who comes to the world naked leaves empty
Without a voice, a throat, a tongue, a mouth
You call the dead in vain.

You and I will depart
To a land of no return
Women and sex will be behind us
Of land, cars, and land, no one can take them along
Of money and gold, all is nakedness
When you depart
It is to the land of strangers
A land without friends, money, relatives.

The sweet world
The honey of life
Death is the killer
Why fear?
You the rich
You the famous
You the wise
Why not write in English to death to have mercy on you?

I am the husband of a goddess
The courageous
I am the most handsome
My plans are foolproof
I am the talented businessman
I am the best politician
I am even the successful crook
You are powerless before death.

Death shames all
The warrior shall stumble
The wise becomes a fool
The genius lacks knowledge

The rich man is gone
You are short or tall, death does not care
Death, the calm and silent water that drowns a man.

What is your *kakandu* [courage]?
What does it mean to be tall?
What does it mean to be short?
What does beauty amount to?
Remember the end
We are all nothing.

Chief, the rich, the mighty
Swallow your house
Swallow the key to your car
Take your wife to heaven
Befriend your children, ask them to accompany you
Hold a party in heaven
Move your savings account to the coffin.

Abuse death
Call it the evil kidnapper
Curse death
Call it the bitterness of life, the comedy of heaven
Death is silent
It responds only to stop you from talking.

Run all over
Reflect about life
Beckon to the far and near
Talk, shout, sing, write
Death is the warrior who does not think
The illness that seeks no permission.

All the wise gathered
All the fathers met with all the mothers
Apprentices and masters converged
All planners prepared
Death dominated all
Thou, master, I salute.

Listen, where are the kings of the past?
Remember the chiefs of old
Love the princesses of old
Death knows no history

The noise it brings must be heard
When death talks, even the blind can see, the deaf can hear.

Death is the genius
What you build, it destroys
What you value, it depreciates
Death cares not about anyone
Man is nothing, just a piece of clay
Mighty chief, the grave awaits.

Pasitor ended on a note of anger. Usually, he would tell stories for people to laugh at. A hymn would follow the song, a reading from a Bible passage, a long prayer, and another hymn to close the service. Pasitor changed the order. Without mincing words, he said that the "wicked would be discovered." He asked for cooperation from all gathered there.

"This is not the time to say that I am a Muslim, child of the god of iron, or a good Christian. This is the time for cooperation. Only God knows the believer." I heard what he said, but I did not understand its meaning. I was probably not being counted in the membership of his group.

I was right in my suspicion of being excluded. "All children and women must leave the church now," declared Pasitor. Without grumbling, I followed the others. It was then that I began to understand what was going on. Pasitor was talking about the chief the man had complained about in the morning. Pasitor meant that the chief was responsible for the family's sudden decision to relocate to nowhere, to exchange their predictable poverty for an unfathomable world of misery. As I later grew to learn and appreciate, the use of death as the conqueror was the most powerful device to appeal to the powerful, to warn them that death is a leveler. The powerful witch would die as well as the knowledgeable charm maker. Even Leku the herbalist could not overcome death. The threat of death was to impress upon the living the necessity of good conduct and appropriate morality. Death, always spoken about as a living being, was so powerful that even the most successful person became a coward before it. As Pasitor said, death neutralized the importance of wealth and life itself. To obtain sympathy from the overwhelming might of death, a wise person must be patient, generous, and always "walk gently."

The chief, in bringing about the downfall of another man, was "walking hurriedly," using his power in such a way that the intervention of death became necessary. It was the women who revealed the "secret" to me. If Pasitor was talking in code, using poetry and didactic stories to allude to the chief without mentioning any name, the women were more direct. As they left the church, they praised Pasitor for bringing them together to talk about the "wicked chief." They even mentioned his name, a name that had been repeated on the radio and in newspapers many times. I had seen him in his black car, which had passed along our street on many occasions. His neck was heavy, much bigger than that of a ram, as I could see, but he needed it to carry his big head, which was slightly smaller than that of a cow. The women added other features, definitely not in praise, as they spoke about his big stomach, which could take a goat, except that the chief stored wickedness in it. I had heard of "evil men" being able to manifest evil, and the chief was being described as one of them. As the women spoke, they mentioned another set of evil people, the osomalo, "the ones with the red oil in the company of those dressed in white." Either out of envy or due to provocation, the osomalo can spill the oil on a dress to damage it and turn the joy of the owner into sadness, a sweet orange turning sour all of a sudden. I was not sure I had seen an osomalo before, but the attack on them was vehement.

Pasitor communicated his anger in his tone; the women used curses. The curses were harsh and new to me. Curses as a manifestation of anger were not new, and my schoolmates used them in conflicts and anger, posing them as a probability: "If you don't return my stolen money, the dog will eat your corpse." "If you do not stop talking to me like that, you may have a car accident." "If you want to succeed in life, never abuse my mother." The Elepo women heaped extreme curses on the chief and osomalo, and they said "Amen," which we did not add at school. "The wives and children of the chief will die in succession, all to be buried by the chief." As they said "Amen," another added, "The chief himself will commit suicide." "The osomalo will use the darkness of the deep night to escape," one person added to remind the others about another category of wicked people.

I gradually understood what was going on. By the time I was able to analyze it, I was annoyed that Pasitor and the women had not cursed the British in addition. Without a crack in the wall, insects and lizards do not have an easy passage. The anger and resentment directed at the osomalo were caused by the intrusion of capitalism and credit into the villages and farms. The osomalo were active traders, mainly of Ijesa-Yoruba origins. Tough with money and debt collection, the osomalo relied on the use of credit to make huge profits, to the extent that the name described both a trading practice and cruel habits. The stories told by the women at

Elepo were consistent. The *osomalo*, well dressed, riding a bicycle or walking in the company of his carriers, would visit during the dry season when people were short of cash. Full of good humor and sympathy, the *osomalo* would tempt the villagers to buy all sorts of goods on credit, promising that they could repay him in the next season, some four months later. As the villagers explained in anger, the *osomalo* would break his promise, coming back at an earlier date to demand payment of the first installment. When the debtor had no money, the *osomalo* showed his true colors, using force and verbal attacks to obtain his money. The name *osomalo* itself derived from the statement, "I will squat down until I collect my money." The itinerant trader became a sedentary debt collector, taking control of the debtor's life. The *osomalo* did not require the police and the law to enforce payment, only the use of insults and force to humiliate the debtor. As the women at Elepo said, the *osomalo* was so "wicked" that he could constitute a nuisance. He could prevent the debtors from eating, use foul language on house members, turn their living room into a toilet, and block the entrance to prevent people from moving in and out. By avoiding the use of law and intermediaries for debt collection, the *osomalo* reduced his management costs. To the *osomalo*, there was no "bad debt" to be forgiven. Rather, all debts must be collected to send a powerful signal to the Elepo debtors and others that they must always pay or get into serious trouble.

If we took the position of the *osomalo*, the story would be one of trade and business management. The *osomalo* obtained imported items, mainly textiles, from bulk dealers such as European and Indian firms. He divided the items into smaller pieces, carrying them to villages. Knowing very well that the clients did not have money for much of the year, the *osomalo* sold on credit. The Elepo women and the *osomalo* agreed that to buy on credit one had to pay at least three times more than the cash payment. The Elepo women could go to the city to buy from the Indians and Lebanese. They knew the place, as I did. The problem was that they did not have ready cash, thus making them easy victims of the *osomalo* traders. The women knew the *osomalo* was not doing them a favor, only ruining them. They understood the extortion, as many of them were small-scale traders themselves. What they and the religious-minded Pasitor did not appreciate was what they regarded as the *osomalo*'s excessive love of money, papers, and coins, which one could not carry to heaven. "They love money more than their eyes," my grandmother once told me. And the Elepo women did not know what the *osomalo* did with that money, since they also cultivated the image of miserliness.

The values of consumption and savings always clashed: for the Mesiogo, the purpose of acquiring money was to spend it. Indeed, one of the lorries that took me to Elepo had a bold sign on its side, "Nina Lowo," which enjoined people to spend money whenever they had it. The *osomalo* was saying something different: conserve money to make more money. If they had been able to conserve, then why torment the poor villagers? Those at Elepo could not answer this question in any positive manner. Even Pasitor could not take a positive attitude toward the *osomalo*. Villagers knew about wealth, and they could even be conscious of its power, but they had limited means of accumulation. Pasitor told me that my father could buy the entire village and farm, and he was always praying that his son-in-law would not be so "wicked." The distinction between a bad person and a wicked person was clear: a bad person could be redeemed, persuaded to change his ways. The "wicked" person was evil, headed for hell. Rather than praying for the "wicked," it was easier for Pasitor to torment them with the threat of hellfire.

The *osomalo* violated the code of honor in the village. Before I knew who the *osomalo* were, I had seen adults running away to hide on farms when they approached. Some even slept for days in tents on their farms, enduring cold and mosquitoes, a really agonizing experience. The *osomalo* trusted the villagers with the goods, which was why he sold on credit. But the villagers misunderstood the friendship and jokes of the *osomalo* to mean that he would be kind when they defaulted. If the teeth can smile, what about the heart? The friendship of the *osomalo* was transient: a strategy to sell. The strategy had to change in order to collect the debts. The *osomalo* believed the Elepo women should till more land, produce more palm oil, and crack more palm kernels to raise the money to pay. As the *osomalo* descended on them, blocking their doors and announcing to the public that debtors lived there, he became nothing but an enemy. As the debtor agonized, he or she looked at the cloth purchased many months ago: it had become a rag or gone out of fashion. The debtor finally realized that being well dressed does not solve the problem of poverty. The debtor hated himself, the item purchased on credit, and the *osomalo* who had sold it. The debtor could blame the rag or kill himself, but he could castigate the *osomalo* as evil. The fates of the poor villager and the rich *osomalo* were bound together, but it was like putting gunpowder and fire in the same bed.

But nothing could be more evil than the chief, as manifested in the anger of the women and the depressing sermon on death by Pasitor. It took me several years to fully understand that the violence and curses directed at the chiefs were created by changes in the land tenure system.

For centuries, the Yoruba, like the majority of African groups and nations, did not sell and buy land. Whoever wanted a piece of land to build or farm on could obtain one through a process of identification with a clan. Then came cocoa, that lucrative crop that was taken to Europe to manufacture beverages. Candies and drinks that others enjoyed in faraway lands began to produce bloodshed and conflicts in the cocoa-growing areas. Ambitious farmers and entrepreneurs grabbed as much land as they could lay their hands on. Those in areas where cocoa would not grow moved to the cocoa belt. They became tenant farmers, living on land on which they paid heavy rent. Even citizens became tenants on their farms when they pawned their cocoa trees to raise money. The chief belonged to a group of city-based landlords with farms in the villages. Always busy from dawn till dusk entertaining guests and running from one meeting to another, they had no visible jobs for all to see. They were rich, but the money was made for them by a large number of tenants, who paid rent. If the government was broke, it raised taxes on farmers; if the chief was broke, he raised the rent on land. Thus, the government and the chief created an alliance that turned the people of Elepo into mere laborers, toiling so others could reap the reward. Those, like Pasitor, who controlled their own land could minimize the agony. Those, like the tenant farmers, who were paying rent to the chiefs, were always on the edge. If the chief collected rents and the osomalo collected debts on overpriced goods, they had no means to overcome their poverty or educate their children. A vicious circle emerged, and they knew that they were reproducing poverty from one generation to another.

In talking about the chief and the osomalo, the village people were also talking about the larger issues of life and values and the attributes expected of a successful person. The fault lines between the village and city became clear to me. The tension between the rich and poor was even more clear, with neither able to control an emerging division: when you are poor, you are despised, when you are rich you are hated. As Africa marched forward in time, the village gradually lost to the cities in importance, access to amenities, schools, and jobs. The villagers lost power as well. No one represented them in Lagos, the center of federal power. No one was interested in them in Ibadan, the regional capital. They only had God and Pasitor to look to, confirming the idea that religion is the opiate of the poor. Over time, a class of previously contented farmers became angry, regarding the government, the chief, and the osomalo as enemies. They saw the rich as always complaining. The ruin of a nation may begin in the homes of the people. Songs, sermons in churches and mosques, and moonlight stories began to communicate anger. It was in the village that I heard many bad things, in very bad language, about the social order, power, and stratification. The villagers were always talking about the *aiyero* (tough world) and the *aiye baje* (degenerate world). Pasitor and his wife told me many times to be polite and generous to people without explaining the reasons. When elders intervened in the discussions among youth, it was usually about the values of honesty and charity. They never said that one should not seek a fortune but that one must always engage in a culture of sharing.

The villagers probably took a large overdose of the opiate on the Sunday that Pasitor preached about death. Immediately after the service, he turned the church into a public assembly to discuss the chief. I never knew the details of what they said, only the conclusion. They sent for the chief to appear before them a week later, using the church premises as the venue. I knew that they sent for the chief, as no one had anything to talk about except the impending meeting. Time flies! Sunday came quickly and the people gathered, but the chief did not show up. He who begins a conversation can never foresee the end.

The curses directed at the chief on that day were many and bitter. I heard the first barrage of antirich, antichief, and antigovernment statements of my life, contradicting all that the big boys at Agbokojo had told me and the gains that the teachers had promised we would achieve by working hard and going to school. Believing the chief to be already rich, some asked God to make the chief wretched, visited by *agbana*, a deadly social disease that would make him waste his entire savings on irrelevancies, visited by the "father of losses," who would turn him into a rat in the church. Joy and contentment would not come near him, and he would be detested "at home and abroad." May the angels and all intermediaries not take his message to God, and if they did may God never listen. I heard more, and no one stopped them from cursing, not even Pasitor. The crowd dispersed, and each cursed the chief on his or her way home. There is no medicine to cure hatred.

The chief received the summons to visit the village and actually kept the appointment, only he chose his own time. He came on a Sunday, but at dinner time, before it was too dark. His black car was followed by a police truck carrying eight officers of the Native Police Force, with guns and batons. As their vehicles could not reach the interior of the village, they stopped on the main road. People spotted them, and everyone trooped out, including myself and Pasitor. The chief walked slowly, and the police walked behind, without anyone knowing their intentions.

They headed for one of the chief's houses, where the man who had complained about him lived. He and his family were home. The chief requested a chair, and he sat, the only one sitting among the large number gathered there, not knowing what he would do. To sit is to be crippled, but not for this chief, whose action came quickly. Pointing to the tenant farmer, the chief said something close to the following:

"You poor thing, who should have been used as a sacrifice to the gods, but now with a useless mouth to complain with. You think that the fools who live in this village can save you?" He pointed to the crowd, including Pasitor, who was quiet, and asked the tenant farmer to request their help. The tenant farmer said nothing, as he could not follow the golden rule: if you offend, seek pardon; if offended, forgive. The tenant farmer was the one who had been offended, but he was also being punished. The chief became more pompous: evil enters like a needle and spreads like an oak tree.

"Look to the sky, look to the earth, today is your last day here, today is your last day of freedom." The chief made a signal to the police, probably prearranged. In any case, evil knows where evil sleeps: the police promptly arrested the tenant farmer. The police obeyed the chief to the letter: a fool and water go the way they are diverted. As the chief stood up and followed the police and tenant farmer to the vehicles, he told the man's wife not to sleep in that house. With the power of the government, and the guns purchased with the farmers' money, the tenant farmer was whisked away. The chief greeted no one, but he looked at the crowd in an arrogant manner. He actually spit on the ground, a way to indicate contempt for one's enemy. A wealthy man will always have followers, but this wealthy chief was accompanied only by the agents of the government and a man who could kill him. He moved hurriedly, as if rushing to another village to arrest another tenant. Or he might be thinking that if he spent too much time there the villagers might gain the energy to resist him: if one is not in a hurry, even an egg will start walking. No one clapped for the chief for dealing with the situation so quickly: where there is no shame, there can be no honor.

The women were sobbing; the men were silent. A roaring lion kills no game. When the chief disappeared from sight, a series of curses followed: what the antelopes said over the dead lion's body could not have been uttered when the lion was alive. The villagers had to do something, even if it was only to repeat previous curses: a loose tooth refuses to rest until it is pulled out. People could not understand why a rich man would maltreat a poor person to such an extent; simply because the chief wanted more money, he had raised the rent on his land. A local man whom I had seen but did not know brought a pigeon. Moving himself and the life bird in circles so many times that I could not count, he stopped and forcefully smashed the pigeon on the ground, splattering blood on those who were nearby. Then he uttered what sounded like a closing curse: "The chief shall end at the *orita* (crossroads), devoured by vultures." I understood only an element of this, the part about the vulture eating a dead body. But the chief was alive, and I had no idea what the crossroads had to do with it. This was not the time to ask questions.

Pasitor did not eat his dinner. He spoke to no one. He had initiated the rage that led to the decision to invite the chief: the dog he bought had bitten him; the fire he kindled had burned him. The chief had turned Pasitor into a fool who speaks while a wise man listens. He put his chair in the place where my sleeping mat was normally spread to sleep for the night. He wrote down certain things and read the Bible passages until his wife asked him to go to bed. The next day he fell ill, and he refused to eat for days. Could he have been thinking that it is not true that virtue is better than wealth? Or that God would not intervene to punish the chief, that he who has done evil may not expect evil?

The next thing we heard was that the tenant farmer had been arrested for planting marijuana at the Elepo village. I knew the farm, and all that was on it was the regular crops like those of others. The chief had invented a crime to destroy the tenant farmer. The story spread to many other villages and perhaps to towns and cities that I did not know. The chief not only confirmed what the villagers knew, that the rich man and the poor man do not play together, but he gave them yet another lesson: the poor man's mouth is a machete, to be used in clearing the bush.

This was in 1965. Three years later, the behavior of the *osomalo* and the chief, as well as government policies that complicated politics and increased rural poverty, led to the first major peasant uprising in modern Nigeria. The poor realized that even ants can harm the elephant. The government learned that what is inflated too much will burst into fragments. There was a lesson for the rich as well: the strong and the hearty do not live forever. As for Pasitor, he who is free of faults will never die. The chief, the *osomalo*, and Pasitor did not survive this unprecedented rebellion. But they had a chronicler who saw it all and whose life has been shaped by the behavior of the chief and the peasant uprising. If you are not prepared to see evil, never pray for long life.

n groups varying from five to fifteen, they moved around the city, singing, chanting, and making fun of one another. Each group stopped in front of our house to sing loud and clear in praise of sex, in celebration of excess.

Penis times vagina equals penis
Vagina times penis equals vagina.

I heard *keereewu* [a cracking sound]
It is your vagina that is being hit by a long penis.

I heard *keereewu*
The dog is eating your vagina bone.

Three friends
With dangling scrotums
You may abuse me
As your scrotums dangle.

The old man passing by
Your scrotum is dangling, dangling, dangling.

She opened her vagina wide
The lady opened her vagina too wide
The careless one has exposed a vagina.

By now, I and others had blended with one group or another, moving from area to area, mocking people as they passed by. Wood touched by fire is easy to set alight: the bigger crowd only sang more, got bolder. Then we mocked various occupations in sex songs.

The penis of the police is nothing but a belt.

Teacher's penis
Enveloped in chalk.

Mechanic's penis
Full of oil.

The motor driver's penis
Is as long as the sugarcane
The wife of the driver
Deserves commendation for her endurance.

It would be greater fun to see a schoolteacher, as one could repeatedly abuse his penis or her vagina times without number. The song could change either when the group became tired of repeating the same lines or someone came up with another idea.

Give me a grinding stone
I want to break some scrotums.

Just as we had ridiculed the schoolteachers, the sight of anyone with unusual features could provoke a set of songs. How can the hunchback enjoy sex? Why was the man with ten wives so selfish in not releasing one to us? And to the pregnant woman:

Thou pregnant woman
What a pity
Your vagina has gone on leave
For three years
Your vagina is on leave.

The powerful and the rich were not excluded. Indeed, one of the great achievements of the carnival was to use songs to level the playing field, to allow the young and the poor to say whatever was on their mind, using sex and its symbolism as metaphors. As we reached the palace of the mighty king, we would sing until the great man acknowledged us.

Our king, who advised you to stay at home?
Stay at home, stay at home
A load of vagina will fall on you
A load of vagina is about to fall on you
Who advised you to keep silent at home?

Government officials were butts of jokes. Even the friendly mailman riding his bicycle was given a song.

The bicycle rider
Ascend the hill cautiously
For your penis is now erect
Without any available vagina.

These songs were part of a huge one-day annual carnival, usually held in March, to celebrate the spirit force of the venerated Oke (hill), the city's deity. Judging from the many names associated with hills and neighborhoods in the city, one would think that it was full of mountain climbers (Aje Hill, Aremo Hill, Mapo Hill, and so on). Far from it. The landscape was one of hills and valleys. One of the hills stands out, located originally far away from the city center, where the city began its ancient history. I saw the hill, the representation of the deity, many times. A huge stone, larger than many bungalows in the city, standing on a hill became the symbolism of the power of Oke, the hill. Smaller shrines to the hill's deity could be found in several homes, with the belief that they could prevent misfortunes.

The belief was that the hill had offered protection to the earliest occupants, saving them from their enemies, offering shelter and protection. The carnival turned the hill into a god, worshiped as the Okebadan (the hill of Ibadan). A cult emerged around the hill, and the carnival became the annual entertainment for all citizens, whether they worshiped the hill or not. There were many songs to celebrate the hill.

Hold the child of Oke
Robust and handsome
Bring to me the child of Oke.

The child of Oke is peaceful
The child is born today
It starts to walk the next day.

The hill itself did not escape the joy of sexual encounters.

Today belongs to you, the Oke
Today is yours, our Oke
The possessor of the penis who resides by the apple tree
The one with the tough penis
Who cares not whether I wear pants
Hitting me with its big penis
Oke, the possessor of an active penis
Who devours the vagina with energy.

It was an opportunity to bring history to modern reality, with songs praising the warriors of the past, using sex as a communication device to announce victories in wars with neighbors and distant foes. Songs of rapes became the metanarrative of power.

The penis erects actively
I'll insert it into the vagina
Into the vagina of the Osu woman

I will insert it
Into the vagina of the Osu woman
I will insert it.

Sexually explicit songs and dances disguised the goals of the carnival. Vulgarity was used only as a mask, with words that cleverly refused to reveal the meanings of the social celebrations. Vulgarity was accompanied by a rigorous maintenance of social order: the songs could be used on only one day. One must not practice the songs before the carnival, and one must not use them afterward. To do so was to violate the moral code. Used on other days, vulgarities became insults that would attract punishment. One could draw attention to the teachers' penises during the carnival, as I did, but to repeat this on other days was to invite dismissal from school and bring shame on one's parents. Here was a lesson not in moderation but in the recognition of the connections between words, space, and rituals. March must not be confused with May. The carnival was always on a Thursday, which could not be confused with a Monday. And sex songs were not associated with any other event, which meant that no one could plead innocence if they sang them at a wedding. As if to ensure that no one was stupid enough to be confused, the city crier from the palace walked miles and miles around the city to announce the exact Thursday in March when one could use the songs. It used to be observed as a holiday, and many years before my time no trading was allowed. I was told that my predecessors would dress smartly, walking many miles on that day. In order to appreciate what the ancestors had suffered, they would eat cold meals, just as the city founders relied on meager meals of *oro* fruits (*Irvingia gabonensis*) and had only snail shells as drinking bowls.

Some of the goals of the carnival were related to the civic and history lessons offered at school. I was born when the country was awaiting its independence, although its leaders were fighting over the constitution and the distribution of power. I was in elementary school during the years of euphoria, when we all knew about independence and heard the promises of what it would bring. Problems were also developing, and thugs sponsored by politicians burned tires in the streets close to my house and school to terrorize their opponents. The euphoria of independence changed many of the textbooks that students read as well as the stories that were told. Origin stories of ethnic groups and cities became part of the school lessons. By the age of ten, I could narrate the oral traditions of the foundation of my city and provide a list of its early leaders. The Okebadan festival was a reminder of that early history.

But what have the references to penis and vagina got to do with history? The answer confused me in 1964 when I first raised the question, but now it is clearer. Ibadan, like all Yoruba cities, depended on agriculture. For centuries, farmers believed that hard work alone was not enough for the yam to sprout, for the corn to rise, for land to open up and offer its bounty. Nature and the spiritual forces must intervene, with the gods of fertility appealing to the land to show mercy on the farmers. The majority of African groups have gods and goddesses in charge of agriculture. Ibadan was no different, associating the carnival and hill worship with fertility, of both crops and humans. Sex songs were meant to invoke reproduction. As they spoke of penis and vagina, they were seeking the meeting of both to produce yams, cassava, and babies. Devouring the vagina with all energy and passion must translate into population increase as well as agricultural productivity.

Oke, the Oke of Ibadan
Its normal to have seven children
Oke, give me eight
With one as an extra.

The wealthy deity
Lift the robust children of Oke
Carry the plump child.

This song was used to conclude the multiplicity of sex songs, to remind us that we were not just playing, but begging. And the begging was timely. March was the month to inaugurate rain. If rain failed to appear by the end of March, farmers began to panic, anticipating crop failures and the disasters that accompanied them. Sex and rain became linked, in a ritualistic and metaphorical sense. Sex was meant to invoke rain, using pleasing words to beg the hill to ask the sky to release water on the land. Human beings became resigned to their fate, realizing their powerlessness, but communicating words, in a free spirit and communion, that would please the hill, which had to mediate. Even the hill was invited to have sex so as not to become jealous of humans. To encourage her to enjoy the company of her man, further sacrifices were made with animals (cows, snails, dogs, fish, tortoises) and the starchy food to go with them. Now full and happy, the hill would speak well of humans to the forces above the sky.

It was relatively easy to placate the hill. Men had surrendered their power to it, making the hill and the spirit who lives in it a woman with attractive breasts and gentle manners. The pot that contained the sacrificial food for the hill was shaped like a woman. To reach for the pot, as Leku did many times, was not only to pray but to take water from it. One could even buy small quantities of the water from the pot at Leku's store to use for charms to end barrenness, request more children, and cure a variety of illnesses. The hill's breasts were abnormal in size and number. If the normal woman had two, the hill had sixteen because of the large number of children she must feed. And she fed them very well. The hill was presented as gentle, pro-family, kind, and favorably disposed toward women and children. The priests of the hill, though men, dressed like women, with plaited hair, fake breasts, and white wrappers. The priests carried both male and female attributes but presented themselves more as women so that the hill, now of the same sex, would be more merciful.

Even I, as young as I was, knew that God and the sky could be angry with the land, and a mediator might be necessary. The mythical stories of fights were well known, and I could tell them to others by the age of nine. God and the land were said to be in competition over seniority: who was older? The land claimed to have created God, but God said that land was just one of the tiny pieces He had made. Well, to resolve it, the land said that it would never allow God to show up on earth, and if He did He would be swallowed. God tried but was prevented from landing, and He had to struggle back to heaven. In anger, He withheld rain and sun. The land remained, but it dried out. Human beings, now helpless, ran to the hill and other objects to appeal to them to beg God. They offered food, sex, and money to the hill. God listened and released rain. The clever humans now decided not to wait for God and the land to fight before appealing to the hill for help. The hill's big breasts and large vagina will never be left in want, although we do not know the men who moved near them. Rain must come, and it must do so soon after the Okebadan festival. As the first rain appeared, the humans thanked the hill.

We honor thee
The Oke of Ibadan
The one with the biggest breasts.

These were not breasts to kiss or touch but to suck for milk, a sexual metaphor intended to attain sacred closure. Peace and blessings must follow the closure, and as the rain poured down to bless the land conflicts were reduced to the minimum since everyone must now be busy with their occupations and abundant food was expected. Peace and lack of war were also attributed to the power and kindness of the hill. The absence of locusts to destroy the farms, of pestilence to destroy people, and of diseases to damage animals and humans were all attributed to the protective power of the hill.

The Okebadan festival was my earliest experience of the public display of loyalty to the city, and it has remained such a display ever since. It was a peaceful carnival, one that pushed people of all types into the streets in the thousands. I was always in a group of strangers, but the songs united us. I walked to new places, various locations, and compounds. We interspersed the sex songs with those on power and wealth. And as the large crowds approached the grove where traditional rites would be performed by the *aboke*, the chief priest of the hill, the songs changed to those of praise and gratitude to God.

> All evil will be transferred to distant lands
> We shall not experience evil in this land
> All evil will be transferred to distant lands.

This was not a curse on others, but the notion of citizenship and city identity is one of selfishness. While sympathy was shown in case of disasters in other lands, there was always relief that it was not close to home. The other lands were not necessarily in faraway Japan or Australia but could be those of the Ijebu or Egba, Yoruba neighbors. They, too, had a similar prayer, intended to divert their evils and disasters northward, in the direction of Ibadan. All Yoruba cities have the equivalent of Okebadan, and many are far more elaborate, such as Odun Oba at Ondo, Oke Olumo at Abeokuta, Oke Asabari at Saki, and the Agemo among the Ijebu. The motives are the same: to attain community identity and to ask the gods for more blessings. And wherever a hill is involved in the worship, as in the case of the Olumo rock at Abeokuta, it is always in the context of security: the hill provides a hideout, a place for the army to retreat to before staging the final battle to destroy the enemy. At Ibadan, the sex songs connected us closely with past histories, without having to narrate extensive details. The songs also brought traditional power close to the public, without the people having to pay dues and tributes before speaking with the king and chiefs.

I did not know as a child that there was an elaborate ritual side to the carnival. I knew that we all awaited the presence of the *aboke*, and when he appeared the noise was thunderous. What I saw was the carnival, just a small part of the worship of the hill deity. What I learned later provided me with a deep knowledge of rituals, connecting kingship to priesthood. On the Wednesday before the carnival, the stones representing statues of the deity had to be cleaned with water and leaves. A huge cost was borne by the king, who had to provide the objects of sacrifice, a staggering figure of two hundred of each, a number that symbolized abundance. The birds were in danger, for the king had to look for fowls, pigeons, and guinea fowl. Innocent snails were added. Thanks to its size, only a single cow was needed. The hill consumed all of these in addition to palm oil, kola nuts, food items, and even wine. I have no idea what a drunk hill was supposed to do to its worshipers. I never saw the actual sacrifice in those days.

What I saw was the inspiring return home of the *aboke* and the core worshipers. They were happy to announce that the hill had spoken to them, assuring them that the sacrifices had been well received. Christians and Muslims also believed in them, with many joining the procession, moving from the house of one chief to another, singing and praying. Some of the prayers that the *aboke* made to the hill were repeated in public.

Oke, save me, please save me
One who asks for succor is always saved.
Oke, save me, I shall worship you.

Oke, please do not make my problems unsolvable
Oke, to whom people pray in troubled times
One who frequents the house of those who worship.

Oke, save me
Oke, the one with large breasts
Oke, I hail you
Atage, the one with large breasts
The mighty one who takes care of mothers and their children
The mighty one who protects fathers and their children.

As we moved in huge crowds, the prayer was repeated, then replaced by the sex songs to generate more noise, as if a goal had been scored on the soccer field. The king received a special blessing, based on the belief that his health must approximate that of the city.

Okebadan, give long life to the Oba
Bless him, as he has provided the objects to worship thee
Let there be no disaster in the city
Give us peace
Oke, give us children blessed with long life.

Whoever was ready to return home before it was too dark had a closing prayer to make, one that replaced the normal prayers in many homes that day.

Oke, let us witness the next annual ceremony
Prevent the death of children
Prevent the death of husbands
Prevent the death of wives
May we not die painful deaths
May we not die bloody deaths
Give children to those who have none.

Even my church, in recognition of the importance of Okebadan, joined in praying for the survival of the city. In modernizing the city's national anthem, the Christian who chose the lines and the rhythm was aware of history and traditions and tried to blend both the traditional and the modern.

Ibadan, a city on the hill
The city of God's blessing
May the Lord make you a blessed city
For indigenes and foreigners.
 Chorus: Shout joyfully
 And join in the chorus
 In glorifying our God in heaven
 Almighty's blessing is with you
 Ibadan, God will make you a blessed city.
 Ibadan, the city that welcomes visitors
Without forgetting its own
Let love reside here
For citizens and visitors alike.
 Chorus: Shout joyfully, etc.
Ibadan, the city of warriors
Those who make you great
We all the citizens
Will not allow your honor and glory to perish.
 Chorus: Shout joyfully, etc.
I can see from the hill
How beautiful you are
Even if your river is not great
It still crosses the entire city.
 Chorus: Shout joyfully, etc.
Ibadan, the city on the hill
May the Lord bless you
May all thy chiefs

Enjoy long life.
    Chorus: Shout joyfully, etc.

Here is the Christian response to the sex songs. But, just as the carnival songs became popular, so, too, did the Christian song become secularized. I sang it at school, at church, and in the mosque! The teacher and preachers always agreed that we must never behave like the river that forgets its sources and dries up. At home, we even observed the rules of old that no one should make any fire that would make smoke visible on the carnival day. Christian and Muslim leaders reconciled themselves to the carnival. When Christians and Muslims spread their messages or announced prophecies, the traditionalists told us that they were speaking at the command of the hill. By translating Christian and Islamic messages into traditional idioms, reconciliation was attained, stability assured. As fundamentalism grew in later years, Muslims and Christians began to attack the worship of the hill and the carnival songs, while the Christian hymn was dropped from the mosques. As they strengthened their faith, Christians and Muslims slowly but surely eroded the cultural foundations of the city, creating a mess that the visitor can see today.

Before the mess, there was a clean body, not pure but clean. In my day, the anthem of cults that circulated in schools, one that we all sang, was about the retention of the cultures of old.

> We shall perform our rites
> We will obey our customs
> No religion can forbid us
> Not at all
> From performing our rites.

This was a song composed by the first generation of Christians to defend traditional religions and customs. Not many people apologized for being Christian or Muslim and still taking part in festivals, using charms, and looking for local medicines to cure illnesses. The belief in witchcraft and sorcery was ubiquitous, irrespective of education, religion, or social status. No one stopped us from participating in the Okebadan festival.

    The hill and its worship were just part of a crowd of deities, cults, and ceremonies. There were celebrations in honor of many gods and goddesses, notably Ifa, Ogun, Sango, and Yemoja. I did not participate in any of these, although I observed very closely the public performances and the public rituals of two: Omi and Sango. Omi was a water goddess, far less famous than Osun, based in the city of Osogbo, but sharing the same characteristics. A powerful priestess of Omi lived at Ode Aje. This was essentially a cult of women. Their public appearance was marked by the wearing of white cloths and an orderly procession. Each prayer was interrupted with a loud shout of "Omi." The crowd watched the participants without joining in, as they danced round the city. They sang. Twice they stopped in one spot, praying intensely until one of them reached a state of trance. The first time I saw a woman in a trance, I confused it with something else: a seizure. I had seen many children afflicted with seizures, with adults rushing to put fingers, spoons, knives, or any other objects in their mouths. The belief was that if the lower jaw should meet the upper one, they could lock, and the child might die. I had no way to confirm this. Seizures attracted frantic calls for help from the terrified mother: "Help me," "Save me," "Do not allow my enemies to claim victory," "I have suffered too much in life to lose a child." If the child had to be rushed to the hospital or a traditional healer, the mother changed her cries to more depressing ones: "I am dead," "I am ruined," "Punishment and disgrace have come my way."

In the case of the woman in a trance, they were not shouting, calling for help, or panicking. The chief priestess was sober, trying to listen to what the woman in the trance was saying. The words were not intelligible. Then she slumped to the ground, and the members of the cult called out "Omi o, Omi o, Omi o," many times. When she recovered, they burst into vigorous dancing, as if they had heard an important message. This was different from the recovery from seizures that I had seen previously. Unlike the rather slow recovery in the case of seizure, with the victim being forced to rest, the Omi woman recovered rapidly and joined the procession as if nothing had happened. I saw other cases of trance in association with other cults and gods. In later years, I would associate trance with Christian pentecostal churches. Once in a while, the thought has occurred to me that some of those I saw in trances should have been taken to mental homes, unless of course they were faking it.

Of all the Yoruba gods, I knew most about Sango. The reason was simple: this was the god of our lineage. Sango's priests were also very active. I was not a believer, and neither was Baba Olopa or even my mother, who was a testimony to the power of this god. But we had no choice but to participate in Sango worship for two reasons. First, the Sango priests and all the members of their families joined us in all our Christian celebrations. They even attended church when invited. Similarly, they joined in Islamic celebrations, just as I did. The ethics of reciprocity probably gave Muslims and Christians no choice but to participate in Sango worship, at least in the main annual ceremony. Then there was the rule of kinship, which forced all adults to contribute money when the priests called upon them. I myself contributed money in the 1970s and 1980s.

More than anything else, it was the appearance of the Sango priests as women that first attracted me. They made their hair appear like that of women, while they displayed masculinity. The god Sango was not like the gentle hill. Most elementary school kids knew about Sango, the king who became a god, noted for his excessive power as a king and his fury as a god. Decisive, impatient, fast, energetic, and tempestuous, Sango wanted not love but fear. One had to beg the god to escape destruction by the powerful rocks (thunderstones) that he could throw with force and without mercy. His signs and punishments were associated with the powerful lightning and thunder that destroyed homes, brought down trees, and killed people. Even fellow gods were afraid of Sango, as many myths explained to us.

The power of Sango priests had a public face. A few performed magical shows from time to time, using various techniques to change their clothes to make them look like animals, playing with knives as if they would cut open their stomachs, and performing a number of acts that were probably not associated with the original cult. Whenever such actors appeared, we abandoned everything else to watch as part of a crowd that formed a circle. At the annual Sango ceremony, I enjoyed watching those possessed by the spirit, similar to the trance of the Omi people. The difference was that considerable effort had to be made to bring back to life those possessed by Sango. The blood of animals and palm oil were poured on them; at first I was sympathetic but later on indifferent. The priests and unpossessed devotees had to beg Sango to have mercy on the possessed and others, placating the god by praising him. Even when Sango was calm and sleepy, he still had to be appeased.

> The god who kills without using a sword
> The mighty torrent who quarrels with one
> But still shows up in one's compound without fear
> My lord, he makes the wicked lick the soil
> Tough like the bowstring
> Sango dies at home and reappears in the market
> Mighty god, I salute.

Even those in my church were afraid of Sango. God lives in heaven, and He has not announced the day of judgment. Sango, too, is no longer on earth, but in those days he made his presence felt so strongly that Muslims and Christians were afraid of him. They would easily swear on the Bible, even to tell a lie or cheat in a business transaction, but many were afraid of invoking the name of the ruthless god of thunder. Even in school dramas that involved Sango, the character had to be stern looking, showing anger when others were happy. In the drama, a mirror of real life, Sango's advances to women could not be rejected and his requests for tribute could not be turned down. I played the role of an appeaser, memorizing long lines collected from the priests of the god to ask Sango to forgive others as I pleaded my own innocence, attributing my recitation to the task assigned to me by forces more powerful, more threatening, than those of the schoolteacher.

> The Lord of the house of fire
> The murderous power that strikes the ground with resounding force
> I pay homage
> The husband of Yemoja
> Spare me.

> I was only sent to talk
> I did not send myself
> Authority belongs to those who sent me
> Sango, I never said that you committed suicide
> I plead for those who said that Sango killed himself.

> The Lord of the storm
> Hurler of thunderbolts
> The Master of Yemoja, the goddess with the longest beard
> The rushing tornado that tears down houses and trees
> Sango, I am not the one who called your name in vain.

> Oba Koso, I conspire not against thunder and river
> It is not until trouble comes that many acknowledge you as
>   the savior.
> Sango, I accept thee
> In dry and rainy seasons, you can kill
> Spare me, my lord, slayer of men.

It was when one heard people in the audience saying "Amen, Amen," that one hoped they were not confusing the drama with real life. They probably were. The teachers even had to remove from the drama any reference that seemed like a betrayal of the god. So-called real aspects, close to the history and behavior of Sango, were cut out, with the excuse that we needed the permission of local priests. The teachers told us that without this permission the priests and Sango could be angered and might conspire to punish the school.

The teachers were no fools. Even regional and local governments often set aside money to appease Sango and other gods. A successful chief who planned a big party could be prevented from hosting it by a heavy downpour of rain. Then and now, rainmakers and powerful priests of Sango were asked to stop the rain from falling whenever there was an important ceremony. Even devout Christians would secretly send someone to pay Sango priests to control the rain, to stop thunder and lightning. I knew they did, since I carried a few of their messages. So important was the image of Sango in life and drama that the entire modern project of the colonial era in the first half of the twentieth century did not damage him.

Why did Sango survive for so long, as a god, an idea, and a belief system associated with rain? Sango behaved like a leopard who was beaten by rain but refused to change its spots. I think that the first answer probably came to me in 1963, narrated in origin stories of the Yoruba. Sango was one of the most powerful figures in early Yoruba history, presented in various myths and sayings. The schoolteachers believed strongly in the myths, presenting them to us as histories. Indeed, history lessons, whether of ancient or modern times, were presented as myths and stories. When the schoolteacher and the students believed the myths, they had no option but to believe Sango, one of the early kings of the famous Oyo Empire. The Oyo Empire existed as a historical fact, but Sango existed as a recorded legend, one of the kings mentioned in a long king list. The narrative about him is long and often confusing, but the conclusion is that his highhandedness cost him the throne and he had to commit suicide. The stories may be many, but one thing is clear from them all: Sango had a stern, autocratic personality. His main power, according to all legends, was the ability to vomit fire at any time, so that he could burn his enemies and their houses, even entire towns. A master of intrigue, Sango was alleged to have set one chief against another until he met his match in a war chief who discovered his game. The victorious war chief overthrew him, and Sango was forced into exile. Abandoned by his retinue, except for his wife, Oya, Sango chose to commit suicide.

It was in death that Sango became more famous, as the popular legend makes clear. He did not go to heaven to rest in peace but remained to exercise more power. Sango in death was still restless: the man who has too much ambition has murdered sleep and peace. He left a number of wives behind, but one of them, Oya, became the goddess of the river and sea. "Sango, the husband of Oya," has become a popular cognomen for this god. No other god had such a powerful wife, and it is a wife who knows her husband the best. To believe in the wife was to believe in the husband. Oya was more gentle, more approachable, and slower to punish transgressions than her husband. School dramas captured the myth and the image of Oya, but what we called a play the larger society called reality. The most liberated minds of the time did not dismiss the gods. Not many people could have dismissed Sango.

> The fearsome one who frightens a Muslim so that he urinates in the mosque
> One whom the Christian sees and forgets to look unto heaven
> Sango, he falls upon people like the blacksmith's hammer.

This was not a god with whom young boys wanted to joke. I think that many of us believed the propagated view that Sango was permanently angry, sending his messengers to burn down houses and powerful winds to give power to the fire. Anyone who said that Sango had committed suicide was in trouble. To ensure this, the god attracted many devotees and loyalist priests, the Adosu-Sango. As I saw the devotees and priests dance even in the rain, I felt like joining them, only they were not ready to play. They loved the rain, telling us that they brought it about as well as the loud thunder. I never saw any case of this, but I was told that in the event that thunder killed anyone the priests would attribute it to Sango and extract fees from the dead person's family before they would bury the corpse. They even claimed to be responsible for the rainbow. They prayed for everyone and received gifts from members of our household and others. Whether one believed in Sango or not, the drama and dances, with intense drumming, were impressive and attracted large crowds.

Fortunately, we all have dead fathers, ancestors in heaven. If Sango terrorized us on earth, our ancestors would plead for us in heaven, saving us from the dangers of heavy rainfall and thunder. I had a father in heaven, not the same one whom Christian prayers always asked for our daily bread, but the one who gave life to me. I doubt whether he asked anyone to venerate him, but his name was invoked many times: "May your father not sleep in heaven" was a prayer I heard so many times that I stopped attaching any significance to it. My lineage, like all the others in the city, had an egungun (masquerade) to represent the ancestors, and each had a name to distinguish it from the others. Many regarded egungun as part of the plethora of gods, but I grew to regard them as just an annual entertainment. When the masquerades appeared in their season, for a whole week in the famous month of June, the stories of their meaning and representation also became widespread for almost an entire month. I never believed it when I was told that the egungun were from heaven and were even greeted as Ara-orun-kinkin, "nice visitors from heaven."

Whether I believed they were visiting from heaven or not, the egungun were heavily embedded in the culture. More than half my classmates believed that egungun were not human. The foundation of this powerful belief was based in another idea: the nearness of the soul (emi) and reincarnation. The soul of the dead was believed to be within a short distance, only we could not see it with the naked eye. However, the soul could see we humans. Not only that, but the soul could disguise itself and visit the world at any time. Not only could ancestors appear in animal skins, but iwin (spirits) could also do this. A story that terrorized the girls at school was one that we loved to tell. A girl had many suitors but declined them all. When she was ready, she chose a spirit in human skin, who revealed itself when it was too late. Big markets, motor parks, and cities were believed to be full of such agents in disguise, and they could always create problems for the unsuspecting.

The spirit of the egungun was a positive one, most welcomed, and associated with all the good things of life. It was not that the dead corpses voluntarily chose to move from their scattered graves to revisit the earth. On the contrary, it was human beings who appealed to the dead to visit them. The flesh and bones of the dead were already rotten, and their souls were invisible. To overcome the problem that the dead were unable to be physically present, human beings chose from among themselves the people to represent the dead. Once they put on the masks and garments that covered their entire bodies, following a ritual performance in a secluded grove known as igbale, they were no longer humans but guests from heaven. The man in a mask, now a reincarnated soul, became more powerful than those who chose him in the first instance. We now had to beg the man in disguise to have mercy on us, to bless us, to forgive our transgressions.

The fear people had of the egungun was real. I saw it at home, at school, and on the streets. Many people regarded the person inside the mask as very powerful in spiritual and symbolic terms. To me and thousands of others, the motivation to see an egungun, to accompany one, to dance on the street, was to play. Egungun, during the week of their appearance, broke our routine, both at school and at home. When the powerful egungun passed by the school, the teachers lost their power to contain us, as we abandoned the classroom to look at the masquerade. A vindictive teacher would punish an entire class. It was also hard for parents to ask children to stay indoors. Many of us would break our curfews, preferring to accept punishment later on.

Adults participated in equal numbers. Many also wanted to play, thus providing intense interaction between adults and children. A large number of people stayed in front of their houses to watch but also to receive blessings. The egungun prayed for many, and his guides (the atokun) collected gifts in cash, kola nuts, and other items. Some people even sent food and livestock to the household of their egungun. For two consecutive years, I carried such gifts to the egungun of my lineage. When the egungun was not in season, one could approach the room where the garments and mask were kept. I did so, to discover that they were very heavy. The garments were in multiple layers, as if made over many years with cuts from many fabrics. When I tried to lift the garments, it was almost too difficult. Since then, I have had a better appreciation for the man in the mask in terms of the sheer energy needed to wear all the garments and still move about. In some families, they used lighter garments, but even then only a physically strong person could volunteer for such a task.

At Ibadan, the real fun of the egungun festival was the street fights. There were "gentle" masquerades, followed mainly by women and a few men. Their dances and songs impressed only people like me. The really remarkable one, the Alapansapa, drew thousands, each holding strong whips. At intervals, men engaged in serious contests of intense stick fights, and severe pain forced the loser to run away. As he ran, blood could drip, but he would never cry, as this would portray him as a child, a woman, or a feeble old man. To minimize casualties, many wore layers upon layers of cloths, including caps to cover their ears. It was better to endure the tropical heat than the whip. When courage without reason led me to join the Alapansapa, I was unable to endure the street fight for more than five minutes. My weakness attracted the aggression of many people, who whipped me badly.

An egungun in its own class was the Ololu, based in a lineage about a mile from us. It chose its own days and times when no others could compete. Ololu was the personification of patriarchy and fear. Patriarchy because women must never see him. The belief was that any woman who did would die. Over time, even when no one remembered when a woman had actually died, the belief became stronger. When the Ololu moved close to the school, all the women hid their faces on their desks, waiting for us, the proud "men," to tell them when they could rise and look at us again. As Ololu moved from one neighborhood to another, the shout of "Oluoooo" sent women into panic, as they ran inside, even into other people's homes. When classes were over, my friends and I followed the Ololu all over the city, till darkness came. His mask included the skull of a human being, which was the basis of the fear. Ololu himself carried a club, allegedly to kill any woman who came into direct contact with him. The talk in my school was that previously the club had been used, and one could see on it evidence of old and new blood. The children from the Ololu family in our school did not deny the use of the club. They all enjoyed the power and fame that the Ololu gave them, adding more pro-patriarchy stories to our extensive collection.

As the masquerades disappeared in June, yams were harvested in the villages and city farms. A season of cheap and plentiful food followed. Human beings were happy, the ancestors were blessed, and there were resources to show generosity, sponsor wedding ceremonies, and announce successes. Many people suddenly became beautiful, not because of their possessions but because of their entertainments. Students joined in, celebrating with adults while retaining their own spaces. My school did not have a long summer break, since the school year was divided into three terms of equal parts, thus allowing us to have more moments to celebrate and blend into various seasons.

Ibadan had more Muslims than Christians. The lineages included a blend of all religions. Indeed, there were even extreme allegiances, as in my own case. My mother's father was a Christian; my mother's mother was a Muslim. The Christian and the Muslim grandparents, after unfulfilled prayers based on the Bible and the Quran, ran to Sango, who delivered, and with the sanctions that one would expect. I attended the three major Islamic ceremonies: the Id-el-Kabir, when a ram had to be slaughtered to give praise to Allah and atone for sins; the Id-el-Maulud to mark the birth of the Prophet Mohammad; and the Id-el-Fitri to mark the end of the Ramadan. The Muslims shifted their own festivals more regularly than others, waiting for the moon to give them the signals to begin and end. Christians would joke that Muslims had no respect for any particular month, by which they meant in the Gregorian calendar. But they had their own specific month in the hijrah calendar, known only to a few, based on lunar calculations. If you insisted on knowing when, you would get only a rough guide: the Id-el-Fitri came after at least twenty-nine days of fasting (it could never be twenty-eight days), and Id-el-Kabir was the day following the day of the climbing of Mount Arafat during the hajj. The wait for the moon became part of the fun of the celebrations.

Other than the Muslims in Sabo, a quarter inhabited by Hausa from

Northern Nigeria, Muslims were not separated from mainstream culture. Christians knew not to tempt them with pork, and everybody agreed to eat only the cows slaughtered in the Islamic way, with short ritual prayers before the knife was used. Quranic schools were many, within walking distance for anyone who wanted to receive an Islamic education. Some girls and boys in my school attended Quranic schools in addition, and they always complained that it cut down on the time they had to play. On the few occasions when I spent vacation days with my mother's mom, she sent me to a Quranic school as well, not because she sought my conversion but primarily to minimize the excessive time I devoted to play.

My greatest love for Islam came during the Ramadan fasting period, when for thirty days they had to abstain from food, drink, and sex during daylight hours. Not that I fasted. Never! Indeed, free food was everywhere to be had, so the end of Ramadan brought sadness to my friends and me. Boys who had been forced to fast would come to our house to secretly break the fast, as we all joked that only the unwise suffer from the hardship of a fast. My real pleasure came from drumming and singing the *were* songs in the early hours of the morning. *Were* was primarily meant to wake people, to remind them to fast, and to entertain them as they prepared and enjoyed their breakfast. Less organized than choral music, *were* later evolved into a respectable genre in the 1980s, transformed into *fuji* now globalized by Sikiru Ayinde Barrister and Alhaji Kollington Ayinla. Both Ayinde and Ayinla started their musical careers as I did, only while I went to school they continued to sing and improve until they became superstars and extremely wealthy. It never occurred to anyone in our makeshift band to turn professional.

Were was youth music par excellence. A band of four could acquire fame with an excellent lead singer, one drummer, and gongs. When my group was unable to steal the school instruments, we used gongs, beer bottles, even buckets until we could purchase our instruments. The leading *were* bands even organized serious competitions, but this was more to encourage conversion to Islam than to attain musical excellence. I infused *were* with Christian hymns and traditional poetry. I could compose songs very quickly, and I was actually trusted to compose new ones, and join in the chorus, in addition to my playing a variety of musical instruments. Because we had limited time to practice, the lead singer did most of the singing, while others invented the choruses. The boys were so talented that they could sing along, add their own lines, immediately create follow-up verses, and take over when someone was tired. Everyone could sing, and the failure of a person to show up at the appointed time and venue did not mean much. Even latecomers knew to run and join the others, blending perfectly well within seconds.

Were is an eclectic genre, a combination of storytelling, morality tales, praise singing, and devotional songs in very long chants. We were capable of short songs, but the talented songwriter must be a master of words. Spontaneity was critical, as songs must change quickly to reflect changing circumstances. Within a space of five minutes, one might have to praise the poor and the rich, the tall and the short. *Were* could be nasty as well, a brutal condemnation of the miserly. We defined the misers in our own way—those who did not give us money or food. Our lampoon was very direct, as we would stand in front of the miser's house and sing bad lines about him. When we had no other theme, we simply praised ourselves.

I still remember many of the songs I created that made the night rounds, although the translations do not show the play on words, the powerful similes and metaphors. I could create lengthy songs of praise, drawing from traditional sources.

> Here are the kings of the night
> The singing birds
> The kings of music
> The master voices
> We can sing all night for a year
> The bank of our songs is full
> Who can compete with us?
> Is there any food that is superior to the pounded yam?
> What can be sweeter than honey?
> Have you heard any music better than this?
>
> We sing for all
> For the rich and poor
> Young and old
> The blind and the deaf
> Even the ungrateful are not denied
> Look through your windows
> To see the glories of the early morning
> We are for you to appreciate, to glorify
> We have the voice, the words, listen.
>
> When we sing, our energies are full
> Our fingers are fast with the strings
> Our songs are daily dishes, fresher than your vegetables

Our talents have no match
Songs as young as the singers
Chorus sweeter than the best honey.

We are not the shrubs that a river can wash away
With songs we can befriend the sea, placate the lagoon
And for speaking the truth
We expect no persecution.

My praise of the generous was abundant, exaggerated.

The success of the famous rubs on others
Thou hath kind, open-minded, helpful
Stay with Allah
The Prophet will carry His benefits to your house
May you live long
Older than rocks.

You are the prince of the world
The darling of the universe
The big spender knows what he is after
You are generous, you are wise
As you give us, so do you get more
As you feed us, so does your barn increase
The generous one, you are not careless
More blessings will come your way.

The generous do not suffer
If they stumble in December they rise in January
We can seal the mouths of your enemies with tape
We carry a rope to tie them to a tree
For the hyenas to find and eat
The enemy's meat is a delicacy for the wild animals
What is bad luck for someone else is good luck for you.

Money is no disease
Money shoots better than guns
Money is sharper than a sword
You can feast and be rich
Just remember us, your humble followers.

Those not generous to us should expect condemnation.

Your eyes may change their location to the back of your head
Your mouth stays the same, but the jaws will not open

The throat will wage a war with your tongue to destroy your stomach
Your enemy will receive commendation from your friends
Only the music of frogs do you deserve
The music without knowledge, lacking wisdom.

We will not curse the miserly
Only to say that your goals should be far away from you
Contentment may live in another land
Your influence may reside in the sea
We will not insult you either
Only to say that you will use both feet to test the depth of the river
Buried before your death.

We had to praise God, encourage religious devotion, and preach the virtues of good living.

Praise Allah, you devout ones
God creates only those He is capable of destroying
Devote your life to Momodu
If you want to prosper
The stream does not compete with the sea
May Allah not regard you as an enemy.

Expect nothing bad to happen
Allah and Momodu are solidly behind you
Have your fingers ever missed putting food in your mouth?
Has the death of God ever been announced to you?
Have you ever been told that the Angel Gabriel is ill?

Doubt not Allah
Heed the warnings of the Prophet
The last of the prophets
The messenger of God who wears the crown
Fear Allah
The forest that hides you must not be called a jungle.

Be good, be just
Ignore evil and its perpetrators
Be just, be good
If only because of the day of judgment
Promote peace
Promote order
The world is fragile
You can break it with bad manners.

What Allah wants to repair, no man can damage
What Allah wants to damage, no man can repair
Whoever is cursed by God
Cannot be saved by the Prophet
No power surpasses that of Allah.

Adult singing groups were territorial. They wanted to dominate the areas populated by people with money and move speedily to the houses of the wealthy. They could not win with better songs. Rather, they preferred the use of physical force. A night before their arrival, we would receive messages to avoid certain streets. Singing was not like mourning—if we disregarded the threat, the music would expose our location. You cannot light a fire when in hiding. Clashes were not uncommon, as we turned musical instruments, except for bottles, into fighting tools. We never could win the physical fights, and we turned to songs to insult adult groups. When we met, we crossed to the other side of the road to engage in musical competition. As we sang, they replied with their own songs. All knew that not to move on was to lose cash. Conflict was always good for songs, providing the motivation for the use of insulting language.

Age is useless
The voice changes to that of the toad
The fingers only bring out bad beats
They cannot change their dead voices, alter the rhythms
Where is the sugar in your voice?
When we get to your age
We will carry with it our youth and voice
And we will have too much money
As the young play music for us.

The hawk plays with the pigeon
The pigeon is happy, but he is playing with death
We can run faster, sing better
We cannot run out of talents
The carpenter is not working on our coffins.

Witches will pursue you
Driving you to the hands of the sorcerers
On the day that someone needs a human skull for charms
Your head becomes the powder
Swallowed with rainwater into the stomach of the wicked
Later excreta in a pit.

Compare us not with mediocres
Banana and plantain are not the same
Catfish and whales are no kin
Cat, lion, and tiger may look alike
But know the one to befriend
We have no big fists but big mouths
Our wisdom does not lie in killing
But in saving, singing, talking.

The pot boasts about holding too much water
Can it compare to a stream?
The stream glories in holding water
Is the stream a river?
The river and its goddesses
All will be swallowed by the sea
We are the two antelopes that beat a big one
Without the elephant in the jungle, the buffalo becomes a big animal.

As we headed back home to end the performance and allow people to nap after their Ramadan breakfast, we closed by praising ourselves, singing faster than you could ever hope to read the lines, shouting louder, beating the instruments with more intensity, and announcing that we would return the next day with new songs. We turned more creative, as we were now playing for ourselves, not for small cash.

We are the desirable fruits and vegetables
But you cannot eat us this morning
We are the velvet fabric that no tailor can shame
If you cause a war, we will not serve as soldiers
Do not compare us to those other bands
We are the train that can never bow to a car
The elephants that cannot be stopped by vines
We will grow faster than you think
If we cannot add to our age too quickly
We can add to our songs, to our wallets.

We had already added to our wallets, and we had to share the donations and gifts before we parted ways. We always split by numbers. The boys with the talking drums wanted more, claiming that they were the most talented and without them the songs had no "sugar." We always yielded, as even the best singers knew that without the drummers *were* could not be performed. We also had to subsidize the purchase of drums that they just wanted to use for thirty days before we parted ways. Without the creative use of instruments, a song became a poem that no one wanted to listen to at 4:00 A.M. There were solo poets moving about at the same time, but no one paid much attention to them.

December came too quickly. In enjoying all the various seasons, playing soccer and using the rest of the time for school, one did not know that time flew so quickly. December brought more rice to the table, new shoes, new clothes, and elaborate events to end the school year. It was time to memorize new plays at school and to volunteer for the choir in the church. The brain could hold a lot. Adults enjoyed Christmas Eve more than I did, as I had to stay in church till midnight. As we walked back home, I would envy those who were congregating for all-night parties. In areas with nightclubs and drinking places, usually those in the new city, they were usually packed full. Another service followed on Christmas Day itself. Large pots were needed to make the large meals that were distributed to friends, neighbors, and relations. We dressed in new clothes, which we soiled as we enjoyed excessive meals. As we carried trays of food to give to others, we collected small cash gifts. More fun followed on Boxing Day, as people trooped to the zoo and amusement places or simply wandered about on the streets, playing with peers. A week later the events were repeated to mark the beginning of the new year but without the gift of clothes. Christian families who did not entertain at Christmas chose the religiously neutral first day of January to bring together families and friends.

My city created religious harmony and balance, providing pleasures at creatively spaced moments. It balanced the interests of the genders: Okebadan was a goddess, giving power to women; Ololu was a god, giving power to men. Sango was a masculine god, but his wife Oya was equally powerful, and the cult of Omi also represented women's interests. Islamic and Christian ceremonies cut across age and gender lines. Even the world of the living was united with those of the dead, with the *egungun*, "the spirit of the ancestor," providing powerful lines of communication. As one moved away from Ibadan, in space and time, things became different, with new forms of pleasure making the old appear like living in heaven. A time came when I could no longer watch the masquerades. The carnival in March has been replaced with silence in an age of political correctness. Ramadan blues have been turned into different, alert colors to terrorize a frightened public. The rice and clothes of

December now have to be purchased in November to prepare the way for battles with the powerful cults of credit cards that demand their sacrifices in January.

Ten kings, ten seasons
Time does not walk in a straight line
Today's wisdom rots
Turning into "yesterday's madness"
Eras come and go
The best clothes will one day turn into rags
A future without December will surely come
What one hopes for is better than what one has.

CHAPTER TEN : : : THE PASTOR'S ORDEAL

"want you to follow me to Chief Akinloye's house to tell him what you saw" was not put as a proposal to be negotiated but a definitive instruction given by my grandfather one Saturday morning in 1965. I knew what he meant: the encounter between the chief, the police, and the poor tenant farmer at Elepo. I said nothing, just following him as he directed. We stayed at the side of the street waiting for a cab. One did not call a cab with a telephone. The cabs drove around the city waiting for passengers to flag them down. As a cab slowed down, one shouted the name of the intended destination. Once the driver heard, he either stopped or drove off, without words being exchanged. We did not wait long. My grandfather sat in front, the prestige location in a taxi, and I occupied the back seat, which was to be shared with others, usually complete strangers. It was then that I noticed that I was wearing shoes of different colors and sizes. As I hurried to follow my grandfather, I had not even paid attention to my shoes or clothes.

We arrived at the sprawling residence of the chief at Oje, a huge place. People milled around, in front, inside, everywhere. Akinloye was an attorney and a prominent politician. He had served on the city council and was one of the country's pioneer politicians. He had by then become both famous and notorious. No one could anticipate even then that he would live long and gain even more fame, rising to become one of the country's most powerful politicians. The peak of his glory was in the late 1970s when he became the chairman of the National Party of Nigeria, which controlled the federal government until the coup of 1983 sent him into exile in the United Kingdom, where he lived for many years before returning to Nigeria to a hero's welcome by his loyalist followers and political allies. His fortune was incalculable; his gift for deception was legendary; and his ability to foment intrigue was matchless. A master politician, his colleagues spoke of him in awe.

Pasitor and I sat in his waiting room for about six hours. On three occasions, Pasitor went outside to get me snacks of roasted plantain and peanuts. I was bored to death, but I could not complain. I fell asleep many times. I did not know the purpose of my mission. Then Chief Akinloye gave the signal that he would be appearing shortly from his living room, whose location I did not know. I had no knowledge of how it worked, but the signal came from outside the house itself. Drummers and poets began to praise the chief's name, outbidding one another to receive his attention. One poet called him *ekun* (tiger), and the drummers appealed to him to walk slowly, as the wealthy must move with calculated steps. When he approached, I recognized him, as he was a prominent member of my church. The singers became louder, assuring him that the day would be glorious, that there was no danger ahead, and that no one in the city was greater than he.

Now impatient, Pasitor stood up and said that he had been waiting all day to see him. Chief Akinloye betrayed no emotion, and he did not apologize.

"What for?" the chief asked. Pasitor said that it was about his friend, the Elepo chief, and what he had done to the tenant farmer. "I brought my little boy to tell you what he saw."

"It is not necessary to listen to your little boy," said Chief Akinloye. He told Pasitor that he had read the Bible inside out and it was full of wars, kidnapping, slave raiding, wife taking, and land grabbing. There was nothing unusual in what had happened to the poor man at Elepo, Chief Akinloye said, as he adjusted his flowing gown.

"The landowner said that he needed his land back; what is wrong with that?" Pasitor did not answer. "In any case," continued the chief, "the man was discovered to be a criminal." It was this statement that annoyed Pasitor, who now decided to speak.

"No, he was framed. The man and his wife are two godly people."

Chief Akinloye interrupted, saying that all criminals at the Agodi prison said the same thing. "No one ever admits to doing something wrong. I am a lawyer." He was now walking to his car, and the praise singing was drowning out the voices. Others needed his attention, and he also had to issue a series of instructions to a large number of staff persons. Pasitor and I could only get one more statement out of Chief Akinloye.

"Pastor Elepo, this matter is for your *mogaji*, not me." Akinloye's mouth was filled with a razor, and it could only spit blood. The *mogaji* was the head of a lineage at Ibadan, but his power extended to the village as well. In a complicated political system, each village was tied to a chief in the city, who served as its supervisor and represented its interests in meetings with fellow chiefs and the king. While villages had their head chiefs, the large majority of them were denied direct access to the king, the traditional basis of power, and they had almost no contact with the premier and governor, the modern bases of power. The *mogaji* who headed a lineage compound at Ibadan could also double as the head of a village or he could allow the village to have a separate head while the *mogaji* served as his boss. Pasitor knew this power structure, and Chief Akinloye was telling him nothing new, only giving him the coded response that he did not want to help. There could be no doubt that Pasitor knew the *mogaji*, as all villagers did, but by going to Chief Akinloye he was probably thinking that intelligent enemies are better than stupid friends.

If the bull has decided to throw you, it is better to lie down. Pasitor said that we should go home. Akinloye was not ready to assist, and Pasitor was quick to lend credence to the statement that it is better to travel alone than with a bad companion. He probably did not have the money for another cab, and we had to walk more than ten miles back home. I knew the roads all too well, and this was certainly not a case of "he who is being carried does not realize how far the town is." This was not a long walk, by the standard of what my schoolmates and I had undertaken, and I knew the route from Akinloye's house to ours. The Pasitor was taking us by the longest route.

"Why are we not taking the corners?" I asked. *Corners* had acquired the meaning of a shortcut through the compounds, usually shorter than the tarred roads. Pasitor said that shortcuts were good but not on that day. He explained that the *ona moto* (roads plied by vehicles), as the Yoruba called the tarred roads, were safer, as everyone could see pedestrians. All one had to worry about was avoiding cars and motorcycles. Taking "corners," one could be hit by human beings. It took a while for me to figure out that he was saying that the danger posed by pursuers was greater than that of a car accident. He added more statements about corners, saying that the longest route might require more time, but one must pay attention to what one saw. There were many more things to see on the longest route, he said, but the eyes must work well. On the shortest road, as Pasitor explained to me, the brain was asking the legs to be more efficient than the eyes.

Then the discussion changed to why he had asked me to follow him. "Children of your age are believable." I was surprised that he did not coach me about what to say. Even my classmates would practice our statements to the schoolteachers, and we had a long list of excuses to make each time we stayed away from home for too long without an explanation. To Pasitor, only those who had things to hide coached children and witnesses about what to say.

Pasitor did not head home, as I thought he would. We went to another chief, not far from our house. Chief Ajibola was a pioneer politician like Akinloye. Their careers were similar in some ways, as both had served as ministers and abandoned their original political party for another one. When they changed parties, they lost popular appeal, which they never regained, and they became associated with the politics of prebendalism and violence. As we entered Chief Ajibola's house, which was smaller than the one we had just left, we saw a large number of people drinking and eating. I was hungry and was happy when food was offered. Only a fool remains thirsty in the midst of water. Before I could take the food, Pasitor asked them to ignore me, that I had just eaten and that I liked food too much. This was the first lie that Pasitor would tell, and I was annoyed that it was about me. I had not had any major meal for hours, following him on a mission I hardly understood.

We were lucky. Chief Ajibola was home, and there were only five guests ahead of us. Chief Ajibola kept court, and visitors came and went, even when he was not home. More people arrived, and there were food and drinks for them to consume, served by three maids. I asked Pasitor whether Chief Ajibola was celebrating a wedding or naming ceremony, and he said no. "This is normal," Pasitor said, without elaborating, perhaps because others were listening to the conversation. Again he asked me not to eat or drink.

When it was our turn to speak, Pasitor narrated a story that I knew: the case of the tenant farmer driven out of Elepo by his landlord, a well-known chief. It was then that I learned the farmer's real name, as Pasitor kept referring to him as Jakobu, a Yoruba way of pronouncing Jacob. I had previously known him as Baba Laolu, a name associated with his son. "We never thought that driving him out of the village was even a small matter until we heard that he was arrested for smoking marijuana and planting it on his farm," said Pasitor, describing this as "iro nla, iro nla"—a very big lie. Pasitor told Chief Ajibola that I was there to corroborate the story, as he signaled me to step forward to tell my story.

"It started on Sunday before church," I began my story. I had not spoken a second sentence when a woman entered the living room carrying a big bag. Apparently, no one had stopped her or asked her to stay in the reception room. Ignoring Pasitor, myself, and others in the room, she sat next to Chief Ajibola and took over the conversation. It was all about new clothes that she had procured for the chief to make the man happy. When people saw the chief in this attire, she boasted, they would know how important he was and why he was second to none in the entire Western Region. Adding a little bit of drama, she said that many would mistake the chief for the governor and premier, and she hoped that the other chiefs in the land would not be jealous. She opened the bag and brought out three or four flowing gowns made of imported fabric, describing each, its worth, scarcity, quality, and durability. All were *alogbo*, that is, for lifetime use. As if the woman had recruited supporters, everybody in the room except Pasitor and myself endorsed her statement, some saying that the clothes would look good on the chief, making "his body cool" and attractive even to younger women. Chief Ajibola appeared elated. The woman kept talking, praising the chief, identifying all the good things about the clothes. I have heard that with wealth a man can win a woman, but it was new to me that with clothes to sell a woman can win a man. And no one told the chief that one who wears beautiful clothes all the time ends up in rags.

I was waiting to narrate my experience. Chief Ajibola stopped me, changing the topic, asking me questions about my school. "If you do well, you will one day become like us, enjoying life. Do well, you hear?" I said, "Yes, sir." As if the chief believed in the adage that an extensive discussion means a conflict, he turned to Pasitor, saying that he had listened to his entire story, but he was sad that a man of his age, profession, and experience would come to his house to say that a fellow chief and the government were telling a lie about a commoner in a small village. Pasitor got the message: he who runs from the white ant may stumble upon the stinging ant.

When we left the place, I was the first to speak. "Chief Ajibola wanted me to pass my exam and enjoy life. This was good talk." Pasitor said *o ti o* (no) many times, perhaps more than seven. I was not counting, but he said *o ti o* times without number. I must have become the one-eyed man who thanks God only when he sees a man who is fully blind.

"God will let you do well, but God will not let you become like those chiefs," Pasitor prayed for me. This is not a prayer that one can ever forget, as it contains both a prayer and a curse. Many people wanted to become chiefs. Even at school, my classmates were envious of those who played the roles of kings, chiefs, and queens in the school dramas. When boys were asked to play the roles of messengers, slaves, or criminals, many refused to tell their parents when we were going to stage a public performance. Parents, too, would complain to the teachers and the headmaster. "Why couldn't my son be a governor?" one angry mother once asked Mrs. Balogun, my schoolteacher. The teacher, a member of the same church as the angry mother, failed to convince the woman that this was acting, that we were just doing it for entertainment. "It is in lies that truth resides," the woman said, warning the teacher to stop cursing her son. If there must be a messenger in a play, she advised the teacher to look for another student or the teacher herself could volunteer for it. As if cursing Mrs. Balogun or praying that evil would befall the teacher's own child, the woman ended angrily, "Ashes fly back into the face of the one who throws them." She who does not mend her clothes ends up with none: the teacher dropped the woman's son, and the headmaster charged him with controlling the crowd. Thanks to a good mother, the son had moved from messenger to police officer!

"What is wrong with the chief?" I asked Pasitor, but more likely in a question longer than this. Pasitor started by saying that I should never eat anybody's food or accept anybody's drink unless I know the sources of the money used to purchase them. *Atenuje* can kill, it destroys the body, he said. He who lives with an ass will make noise like an ass. I know what *atenuje* means in Yoruba, and I have never been able to translate it into English. It contains an element of greed, a careless desire to consume at the earliest opportunity. *Atenuje* can also mean a person whose soul and conscience can be purchased. I even heard from another source that a man so afflicted would follow his wife to the house of her concubine; as the wife was having sex with her boyfriend, the man would be content with good food and cold beer. As he heard the sounds of sex, all that was needed to make him happy was to be served with additional chicken and cold beer. As he followed the wife home, all the sex-fulfilled wife had to do to calm the husband down was to buy snacks for him to eat along the way. As long as he fills his tummy, more men can have sex with his wife. One may start as a fool and become wise through experience, but *atenuje* prevents the accumulation of wisdom: as the man eats, he does not see the experience that will end his folly. Wisdom may be like the mushrooms that arrive after one has finished eating, but the man afflicted with the disease of *atenuje* never stops eating.

According to Pasitor, the chiefs were entertaining themselves and others with monies meant for villagers and poor people. "You saw the clothes that woman brought," said Pasitor. "They will be purchased with our money, government money. All the chiefs live like this," he added. He told me that they used "small change" (small amounts) to buy food and drinks for fools to consume, praising those whom they should be avoiding. This was new to me. Chiefs collected tribute in yams, goats, and small amounts of cash. Everyone knew this elementary rule from history books. Chiefs were strong, and they fought hard to obtain and hold the land from which the tribute came. This, too, was pretty clear. Tribute for security was not robbery, not connected to the *atenuje* that Pasitor was telling me about. Kola, my relation at home, was a descendant of the great Ajobo warlord. Indeed, Kola's last name was Ajobo, which everyone at school and in the city recognized as a great name. His ancestor was one of the most famous chiefs of the nineteenth century, and his fame made it to our classroom. A strong and warlike general, Ajobo was one of the key figures in the massive expansion of the Ibadan Empire. He no doubt had multiple personalities, as he was both ruthless and generous. He was ruthless abroad in fighting his wars. Back home he was generous, and he became one of the most legendary hosts of his time. Even the visiting missionaries described his generosity in glowing terms. People went to his house to eat and drink, and he never asked them for anything in return.

Pasitor was telling me that Akinloye and Ajibola were not like Ajobo but some other kind of person strange to me. I must have been confusing all the old chiefs in the schoolbooks with the new ones whose names we heard every day on the radio and whom we saw on the television. The little African history that I knew back then, in addition to the extensive Yoruba culture that was already part of me, indicated that sheer success and charisma were needed to become socially mobile. To stabilize one's position if one had climbed to the top, one needed a good character for interpersonal relations. To transfer the status and the wealth that came with it to the next generation, one needed the gods. Ajobo and his contemporaries had to build their fortunes slowly, over time. Ajobo was a warrior, which enabled him to tap into war booty. But the main sources of income for many of the chiefs of old were their farms and their trade. They had to figure out where they would obtain the labor to till extensive lands. They could produce children rapidly, like termites, and they drew additional labor from relations, slaves, and pawns.

I think the point about food interested me more than Pasitor's mission. I asked him whether beggars and poor people were also guilty of *atenuje*. Pasitor's answer was loud and clear: "Yes." Poverty did not mean that one had no right to assert rights and demand respect, only *atenuje* would not allow it. Anyone who was poor, said Pasitor, could stay in the village for the rest of his life, where the land would feed him. It was better to beg the land than the chief for food. To beg the chiefs was to turn poverty into slavery. "The land betrays no one," said Pasitor. "Only man betrays the land and suffers." He told me that many of those I saw milling around in the houses of the two chiefs were betraying the land, running to *awon eniyan lasan lasan* (useless folks) to beg for bananas that the land would give them for free. "Poverty is no illness," continued Pasitor. The sick could go to a diviner but not to obtain the medicine to fill a hungry stomach.

It was clear that no chief was willing to help Jakobu. I myself knew it, and I could see the frustration that Pasitor was experiencing, although I could not estimate the extent of his agony, his anger. Several times, he said to me and others, "Won so mi domode" (They turned me into a child). I knew what this meant, since I, too, had used it when I had problems with my peers. The image of a child was ambiguous. Children like me were regarded as innocent, which was why Pasitor had asked me to follow him to the chiefs to narrate my stories without the need to coach me. If he did not tell me what to say, the description of my experience would be raw, lacking any interpretation that adults would have added to it. It was dangerous, since I could also include what others had said or done, except that Pasitor had done nothing wrong. Pasitor's complaint of being turned into a child was about how the chiefs had ignored him, trivialized his mission, and wasted his time. The chiefs had turned Pasitor into a fool. Pasitor had seen two chiefs in a day, and nothing had happened; the sheep of a fool breaks loose more than once.

Pasitor was equally mocked by others for his approach. "Why report one evil man to another evil man?" was a question posed to him by a few people in my presence. As one of them elaborated, one of the chiefs he took the matter to had made a fortune selling other people's land. He could sell a plot of land to ten people within a week. As each person complained to him, the chief asked the buyer to fight the nine others if he truly valued the land. He would even serve as the buyer's attorney. At the same time, the chief would be negotiating with an eleventh person. A chief with training in law could turn it into a big advantage, taking other people's farms and land, using the language of law to cheat. Land with rich soil suitable for cultivating cocoa was pounced on by chiefs, who used the powers of literacy and government to dispossess the innocent of their most valuable possession. Pasitor was indeed reporting a thief to a thief.

Pasitor had exposed me to power structures rather early. His statements stayed with me for many years after his death. The meanings came too slowly for me to analyze. Even the notes in the margins of his Bible, which I inherited—the most valuable "gift" that he gave to anyone—I have not been fully able to interpret. His handwriting is legible, but his expressions are difficult to decipher. By taking me along with him to the households of the chiefs, Pasitor introduced me to the hierarchies of power in a modern society, although this was not his original intention. He also inadvertently gave me the voice of a narrator. I wish I could be a neutral narrator, balancing all the various interests. What happened to Pasitor, Jakobu, and others ensured that I would only take the side of the poor, not the chiefs. I could understand why the chiefs did what they did, but I could not justify accusing a poor man of planting marijuana just to destroy him and coerce an entire village into submission.

As my understanding emerged slowly, I realized that modern chiefs such as Akinloye and Ajibola not only profited from the traditional sources of power but added education and state power to their credentials, thus making them far more powerful than Ajobo. They carried traditional privileges forward and added newer ones to create a more impressive impact on the landscape. Grandiose houses and conspicuous consumption were there for me to see. A powerful chief needed two legs in government to be able to divert public money to private wallets. Stealing money was quick, much faster than waiting for yams and corn to grow, as Ajobo did on his extensive farms. Once they stole money, they could invest in houses, buy peasants out of their lands, create lucrative businesses for their wives, and use their extensive resources to purchase additional honors by way of titles.

Irrespective of the occupation of a chief, nothing was more important than serving in government. Chief Omololu Olunloyo—a professor of mathematics, a city mate, and an acquaintance—once told me, as the governor of my state, that there was so much available to steal that it takes only a day to steal what one needs for a lifetime. Olunloyo's complaint was that fellow politicians took many more days than one to steal. Never shy of speaking his mind, even in language that would offend his critics, Olunloyo pondered, "Why not steal for one day and use the rest to work for the people?"

No! They needed to steal for twenty-nine days and work for the people for one day. Those who had no wages to live on could go to the houses of chiefs for free food. Those who were angry would be taught the lesson of "power" in various ways. Power, in its raw essence, meant the use of force to obtain compliance, not necessarily the more positive spin that the dictionary puts on it with a stress on legitimacy. The chiefs were smart enough to affirm the traditional basis of power over land and people. But they were even smarter to accept the British idea that power could be obtained through the ballot box. All this small box required was that one be a member of a political party and able to rig an election. Olunloyo rigged an election to become a state governor, aided in part by Akinloye. They both knew this, and Olunloyo would be the last to deny it. When party members pressured him to appoint a fellow city politician to his cabinet, he refused, threatening to reveal to the public how all of them had obtained power.

The translation of *power, ase,* connotes a sort of mystery. *Ase* can mean "amen" as well as a ritualistic yes that can never be converted to a secular no. Olunloyo was an *alase*, someone who possessed the supernatural embodiment of amen and yes. The traditional symbolism of crown and staff that gave the king the voice of the gods was inherited by the modern chiefs. The modern chiefs did not have to pretend that they were agents of the gods, as the kings of old did. The traditional kings preferred to be ranked immediately below the gods, and their people actually referred to them as such. The modern chiefs were agents of the government. Alas! The government was far more powerful than the gods. Regular sacrifices were all that it took to placate the gods. If one god disappointed, one could go to another. Even as powerful as Esu was, he could be neutralized with an appeal to Sango. With the government, it took plenty of taxes, far more than the amounts demanded by all the gods combined. The gods wanted palm oil and kola nuts; the government wanted only cash. When one offered a goat to a god, all that was left for the god was the blood. Even the powerful Ogun, the god of iron, would simply lick the blood and let you take the goat home to cook and entertain your friends. The government took the goat and the blood and asked you to clean up the blood, prepare the goat, cook the meals, smell the aroma, and leave. Tax money made cash flow from the pockets of poor farmers to the wallets of rich chiefs. The collector, the evil intermediary, the real satanic god, was the chief.

Satan was powerful, hard to subdue. Even Pasitor recognized this. All his prayers were always about the conquest of Satan. "When will Satan die?" I once asked him, not as a joke but as a serious question. Pasitor replied, "When Jesus returns to the world." He was unable to tell me the precise time when his Lord would revisit the earth that had sent him to heaven in the first place, but it was clear to me that Satan would be here for a long time. Pasitor saw Satan as an invisible force, but I saw him as a visible energy, manifested in chiefs and the agents of government. Due to Jakobu's experience, my resentment of power grew out of proportion. Even when close friends and allies become ministers or college presidents, while I do not sever the friendship, I reduce interaction to the barest minimum, refusing to stay too long in their houses or eat their meals. No one has ever succeeded in persuading me to accept any position of power, even the most accessible one of chair of a department. Whether because people know that I will reject them or because circumstances force them to approach me, I have been offered positions too numerous to count. Even the governor of my state once told me that he would fund me to run after his term ended, though, as he said jokingly, just to "clean up the mess that he and his bad friends would create."

Having acquired the *ase*, the chief treated Jakobu with the full force of its symbolic and secular essence. No one denied that he was a chief when he came to the village, even requesting a chair to use to insult his hosts. This was the *ase* of the past. He came with the police, the *ase* of the present. Pasitor took me with him to seek help from other chiefs, recognizing their *ase*. Pasitor never queried this *ase*, he only said that the exercise of it should be just and there was no need to lie.

Satan does not have to lie. Even in my school when someone stole a pencil he swore that he did not do it, using the name of Jesus Christ. The humble Jesus, so humble that he voluntarily allowed himself to be led to a cross. None of my schoolmates dared to swear by the mighty name of Satan: "If I stole the pencil, may Satan kill me." Only a suicidal person would say this. Even to try it with Esu was to fail the next exam; Ogun would immediately strike with a car accident, and Sango would send the powerful thunder to crush the house. Satan was very powerful, and he did not have to lie to fool anyone.

The chiefs and the government, as the visible Satan, did not have to lie either. The kings and chiefs of old were clever in justifying their power by attributing its source to mysterious agencies. The kings covered their faces with beads, their heads with crowns, their feet with shoes made of ostrich feathers, and the rest of their bodies with regalia. As they lived in huge palaces, the majority of the public could not easily see them. Kings were not masquerades, although they could appear as such. The new chiefs that I saw did not wear crowns. Indeed, they wanted people to visit them. As they acquired more power and money, people waited in their houses for twenty-four hours and retinues of beggars lined their "frontages." The chiefs loved the beggars, making rounds to give them money, not even bothering to say "amen" to their repetitive prayers. Why would a poor beggar pray for a rich man?

The chief needed the beggars, not their useless prayers. The chief needed the visitors, and he knew that daily feasts would bring more people. The chief did not like his guests, the beggars, the poor, the string of visitors; the chief was only sending a message to fellow chiefs that he had more support than they had. In a traditional setting, the numbers would have been useful on the chief's farms to produce food to feed the crowd in the city. Slaves and pawns in faraway villages worked to maintain city chiefs and their large retinues. The modern chief retained the followers but changed the economic basis of support from farms to government coffers.

All chiefs needed to practice the politics of numbers: how many people could they mobilize in a short time? But they also had to manipulate the culture of numbers. Ajobo, in becoming successful in the traditional milieu, was guided by an entrenched philosophy, that the ultimate success was to be known by at least "two hundred people." Once a person attained this, he became a *gbajumo*, which means that one can count as friends and allies "two hundred people." The figure was derived from a literal translation of the concept, but it meant the same thing in real life: one is known to hundreds of people. I know "two hundred people"; at least I had coordinated a university course of more than three thousand people, all of whom knew me. But my own numbers were useless, as I could not show them to others, I could not buy drinks and food for them, and they would not fight for me. What the chief did with his numbers was use them to justify his power, perpetuate the belief in a man with inexhaustible fortune and wealth with which to display generosity, hint to opponents that he could build an ad hoc army on short notice, and show that if issues of development came to the table he had people who wanted to help or seek benefits.

Only a fool would think that the chief was wasting his money on the two hundred people or was merely dependent on the food he offered to maintain his power and prestige. When the chief went to Elepo, he did not go with rice and fish but with a lorry load of policemen. The villagers did not have to read Gramsci's *Prison Notebooks* to understand what was going on; only their successors, like Toyin, needed this kind of information in order to come across as serious and intelligent. As far as the villagers were concerned, the chief had simply used his power once again. They actually credited him with having that power, but only in its satanic dimension: *ipa*. *Ipa* was terrorism but legitimated by the government. *Ipa* was used to disconnect the spiritual dimension of power from its secular application, to exercise force without the rituals of *ase*. *Ipa* assumed that political institutions on their own could deliver without the morality of *ase*, that the *gbajumo* could disregard the voice represented by the two hundred he knew and instead use a smaller number of policemen to maintain order. To use *Ipa* was to affirm that power did not need consensus to be delivered and that the one with power did not have to seek respect.

The chief who went to Elepo was not seeking respect: he combined *ase* and *ipa* to enforce an order narrowly defined around himself. But in defining this narrow interest he called on the agency supported by the two hundred people and their tax money to obey his wishes. As Pasitor took me about to seek a solution, the assembly of two hundred was everywhere we went, eating and showing respect to their chiefs. It was not Pasitor who told me this but some members of the two hundred.

From an alternative perspective, they saw nothing wrong in accepting the food and water offered by the chief. What was wrong, they said, was to develop any serious loyalty to the chief or eat only the food of one chief and reject that of others. According to them, they knew that for the chiefs to use *ipa* was immoral but that this did not necessarily undercut the chiefs' authority or damage their wallets. I have been talking about a time before the military appeared in Nigeria in 1966; the military subsequently redefined the notion of *ipa* in such a way as to permanently damage the people and their psyche. The chiefs were writing the preface to the military: in the new Africa, physical forces overwhelm the spiritual, power is used to develop private estates, and small change from stolen money is sufficient to satisfy the two hundred people.

Now tired, frustrated, and perhaps angry, Pasitor was resigned to the fate that Jakobu would die in prison. No trial had been called, although charges had been made and so-called conclusive evidence had been obtained. Jakobu was at Agodi, a prison, instead of in a police cell. "Don't give up," advised my grandmother, who always had to be forced to speak. Then she came up with what sounded like a bizarre suggestion: "Talk to Leku, Baba Nihinlola, talk to Leku about Jakobu." I heard the statement, but I was unable to process it. Could this be a case of "if a friend hurts or disappoints you, run to your wife"? What did Leku have to do with a man suffering in jail awaiting trial? I did not pose this as a question to anyone; I was just thinking. Then she said that there was a need to try *agbara orun* when *agbara aiye* had failed. I understood the words but not the application of the concept to what Pasitor was trying to achieve. My grandmother had made a distinction between two kinds of power—*agbara orun*, referring to the "power of unseen forces," and *agbara aiye*, referring to the power of chiefs, governments, and lawyers. For the second time, I heard the story of the birth of my mother. Pasitor was reminded that when they tried to have a baby without luck, they had to beg Sango, who used *agbara orun* to help them. The *agbara aiye* would have been sexual activity by the couple and medicine from local doctors. Of course, I knew about spirits and ghosts, and I believed, as my grandmother did, in the reality of these unseen forces. Pasitor himself believed it, which was why he went to Sango. He had also cautioned me to be careful of angering evil people. To Pasitor, the world was merely a trip to a market (*aiye loja*) and heaven was the place to cook the food and rest (*orun nile*). Heaven, he told me many times, could crash to the earth, and what was preventing it was the desire of God. If God became angry, all He had to do was release heaven to fall to earth.

Heaven was not a vacant space. Pasitor told me that heaven's population was far greater than that of the earth. Not only did it contain all the dead people, whose number no one knew as many people died without telling anyone or leaving a trace, but the dead insects and fish that did not make it to the stomach also lived there. Then there were the angels, the spirits, and the ministers of God. Heaven itself had to be managed. The forces that managed heaven were the *agbara orun*, far more powerful than those who managed the earth. To get the picture, compare God to a king. In each person, there is a small representation of *agbara orun*, as in the idea of *ori* that Alhaji and Baba Olopa mentioned to me. Every human being has a head that he carries about, but unknown to him there is a "shadow head." The problem is that the motives and fortunes of the real head and the shadow head may not be the same. If the shadow head is prone to risk and danger, it will destroy the real head, which is prone to stability and peace. Indeed, there was so much fear of this shadow head that it formed a component of Yoruba prayer when I was growing up: "May your shadow head not destroy you."

Pasitor was being advised to invoke *agbara orun*. He started to dig for a fish, but he dug too deep and caught a snake. A man bitten by a snake can become afraid of a lizard. Pasitor had transferred his stomachache to his feet, becoming lame. Probably no details were known to him, since neither he nor his wife were competent in this powerful domain. They surely believed in the idea, but they lacked the means to achieve it. Witches could kill, and I was thinking that they probably knew the address of one who could destroy the Elepo chief. Why not use the *egbe* that those big boys had told me about years earlier to remove Jakobu from his cell? In addition, the Elepo chief could go mad. The charm to turn a sane person into a madman existed; I had been shown the compound of an herbalist who made the most powerful ones in the city. In those years, I believed strongly that the power of the Elepo chief could be destroyed by this *agbara orun*, and I was thinking of many possibilities. No king or governor had the physical power to fight the "heavenly ones." The Ololu could be asked to use his club on men, if only once. If the Ololu refused, other *egungun* could conspire to take the chief with them to their abode in heaven.

Pasitor did not object to the suggestion, and a few others encouraged him in my presence at his city home where the discussion took place. Everybody agreed that the chief was an *ika buruku*, a very wicked person. But there was a voice of dissent, warning Pasitor to tread cautiously. The elderly woman who urged caution did not say that Pasitor should not tap into *agbara orun* but warned him to first understand the basis of the chief's power in its supernatural sense. An *ika* (wicked person) could be dependent on magic and charms or could have the support of evil witches and spirits. In the attempt to fight this kind of *ika*, human beings could become victims in the power play of the unseen forces of evil and goodness. There was no assurance that the forces of goodness would always win. Many diviners had been defeated by the power of witchcraft, failing to save an *abiku*, preventing miscarriage, or failing to detect a small illness that killed a decent man. The process of obtaining evil and good power sounded the same to me. One could be initiated into both. Some people were automatically good, like the kings initiated into cults to give them power, to turn them into gods after their death. The witches, who demanded respect, could be both good and evil.

Pasitor took the advice, but he chose not to go to Leku, as his wife had advised him, but to a very powerful male-dominated secret cult: the Ogboni. I did not know why he chose this option, and I will never know. I could have found out, but I didn't try early enough. When I asked my grandmother in the 1980s, she said that two-thirds of what her late husband did was unknown to her. Also I did not know all the steps that Pasitor took to reach this cult. I followed him once, and I saw what happened. The Ogboni were very widely feared. No one in my day knew much about them other than the fear associated with the cult. Indeed, we had to whisper when speaking about witches and members of the Ogboni cult. I could recognize those who belonged to the old Ogboni cult invented by the Yoruba themselves but only when they used the public symbols associated with secret societies.

The Ogboni's esoteric nature meant that it did not enter the pages of many books and school dramas. The old Ogboni cult of the Yoruba was discussed as part of indigenous political systems. The discussion tended to be subtle and positive, presenting the Ogboni as a cult of elders and chiefs. I came to understand it as an attempt to merge executive and judicial powers in the hands of a few reasonable people who knew the affairs of the city profoundly.

By the 1960s, the old Ogboni based on Yoruba practices existed side by side with a modernized version, the Reformed Ogboni Fraternity (ROF), which was more open to younger men and later admitted a few women. I know that Pasitor went to the ROF, since I saw the notice in the entrance to their meeting place. The founder of the ROF was an Anglican clergyman, the Rev. T. A. J. Ogunbiyi. He creatively blended the Christian Bible with the traditional Ogboni rites, replacing the prayer to mother earth with a Christian prayer, and making the Bible, placed in a white bowl, the object of worship. Although Ogunbiyi was attacked by other senior priests, he nevertheless went ahead and established the ROF. The organization met every seventeen days, and it kept its meetings and membership secret.

As on the day he took me to Chief Akinloye, Pasitor came to Ode Aje unannounced. There was nothing unusual about this. It was uncommon for anyone to announce that they were paying a visit. He was unlucky: I had gone to play soccer. Perhaps telling them of his urgent need to see me, he asked all available adults to look for me. Even Baba Olopa crossed the road to check whether I was at school. I was at another school, about a mile away. I had to be rushed home, running faster than the person who discovered my location. Even though I was covered with sweat and dust, Pasitor asked me to follow him yet again.

We took a cab to the Oke Ado office of the ROF and arrived when their meeting was already in progress. We were not allowed inside, and we sat on a bench placed in front of the building. After about an hour, a man who described himself as the secretary came to speak with us. It was a rather short meeting, about two minutes. The secretary said that the Ogboni members had refused to consider the matter as the Elepo chief whom Pasitor wanted to report was a member. Pasitor repeated part of what the secretary said, posing it as a question: "Chief is one of you?" The secretary did not even answer him. Only a monkey understands a monkey! He was in shock, in great shock. As if in fear, we rushed to the street to flag down another cab. When Pasitor refused to speak with me, it was always because he was unhappy. I learned not to speak either, using silence to allow him to reflect and regain his spirit. Sorrow has been compared to a valuable treasure that can be shown only to a few friends.

This was the briefest of the missions and the most unpredictable. The head of an elephant is too big for a child to carry: Pasitor was too "small" to negotiate with the ROF. I had no idea how Pasitor wanted to present Jakobu's case to the secret cult and what my evidence would have done. Pasitor was probably ignorant of how the cult worked through a highly successful strategy of networking. A successful ROF had as its members senior police officers, army generals, top administrators, wealthy men, and the cream of other professions. Secrecy was an instrument of network building, their meetings allowing them to talk about land and "criminals," such as Jakobu, who were to be punished, huge contracts that the government was thinking of awarding, and the means of obtaining admission to the universities for their children. Someone must have leaked to the Elepo chief that he was being reported by Pasitor, and he made a move to kill the complaint. Even if the Elepo chief was not aware of what was happening, I could not understand what reporting him to the ROF would have accomplished. Perhaps Pasitor was thinking that the cult was driven by morality and it would defend a poor man. Perhaps someone tricked him into doing this. As far as I was concerned, I learned nothing, saw nothing, and understood not a single bit about the cult other than the location of the building, which was not hidden from the public.

Fundraising to save Jakobu was already under way by the time we went to see the Ogboni people. I did not know how extensive it was, but some people at Ode Aje asked me to give Pasitor money. I recorded the donations in an exercise book. *Owo loya* was what they called it, meaning "lawyer's fee." It was not the first time that I had been asked to collect donations, but they were usually for someone who had lost a mother or father and needed money quickly. I have no idea how much they eventually raised, nor the number of people who contributed to the fund. It must have been impressive, as Pasitor and his associates successfully moved Jakobu's wife and child to the city and sustained her for some years. Again Pasitor dragged me along to the lawyer's office. This time I was able to say everything that I knew, and the lawyer took notes. I could see from his face that Pasitor was happy with me, telling the lawyer that he had not even paid attention to the aspects that I was relating. I added redundant information, noticing points that the lawyer did not write down. He congratulated Pasitor for having a good witness, repeated many times that this was the easiest and most straightforward case he had ever handled, and promised to get back to Pasitor in a few days. He who boasts much does little, and he who speaks incessantly says nonsense. I never went back to the lawyer's office. As with the ROF, I have no detailed information about what happened. All I heard was that the lawyer "chopped our money." In Yoruba, money could take the form of food that someone could "eat." When a person lost money or was owed money, someone was said to have "swallowed" it. How do you recover the money without surgery?

Pasitor came to collect me once more. It was December 1965. He was waiting for me in the office of the headmaster, and my teacher told me to see him as soon as the assembly was over. As Pasitor never brought bad news, there was no need to panic. He was not his cheerful self, but he still called me Abiodun Isola; he was the only one who combined both names and never used Toyin. He was the one who gave me the name of Abiodun, and he ignored my other names. He also monopolized the use of the name; no one competing with him. He took a special liking to me, the only son that his own family had produced for quite a while. Religious differences with his first wife prevented their living together. As he said, he could not be a pastor and have a wife who would not follow him to church at Elepo. His second wife had failed to produce a son. Everybody knew that his love for me was special—he could not produce a son, and only one of his grandchildren was a boy. He had a sense of loyalty and identification with me, to the extent that people believed I was his most trusted friend. I reciprocated because he was gentle with me and because of the way he talked.

As we left the school, we walked in a direction that I knew inside out, even if I closed my eyes. I did not know what his final destination would be. I saw Leku's store some distance away, and I thought we would pay a short courtesy call and move on. No one passed the store without saluting the owner, lest one become a stream that marched past the house without showing gratitude for the use of the land. We walked to the store, and I stayed outside, thinking that Pasitor would just greet Leku and we would proceed. Then he took a seat and asked me to do the same. I sat on the floor.

Pasitor told a long story, half of which I already knew. Then he narrated his efforts to get Jakobu out of jail. He added new information, such as his interactions with the police and the bribes they took from many people. Pasitor believed that the police were unredeemable and that it was no longer necessary to ask God to forgive them. God would ensure that they would suffer much on earth and would continue their suffering in the world beyond. Pasitor wondered: if the police were asked to carry out such unpleasant duties, why did they not resign and become farmers? Then he spoke about chiefs, how he had visited about fourteen of them. He only took me to two, politicians who were also chiefs. He must have tried the traditional chiefs before pursuing the option of the politicians. "Everybody dribbled me," he said, borrowing *dribble*, which had been popularized by soccer, as an alternative to *deception*. The lawyer, too, took the money and said that the "case was a difficult matter o." Pasitor did not understand why a case based on a lie should be difficult. The chief had driven the man away from his farm, but why drive him to jail?

Pasitor asked me to tell Leku what I had seen at Elepo. I repeated my story. Leku concentrated on looking at our mouths, and I was not sure whether she was listening to my story or not. She kept smoking, and would cough occasionally. After I was done, Leku opened a short question and answer session. I remember all the essentials but not the order in which she posed the questions. Leku wanted to know why Pasitor had not told her this much earlier. "It is the running up and down to the others that I mentioned that delayed me," said Pasitor, as he begged for forgiveness. Leku assured him that she was not annoyed, only interested in knowing. Leku wanted to know from Pasitor precisely what he wanted from her.

Pasitor did not specify, simply saying, "Help us." I could have answered the question: "How do we release the man in jail?" But it was not unusual to be nonspecific as a technique for seeking help. To seek broadly defined help was a common strategy to ensure that one did not walk away with empty hands. Leku asked Pasitor whether he wanted her to inform all the other herbalists and diviners in the city and elsewhere. Pasitor said that it was up to her, without asking what impact this would have.

Then she turned to me, asking about my future plans. I said that I had none other than to continue with my education. Without bothering whether I was there or not, Leku scolded Pasitor for involving me, telling him that his enemies would prefer to kill me rather than him. Pasitor looked agitated when he heard this; apparently the thought had not occurred to him. In Leku's view, the chiefs did not bother to authenticate a story, as they believed that they already knew the truth. The chief who said that a farmer possessed marijuana was not expecting a small boy like me to reveal his lies, Leku continued, as the chief himself knew that he was telling a lie. If the end of an ox is beef, the end of a lie is grief.

Then Leku came out with a bombshell: "Why do you bother about Jakobu instead of the chief?" She meant the Elepo chief who had created the problem in the first place. Pasitor said that everybody at Elepo wanted Jakobu out of jail. To Leku, this was a small issue. Hundreds of people were in jail, she said, and hundreds more would follow. I am sure Pasitor himself knew this. Rival political parties had begun to use thugs in large numbers to harass their opponents. Nigeria's independence in 1960 had not brought the good things of life that the politicians had promised. Instead, interregional competition had become intense, and Ibadan was at the center of it all. No political party was strong enough to wield power, and the politicians, many of whom who had bought chieftaincy titles to dignify their names, were playing the politics of "no rules." All means to capture and stay in power were acceptable. Strong factions had emerged, each bent on destroying the other. I saw their fights on the streets, I heard them on the radio, expressed in bitter campaign rhetoric. The newspapers they owned contained virulent poison. Those in power used the police to advantage, hatching various schemes to destroy their opponents. The police would tie a goat in front of an opponent's house and arrest him for theft, just to incarcerate him. Planting marijuana in cars, houses, and farms was done simply to destroy opponents. Jakobu was not a politician, but the Elepo chief was using the destruction machine that he and his fellow politicians had successfully put in place.

"If we bother about the chief, what happens to Jakobu?" Pasitor asked, now speaking like the innocent Toyin. Leku again said that Jakobu did not count, that the key thing was to destroy the chief. If Pasitor released Jakobu, the chief would put another person in prison, maybe Samueli, Leku said, using exactly this name. To Leku, the politicians were *ounjelu*, a concept that translates as "to eat the city." This should be the title of a famous book, and no copyright permission is necessary to use it. Leku had used the metaphor of food and consumption to create a powerful image for what you and I would observe for a decade. The Yoruba word for chiefs and politicians was *oloselu*, that is, "city managers." Instead of managing politics, they turned the city into edible food and began to eat it. In the old-style corruption that the books reported, *ifa* (influence) was the abiding principle, with the politician and chiefs accused of *jefa*, which was benefiting from power and information to take some advantage. *Ifa* was to take not everything, but the little extras, leaving the rest intact. *Ifa* was not robbery, and one critic was even accused of complaining only because he had no access. A minister in charge of education could locate a school in his city, which was *jefa*. He had not stolen any money, only used *ifa* to arrive at a decision. In the eyes of the Ibadan, the Ijebu had electricity, pipe-borne water, and tarred roads because the first indigenous Western Region premier, Chief Obafemi Awolowo, was an Ijebu man who used his office for his people to *jefa*. He was not criticized but envied for using power to benefit his own people.

Leku turned things around, moving to an extreme position. To "eat the city" was to gradually destroy it. In this analysis, Pasitor's concern was misdirected. He could not save one man if all the chiefs were eating the city. Leku was asking Pasitor to "eat the chief." To eat the chief was not to nourish the bodies of some happy cannibals but to completely incapacitate the chiefs, end their influence, and destroy the sources of their power or even of their beings. It was Pasitor who eventually asked how the chief could be destroyed. Leku said she would consult with all the herbalists and *awon aiye*, and Pasitor would have to come back.

Everybody of my age knew what *awon aiye* meant, although we had difficulty defining it. There was a consensus that all witches and sorcerers were included in *awon aiye*, a body of powerful unseen forces. Just go to Ode Aje in 2016 and threaten people with *awon aiye* and they will rush to their pastors, imams, and *babalawo* to seek immediate help. The year 2016 is still in the future; this is just to show you how strong the belief remains, and how persistent it is. If one had said in 1965 that there were no witches, one would have created panic in the household, a mother probably crying that her son was about to destroy her by inviting the wrath of *awon aiye* to visit. At school, some believed that there were three or four girls who were witches, victims forced to inherit the power from their mothers. I knew all of them, and I kept my distance. At the same time, they must never know that one was avoiding them or that we had discovered their membership in the club of witches. It was tricky. *Awon aiye* had no physical characteristics to separate them from others, and they had the gift of blending easily with others. Only Leku and powerful *babalawo* had the "medicine" to discover them.

I do not know whether Leku had to turn into a bird to consult *awon aiye* as she had promised Pasitor. I believed then, from what the school-teachers and other adults had told me, confirmed by storybooks and moonlight stories, that *awon aiye* turned into birds to converge at a secret location for their meetings. They met at night, when everybody else was asleep. The *aiye* transformed itself into thin air to leave the house, the air became a bird, and when it reached its location it became human. Blood was waiting for each of them to eat, and each must supply someone to eat at the meeting. An *aiye* should be ready to donate its son or daughter, cowife, enemies, and husband. When a woman lost many children, this was the first sign that she was a member of a powerful guild of evil forces that needed blood for dinner.

It was probably at this kind of meeting that Leku would present Jakobu's case and ask other witches to "eat the chief." Leku had come up with an answer, so easily, without Pasitor having to pay for a cab or my being dragged to chiefs and lawyers. Leku became my first heroine. Not that I resented Pasitor. Far from it. I was happy that Leku had come to the assistance of Pasitor when others had abandoned him. He had become emaciated, eating less and less and talking to himself even when I was with him. After Leku had consulted *awon aiye*, as she promised us, Pasitor could stop coming to the city and enjoy his church and farm at Elepo. With the Elepo chief now dead, Jakobu would be released, and he, too, could rejoin his family.

When we left Leku, Pasitor promised to return between Christmas and the New Year of 1965. I forgot all about Jakobu and enjoyed the pleasures of the season. I even went to Elepo for four days before returning to Ode Aje for Christmas. The school year had ended very well, and I had collected more awards than everyone, including one for taking the first place in the graduating set. I was presented to the crowd of parents. Elementary school had come to an end but not the friendship with my mates since we all lived within walking distance.

I had no idea that I would follow Pasitor again to Leku's store. This time, he sent advance notice through my mother that I should meet him there. I was so happy. I told my friend to expect a big announcement on the radio about the death of a big chief. "How do you know?" asked Sali. He must have been dead for some days, I told them, but his children and wives needed to save money for a big feast. This was not abnormal. When kings and chiefs died, their relations could decide to keep it a secret for a day or two in order to prepare for the large number of mourners that would descend on them. Or it could be that they wanted some people to hear about the death before some others did. I sincerely believed in what I said, as I was certain that Leku and *awon aiye* had killed the chief.

I got there before Pasitor. Leku and the store had refused to change, even as I grew taller and better informed. My perception of Leku had not changed either. The school and prevailing worldviews had actually made Leku larger than life. In his parting words, the headmaster had said that some of us would even go into the world to discover ourselves, including our spiritual power. He could only hope that those who became witches and sorcerers would forgive him for all "the canes their bottoms had received." A drama closing the school year celebrated the success of a "good witch" who gave a king in trouble the magic to defeat his enemy. I was not responsible for choosing the play. The schoolteacher did and gave me a role. As I sat down at the store, gazing at Leku, I saw the "good witch" at work, ready to save Pasitor. The chief must be dead by now, I assured myself.

When Pasitor arrived, Leku said that she had two important things to say. She had consulted *awon aiye*. And she added that she had also spoken with *awon agba* (the elders). At the previous meeting, she had not mentioned *awon agba*, a concept that I understood to mean a body of very powerful elders. *Awon agba* could be people in Pasitor's category, but they could also be the "unseen forces of goodness." The two "bodies" told Leku two things, and she had been instructed to tell Pasitor.

"They said you must all fight," said Leku, emphasizing the word *fight*. "And they said it would be a big fight." Leku was not giving an instruction, only citing authorities greater than herself, which was why she was using the word *they*. Jakobu and others would be freed, but Pasitor and others had to shed their blood for them. She mentioned the shedding of blood, and I paid attention to this since I was thinking that Leku had consumed the blood of the chief. Now she was telling us that it was Pasitor who had to shed his own blood, as Jesus Christ did. *Awon aiye* had promised their support in the fight; *awon agba* had consented to it. Leku was telling Pasitor that "the heavenly powers" had given the go-ahead to organize a fight. Leku was no longer an herbalist but had become the Angel Gabriel announcing a divine revelation to Pasitor. It remained now for Pasitor to leave the wilderness with the revelation and work on it. He looked sad, as if he had lost the will to live.

Then Leku changed the subject. "Pasitor, your son is in danger and you are responsible." Now she was talking about me, saying things to indicate that when the leopard is away his cubs are food for others. Pasitor was no longer looking sad but worried. Pasitor would prefer the danger to befall him rather than me. "What is the matter?" asked Pasitor. As the wound inflames the finger, so does thought inflame the mind.

"Calm down. There is power to conquer the problem." I have translated what she said into English, but Leku was using the notion of supernatural power, not physical power. She explained that by taking me on his missions Pasitor had exposed me to danger. To Leku, the best way to get to Pasitor, to completely destroy him, would be to "send me to heaven." Pasitor got the message. Yes! My death as a young boy would produce that effect. When my mother died in later years, my grandmother followed within five months because she could not endure the loss of an only child. It was Pasitor now begging Leku to save him, an indirect way of requesting her help to save me. He prostrated himself, weeping, begging Leku to save him, to protect him from destruction by allowing me to live. Pasitor was not running to his Bible to read psalms for my protection; he was begging Leku.

"There is no danger," assured Leku. She had solved the problem. I had to use magic to prevent being recognized by evil forces. As she carefully explained to Pasitor, when the powers of evil looked for me they would see another person. It was not that I would change into something else but that their eyes would see something different. She gave Pasitor a small quantity of powder charm, wrapped in a used newspaper, with the instruction to make a set of three small incisions on my chest. I was not to wash my body for two days so that the incision would dry with the magic inside. She said some magical words (incantations) over the powder. Unlike songs and poems, incantations are hard to memorize, as they contain many archaic words and connections between symbols that may sound illogical. What Leku said so rapidly was all about the conquest of powerful forces. Whoever wished me bad fortune would be visited with the same.

> If a frog invokes rain, the rain falls on him
> Anyone who wishes Isola bad fortune
> Let him carry the misfortune on his own head.

Pasitor was happy. Unknown to me, he had his own agenda. He had actually invited me to the meeting not because of Jakobu and the chief but because of me. Leku, too, probably did not know what Pasitor had in mind until he opened up.

"Iya, I meant to seek another favor," Pasitor said in a subdued tone, trying to regain his composure after the bad news he had just heard. Leku signaled with her pipe that he should talk.

"My son is going to grammar school and I want him to do well," said Pasitor.

Leku smiled, a smile of assurance. "I took care of this some time ago."

"Thank you, Iya, what did you do?"

"I gave him *ogun isoye*." I was in disbelief. I knew what Leku meant. *Ogun isoye* was the magic used to permanently invigorate the brain to attain excellence. Most parents and their children in school believed that Yoruba charms were available to overcome the difficulties of Western education. I never knew of a classmate who did not talk about such a charm. We even acted it in plays. Many of us attempted it on our own, putting *kuluso* insects into a cooked egg that we swallowed. We all knew one of the most powerful ingredients, a plant known as *amunimuye*, which could control one's consciousness. We would go to *oko etile* before examinations to pluck the leaves and eat them, without combining the plant with other ingredients as the herbalists would do. When I beat Sali in a 1964 examination, he told all the others in the school that it was because I had consumed more of the leaves than he. It was true that Sali and I had decided to go to the farm to eat the leaves in order to do well on the examination, but on getting there he had said that he could not eat a lot. The last time we had tried, he had developed stomach trouble. He plucked two or three, but I ate *amunimuye* as a hungry goat would eat cassava.

As Pasitor stood up, profusely thanking Leku, she explained the medicine.

"I gave him the charm to remember. Your son will always remember." Leku was saying that I would never forget, having been given the same kind of charms that herbalists and *babalawo* consumed to remember the "one thousand leaves, one thousand birds, and one thousand incantations." But Leku quickly changed the subject.

"Pasitor, prepare for the big fight that *awon aiye* has sanctioned. A single stick may smoke, but it will never burn. One finger alone cannot kill a louse. One finger alone cannot carry a load." Pasitor said "Yes," thanked Leku, and we left. Pasitor took me to Ode Aje, asked me to pack a small bag, and we immediately headed for Elepo. There is no cure without cost: Pasitor made the incisions as Leku directed, and I did not grumble. I returned to the city in time for the New Year's celebration, when I also turned thirteen. A few days later I headed to a boarding school to start my high school education. Less than two weeks later the military staged a coup, removing the chiefs and politicians from power. Events were moving toward the "big fight" that Leku had foretold, while my own egg was growing into a cock. No one could have predicted that less than three years later I would become a high school dropout, joining Pasitor in a peasant rebellion that created a political earthquake.